Holy Laughter

HOLY
LAUGHTER

Essays on Religion in the Comic Perspective

Edited by M. Conrad Hyers

THE SEABURY PRESS · NEW YORK

ACKNOWLEDGMENTS

Grateful acknowledgment is made to the following publishers and authors for permission to reprint copyrighted material from the titles listed—either in original form or slightly adapted to the purposes of this book:

Chapter 2, "The Humanity of Comedy," is from William F. Lynch, S.J., "Comedy," in *Christ and Apollo: The Dimension of the Literary Imagination* (New York: Sheed & Ward, 1960). © 1960 by the publisher.

Chapter 3, "The Bias of Comedy and the Narrow Escape into Faith," is from Nathan A. Scott, Jr., *The Broken Center: Studies in the Theological Horizon of Modern Literature* (New Haven: Yale University Press, 1966). Copyright © 1966 by the publisher.

Chapter 4, "The Clown as the Lord of Disorder," by Wolfgang M. Zucker, and Chapter 5, "The Clown in Contemporary Art," by Samuel H. Miller, are from *Theology Today*, Vol. XXIV (October, 1967). Reprinted by permission of the publisher.

Chapter 6, "The Rhetoric of Christian Comedy," by Barry Ulanov, is from Francis X. Connolly, Martin D'Arcy, and Barry Ulanov, *Literature as Christian Comedy* (West Hartford, Conn.: St. Joseph College, 1962).

Chapter 7, "Christian Faith and the Social Comedy," is from Peter L. Berger, *The Precarious Vision* (New York: Doubleday & Co., 1961). Copyright © 1961 by the author. Reprinted by permission of the publisher.

Chapter 8, "Humour and Faith," is from Reinhold Niebuhr, *Discerning the Signs of the Times* (New York: Charles Scribner's Sons, 1946). Copyright 1946 by the publisher. Reprinted by permission of the publisher.

Chapter 9, "The Traditional Roots of Jewish Humor," by Israel Knox, is from *Judaism*, Vol. XII (Summer, 1963).

Chapter 10, "The Humor of Christ," is from Elton Trueblood, "A Neglected Aspect," in *The Humor of Christ* (New York: Harper & Row, 1964). Copyright © 1964 by the author. Reprinted by permission of the publisher.

Chapter 11, "Eutrapelia: A Forgotten Virtue," is from Hugo Rahner, S.J., *Man at Play*, trans. Brian Battershaw and Edward Quinn (New York: Herder & Herder, 1965).

Chapter 12, "Zen Humour," is from R. H. Blyth, *Oriental Humour* (Tokyo: The Hokuseido Press, 1959).

Contents

Introduction

Titles are frequently as confounding as illuminating. The announcement of a species of laughter called "holy" is no exception. It is not particularly obvious what "holiness" has to do with laughter, any more than it was obvious to Tertullian what Jerusalem had to do with Athens; for holiness and laughter, like the sacred and the profane, seem to be opposite, if not in opposition to, one another. Nor is it especially clear whether the reader, confronted with such a hybrid, should prepare himself for laughter, or brace himself for holiness; whether, in fact, he is expected to laugh in a holy sort of way, or perhaps to become holy in a laughable sort of way. It is not even apparent why the object of inquiry should not be labeled instead *"unholy* laughter" in recognition of the element of profanity inherent in all laughter with respect to holy things.

For that matter it might be questioned whether the word "laughter" is appropriate at all, seeing that the central concern of the book is with an analysis of the place of the comic spirit and perspective in religion, and not with some sort of sanctimonious giggling. Laughter has been emphasized in the title, nevertheless, rather than other qualified candidates such as comedy or humor, precisely because it represents a category

of human emotion and expression seemingly the furthest removed from the so-called religious affections. The domain of
laughter and that of those motley associates who symbolize
and provoke it—clown, jester, joker, trickster, or comedian—
are generally relegated in both theory and practice to the
periphery of the religious consciousness, if not more or less
half-way between the sacred and the demonic. And when ad-
mitted to the inner sanctum of piety, it is usually only in the
most guarded and restrained form of the nearly imperceptible
saintly smile, as in the myriad Christian representations of
Madonna and Child, heavy with divine solemnity and messianic freight, or as in the careful insistence of Buddhist
scholastics that, of the six degrees of laughter, the Buddha
was only "guilty" of indulging in the first: the faintest of
smiles.[1] To the puritanism of the pious imagination, it is unthinkable that the Christ or the Buddha should have stooped
to the vulgar level of openly displaying the teeth in a jovial
grin, or of emitting even modest chuckles of amusement, let
alone the more extreme forms of hilarious abandon: doubling
over in laughter, tearful hysteria, convulsions, and the like.
The humanity of Jesus, however, or of Gautama, points to a
larger understanding of man and the sacred than that which is
isolated by devotion and veneration alone; and it is to this

---

[1] The scale of laughter moves from what is seen as the most spiritual to
the most physical species: (a) *sita,* the subtle and serene smile manifest
in a barely detectable facial expression; (b) *hasita,* a smile that slightly
reveals the teeth; (c) *vihasita,* a smile accompanied by a modicum of
restrained laughter; (d) *upahasita,* pronounced laughter associated with
movements of the head, shoulders, and arms; (e) *apahasita,* laughter that
brings tears; and (f) *atihasita,* uproarious laughter accompanied by boisterous bodily expressions. By definition, therefore, the fullest and most enjoy-
able developments of laughter are the furthest removed from holiness.
Cf. Shwe Zan Aung, *The Compendium of Philosophy,* a translation of the
Abhidhammattha-Sangaha, rev. and ed. by Mrs. Rhys Davids (London:
Luzac and Co., 1910), pp. 22–25.

that the holiness of laughter, and the laughter of holiness, refers.

The anthology is not, however, as the title might suggest, a book of religious jokes with laughter in any sense as its immediate goal. It is not even a collection of recipes for the successful creation, transmission, and consummation of religious jokes. This is a book *about* the comic dimension in religion, about the holiness of laughter—indeed for that matter the profanity of laughter as well—which should not be taken to imply that it is intended to be funny or calculated to precipitate laughter. It must, of course, be granted at the outset that the choice of a book *about* humor rather than a humorous book, and in particular a book about humor in the context and style of the academic tradition, immediately plunges the enterprise into an apparent contradiction with a certain humor of its own; for what is advocated in theory is not openly displayed in practice—suggesting what is already suspected anyway, that the only people capable of studying humor and turning it into an academic problem are people without it. The dilemma has a comic awkwardness about it: How does one write seriously about humor? Either the result is not taken seriously because it is about *humor*, or it is not taken seriously precisely because it is *serious* about humor.

There is also a certain precariousness from the religious side; for while, on the one hand, the project seems to err in undertaking to treat the comic too seriously, if not with scholastic humorlessness, on the other hand, it seems to err in suggesting that sacred matters ought to be treated comically rather than with the appropriate sincerity and piety. The underlying thesis of this collection of essays, however, is that there is not only an important, but necessary, interrelationship between the comic and the sacred, apart from which both the sacred and the comic are subject to distortions of far-reaching consequence, and that this interrelationship is far more significant, indeed more crucial, than the occasional and often quite miscellaneous attention afforded the issue would appear to indicate.

Though considerable attention has been devoted to the comic from the standpoints of psychology, philosophy, and literary criticism, proportionately little analysis has come from the various disciplines that comprise religious studies. There is a curious oddity about this virtual silence considering the major role performed by the many forms of comedy and humor at all levels and in all contexts of life, including those of what on any definition might be called the moral and religious categories of life, and also considering that, in a very real sense, human existence as such may be defined as a running interplay between seriousness and laughter, between sacred concerns and comic interludes. When half of the life of man, as it were, is lived within the province of laughter, humor, and comedy, the ecclesiastical and theological obliviousness to it is truly a remarkable phenomenon. For all the wealth of material produced on the general subject of religion, the amount of attention devoted to the place of humor in religion, and to the manifold relationships between the sacred and the comic, is almost infinitesimal by comparison. If the purpose of the various disciplines within religious studies has been to present an accurate picture of the religious situation, then that picture has been seriously falsified by the presentation of but one side. Even granting both the ontological and psychological priority of the sacred and the serious, to have presented only one term of what is clearly a polarity is to have been unfaithful to the professed object of inquiry: man and his responses to the sacred. As Peter Berger has indicated with respect to the field of sociology, the overwhelming tendency among professional academicians has been to depict human relationships solely in the *dramatic* mode, to the exclusion of the *comic* mode, thereby giving a very distorted and misleading view of the actual character of man and his existence.[2] Nowhere has this been more true or more debilitating than in the scholarly study, as well as official espousal, of religion.

The following essays are a parenthetical reminder of this "other side," a corrective footnote in defense of nonsense and play, in particular the nonsense and play of the comic spirit. The criteria of selection have been, first, to present the best formal treatments of the relationship of the comic to the sacred written in the past two decades, second, to present as many different facets of the relationship as possible, and third, to present analyses written from the perspective of a variety of disciplines within or bordering on religious studies. In this way it has been possible to encompass at the same time both various dimensions of the dialectic of the sacred and the comic, and various types of approaches to it. The essays by Niebuhr, Berger, and Rahner, for instance, not only reflect the standpoints of different disciplines (Social Ethics, Sociology of Religion, History of Doctrine) but also bring to light different aspects of the problem. Other approaches represented are Phenomenology of Religion (Hyers), Biblical Studies (Trueblood), Theology and Literature (Scott, Lynch, Ulanov), and Theology of Culture (Zucker, Miller). Though the primary focus of the essays is upon the Christian tradition, essays on Jewish humor (Knox) and humor in Zen (Blyth) have been included as an indication of the possibilities of analyzing the role of the comic spirit and perspective within other religious contexts. The Afterword by Chad Walsh rounds off the anthology in a lighter vein that points beyond

---

[2] *The Precarious Vision* (New York: Doubleday and Co., 1961), pp. 67 ff. Cf. the similar complaint of William B. Cameron, *Informal Sociology* (New York: Random House, 1963), "The Sociology of Humor and Vice Versa," pp. 79–94.

an analysis of the comic to the spirit of the comic itself, something perhaps that comes more naturally to one who, as a
poet and lay theologian, is not so caught up in the official style
and reserve of the academic establishment. An excerpt from
Robert Barclay's *Apology for the True Christian Divinity*
(1676) has been added as an appendix in that it represents a
classic, and in many ways characteristic, repudiation of comedy
and humor in the setting of a "Christian sobriety." The absence from the collection, however, of any substantial treat-
ment of the subject by a systematic theologian is perhaps the
best illustration that could be given of the power of the taboo
against the comic that so commonly surrounds the sacred.[3]

The use of the terms "humor" and "comedy"—sometimes
interchangeably—should receive at least a preliminary clarification; for though overlapping, they are hardly synonymous.
In other contexts very specific differentiations may be made
between comedy and humor, and the various types of each
(e.g. "high" and "low" comedy). It will be sufficient to the
present purpose, nevertheless, to use the terms correlatively,
and in the broadest sense, to refer to the same general
phenomenon. If a distinction is made between the terms, it is
that humor represents those attitudes and moods—identified
by such words as caprice, frivolity, levity, jest, and facetious-
ness—that are expressed in the various types of comic structure: farce, burlesque, buffoonery, joking, clowning, etc. In
the comic spirit, humor is the spirit, comedy the form; and
laughter is its overt expression.

[3] Karl Barth, in his monumental twelve-volume dogmatic work, did at
least grant a page to humor as something theologically mentionable. Unusual though even this might be in a systematic theology, however—and
granting that Barth's undeniable sense of humor often found its way into
his prodigious labors—it remained almost completely undeveloped and
unexplored in doctrinal terms apart from a brief correlation with humility.
See *Church Dogmatics* III/4 (Edinburgh: T. & T. Clark, 1961), pp.
662 ff.

Focusing upon these terms, on the other hand, is not intended to suggest that all manifestations of the comic spirit are hilariously funny, or necessarily provoke laughter. Laughter is not always a reliable signature of the comic spirit; nor does the comic spirit always reveal itself in laughter. The comic spirit is fundamentally a certain attitude toward and perspective upon life. The essential element in relation to the sacred is the periodic suspension of seriousness and sacrality (the comic spirit) and the realization of the playful, gamelike quality inherent in all human enterprises, however holy (the comic perspective). The spirit of comedy is kindled by that same spirit of play that lies within the very nature of things themselves, from atoms to "little creeping things" to whirling galaxies to *homo sapiens,* who nervously tries to comprehend the whole in neat little packages of rationality, order, and meaning—the element of indeterminacy and randomness, of vitality and spontaneity, yes, of purposeless being and becoming for the sake of being and becoming.

Comedy is not simply a response to the incongruities and absurdities of life, or the lighter side of tragedy—a correlation which some interpreters of the comic never get beyond. In its own right, and in its own terms, comedy points toward, and even creates for its own plaything, incongruity and absurdity. Sense is turned into nonsense, the sacred into the profane; seriousness becomes frivolousness, and the sober drama a merry farce; and the Fool is crowned King for a day. Comedy in fact plays with both the categories of reason and irrationality, of order and chaos, of meaning and meaninglessness, and in so doing opens up the playfulness at the heart of reality itself—the playfulness which characterizes both Creator and creation alike.

M. Conrad Hyers

Department of Religious Studies
Beloit College

ONE

The Comic Profanation of the Sacred

M. CONRAD HYERS

> For the name of these gods there is both a serious and a
> humorous explanation; the serious explanation is not to be
> had from me, but there is no hindrance to my offering the
> humorous one; for the gods too are fond of a joke.
>
> Socrates, *Cratylus*

One of the significant weaknesses of all analyses of the
sacred[1]—whether Otto's *The Idea of the Holy*, Durkheim's
The Elementary Forms of the Religious Life, Van der Leeuw's

[1] Although the term "sacred" is being used primarily in the narrower,
religious sense as the sphere that has its focus in ultimate concerns and the
ultimate questions of meaning and value (Tillich), it is also applicable in
the larger sense to any sphere of concern, meaning, and value, to any space,
time, object, person, act, order, or idea that is set apart and surrounded
with an atmosphere of seriousness and importance. A committee meeting,
for example, is a sacred time and space set apart from the ordinary time
and space that precedes or follows it, a sacred zone having its own rituals,
officiants, and taboos. In either context one may speak of the necessity for
a comic profanation of the sacred.

Religion in Essence and Manifestation, Caillois's *Man and the Sacred*, Tillich's *Dynamics of Faith*, or Eliade's *The Sacred and the Profane*—has been the failure to treat, as an integral movement within the experience of and response to the sacred, the dialectical interrelation of the sacred and the comic, of holiness and humor. In his classic treatise on the nature of the holy, for example, Rudolf Otto analyzed the sacred in terms of the fundamental experience of awe and wonder, with its ambivalent movements of attraction and repulsion, the *mysterium fascinans* and the *mysterium tremendum*. This, however, is but one side of the human response to the sacred, albeit the primary and more important side. The other side, the shadow side, which Otto did not explore, and to which only negligible attention has been given in subsequent interpretations of the sacred, is that of the comic. The dialectic that Otto so brilliantly investigated has its counterpart in a comic dialectic of withdrawal and aggression, and is part of the larger dialectic of the sacred and the comic. Equally as universal as awe and wonder before the sacred, and as the more sober moods of religious devotion and moral commitment, is the response of the comic spirit that, secondary and derivative though it might be, stands in its own interior relationship to holiness and mystery.

The Seriousness of Humor

The critical importance of understanding, and religiously appropriating, the dialectic of the sacred and the comic was posed a century ago by Kierkegaard—one of the first moderns seriously to examine, and self-consciously employ, the comic mode in religious thought and life: "The more thoroughly and substantially a human being exists, the more he will discover the comical. Even one who has merely conceived a great plan toward accomplishing something in the world, will discover it. . . . But the resolution of the religious individual is the highest of all resolves, infinitely higher than all plans to transform the world and to create systems and works of art: therefore must the religious man, most of all men, discover the comical. . . ." [2] G. K. Chesterton, another modern master and prophetic voice of the comic spirit, once suggested that the religion of the future would be characterized by an increased appreciation of humor and comedy as intrinsic elements in the experience and expression of the sacred. And, as he himself demonstrated, there is a plane of spiritual and theological freedom, liberality and humanness, as well as personal maturity, that is not to be achieved apart from a refined sense of humor and sensitivity to the comic perspective.

In some respects, Chesterton has already proved to be right in his prophecy, as evidenced in the accompanying essays by the growing attention to the subject on the part of students of religion, and the even more dramatic use of humor and comic insight in religious writing in general. Whether there is something qualitatively distinctive about modern man's analysis and employment of humor in religion is a matter for historians to debate. Certainly a line of demarcation of some sort is visible in individuals like Kierkegaard and, later, Chesterton.[3] Such a development may, of course, be interpreted as a sign

---

[2] Søren Kierkegaard, *Concluding Unscientific Postscript* (Princeton: Princeton University Press, 1941), pp. 413–414. In the *Postscript,* Kierkegaard repeatedly returns to the problem of the relationship between humor and religion.

[3] Kierkegaard has been chosen, rather than an earlier figure such as Voltaire, in that Voltaire stands largely outside of a faith and religious expression which have become for him the external objects of humor, whereas, though Kierkegaard was equally adept at using humor as a weapon in relation to other points of view, he stands essentially within the act of faith and the existential situation of the man before God, and in this context attempts to analyze the inner relationship between faith and humor.

of spiritual decline and loss of religious conviction in a rising
tide of secularism. It may be understood as a pale substitution
of comic detachment for all ultimate concerns and commitments in an atmosphere of moral and theological relativism. It
may be seen as a questionable device resorted to by popular-
izers of religion to attract prospective proselytes or endear
skeptical audiences. It may even be viewed, in William
Hamilton's words, as "a pathetic attempt to keep in step with
a secular culture that has nothing else." [4] But though at
first sight the comic spirit seems inappropriate to the seriousness of one's most fundamental ethical and religious persuasions, and even though humor can easily degenerate into
frivolous diversion or cynical sarcasm, it is nevertheless the
special virtue of modern spirituality, if hardly to have discovered comedy, at least to have begun more self-consciously
to use and understand it out of an awakened sensitivity to its
moral and religious imperative.

This is not to say that the phenomenon under question is
peculiar to the modern period. On the one hand, it is not
peculiar enough if the enormities perpetrated in the twentieth
century in the name of holy causes and sacred ideologies, and
in the proud boast of national, political, and technological
superiorities, is any index. On the other hand, instances of the
phenomenon are to be found in every culture and every
period, however weakly and imperfectly that culture and
period may have appropriated the comic spirit and perspective.
And it is to an analysis of such instances as these that one
must turn in order to understand the special role that humor
can play—and indeed must play if the prospect of even more
demonic forces being unleashed under the righteous banners
of militant revolutionaries and reactionaries alike is to be
averted. There is a contemporary urgency about the question

[4] "Humor: Plausible and Demonic," *The Christian Century*, Vol. LXXVI
(July 8, 1959), p. 807.

of the function and place of the comic in relation to the sacred which constitutes a part of the seriousness of humor. As Konrad Lorenz indicated in concluding his important study of the phenomenon of aggression among animals and humans, the survival of mankind depends to a significant degree upon man's ability to develop, individually and culturally, the capacity for humor, both as a ritualization of aggressive impulses in substitution for the more violent and destructive expressions available to him, and as a vehicle for achieving perspective and humility in relation to his scientific capabilities and his ideological convictions—whether religious, moral, political, or socio-economic.[5]

The criterion by which one judges the seriousness and sacrality an individual attaches to something is not, as is often supposed, the degree of his unwillingness to laugh about it, to profane it, to make it the grist of comedy or the target of puns and anecdotes. Though such an attitude has been a common prejudice surrounding the sacred, and a prejudice that spills over from religious sincerity to sincerity in general, it is the mark of pseudo-seriousness, in fact the mark of what often becomes a demonic seriousness. There is a qualitative difference between taking something humorously and taking it lightly. Genuine seriousness is human; and insofar as it remembers its humanity it finds the profane act of humor not sacrilege but a moral and religious necessity. The endemic weakness that accompanies the intensity of sacred concerns is a predilection for translating itself into intolerance, aggression, and violence. In this lies the "seriousness" of humor. The barbarous chronicle of inquisitions, heresy trials, witch hunts, religious persecutions, holy wars, book-pyres, and martyrdoms, justified by the most respected elements of society and sanctified by pious interests, is sufficient testimony to the

[5] *On Aggression* (New York: Harcourt, Brace & World, 1966), pp. 293 ff.

stark possibilities of sincerity without humor, and the sacred apart from the comic. The same debility besets the radical enthusiast of whatever persuasion who, in fanatical certainty over the righteousness of his cause, zealously pursues some ideological program. Whether a fiery exponent of Marxism, Democracy, Free Enterprise, Black Power, Segregation, or Minority Rights, the predisposition of the advocate—rebel, moderate, or reactionary—is to absolutize his schemes for saving the world and rectifying the ills of society. Ideologies, like dogmas, have a high level of missionary, and often military, zeal, but a low level of comic awareness.[6]

In this regard, there is a marked affinity between religious absolutism, ideological radicalism, and political tyranny. Theological dogmatism shares with its socio-political counterparts in the attempted abolition of humor in relation to itself. A common trait of dictators, revolutionaries, and ecclesiastical authoritarians alike is the refusal both to laugh at themselves and to permit others to laugh at them. In totalitarian countries, for example, humor and satire directed at the sacrosanct ideology or official program is the nearest equivalent to treason. The humorist or cartoonist or playwright who engages in caricature of the functionaries and policies of the ascendent regime is open to the charge of unpatriotic, if not subversive, behavior, as in the religious sphere he is open to the charge of heresy or blasphemy. For a part of the pretension of orthodoxy of whatever type is the claim to have transcended the dialectic of the sacred and the comic, to have elevated itself beyond the requirements of humor. This, however, is equivalent to the claim to have transcended the hu-

---

[6] E.g., it is difficult to imagine anyone with a profound sense of humor in relation to his own most ultimate convictions participating in the burning of another at the stake because he failed to subscribe to a certain formulation of the doctrine of the Trinity, or engaging in violent acts of aggression in order to convert others to one's own ideological persuasions.

man condition, to have become "as God" knowing in some final sense the difference between good and evil. Various attempts have been made historically to minimize the human element in matters of ultimate concern, and thereby the necessity for the comic perspective, through infallibilist presumptions; but like the proud man who stumbles in his moment of glory, or the foolish man whose disguise fools no one but himself, the very claim to have risen above the finiteness and folly of the human situation is itself comic-pathetic. It is in this sense that, far from humor being a sign of the fall of man, and a trespass upon the holy ground of the sacred, the absence of humor and the loss of the comic perspective signifies the pride symbolized by the fall, and comedy a reminder of paradise-lost.

The Phenomenon of Comic Profanation

Contrary to Auden's comment that "primitive cultures have little sense of humor; firstly, because their sense of human individuality is weak . . . and, secondly, because, as animists and polytheists, they have little notion of necessity," [7] the dialectic of the sacred and the comic, with its various nuances, is visible even in the more primitive societies where taboos are often most rigid and inviolable, where the sacred is dramatically differentiated from the profane, and therefore —for these more than for Auden's reasons—where one would least expect to see a deliberate profanation of the holy. A common phenomenon in many such societies, for example, is the symbolically re-enacted return of cosmos to chaos, a phenomenon that has its own peculiar relevance to the correlation of the sacred and the comic; for the comic is a form of periodic profanation. Several lines of meaning and function

[7] W. H. Auden, *The Dyer's Hand* (New York: Random House, 1952), p. 372.

intersect in this seasonal drama, one strand of which is the recurrent relaxation of the rigid structures of society, the lifting of certain taboos, and the profanation of the sacred order. Sexual restrictions may be temporarily suspended, as in the festival orgy; the sharply distinguished and alienating culture roles of the sexes may be reversed (through the exchanging of costumes and activities, often in humorous mimicry); even acts bordering on sacrilege may be permitted.[8] In all this, one can see not manifestations of so-called pagan degeneration or desecrations of holy concerns but essential qualifications of the absoluteness of the sacred. By such acts of profanation, frequently having comic overtones, a reversal takes place through which certain necessary and healthy functions are performed: psychological release is given to pent-up emotional forces; the rigidities of the social system (the human cosmos) are rendered tolerable; culturally acceptable expression is provided an innate rebellion against monolithic structure and order, however sacred; purgation takes places through a dissolution of forms; the divorce between male and female, and the distances and hostilities created by other societal differentiations, are tempered; the dualities and hierarchies of existence are momentarily overcome; and what might otherwise be an oppressive tyranny of taboo is ameliorated. At the same time, a restriction is imposed on the ultimacy of the sacred, preventing it from becoming relentlessly and irrevocably absolute. The profanation of the sacred keeps the religious cosmos and the moral cosmos, on the one hand, psychologically human and, on the other hand, ontologically human.

Ethnological literature abounds in more specific instances of the comic profanation of the sacred. Among the Navaho, for example, in the Night Chant ceremony—essentially a serious religious ritual—the Water God (*to ninili*) is imper-

---

[8] Cf. Mircea Eliade, *Patterns in Comparative Religion* (New York: Sheed and Ward, 1958), pp. 358–359, 398 ff.

sonated in the sacred dance by a clown, dressed in inferior clothing, perhaps rags, and playing the buffoon. While the other masked dancers, also personifying various Navaho deities, are intently and meticulously pursuing the intricate rhythms and patterns of the ceremony, his function in relation to the rest is to mimic the entire proceeding. He dances out of step with the others, staggers, trips, and falls to the delight of the audience, presents comic exaggerations of their gestures and movements, sometimes stumbling or leaping out of the prescribed arena, or dashing into the crowd and indulging in pranks, taunts, and teasings.[9] He is clown, comedian, trickster, jester, and fool all in one. Here the comic profanation of the sacred, rather than following the sacred drama, or appearing as a lighter interlude between sober ritual sequences, and far from being performed to one side in the shadows, or in a more profane time and space, is incorporated within the religious festival itself. The dialectic of holiness and humor, of sacred ceremony and profane comedy, is openly enacted.

In modern Haiti the same phenomenon has taken the form of a good-natured ridicule of religious matters, as in the "catechism of the Guede," in which Roman Catholic devotees, catechetical instructions, and ecclesiastical functionaries are parodied. At the end of a ceremony in honor of ancestral spirits (the Guede), the participants are commanded by the leader to form a line and are given a mock catechetical examination, the answers to which are facetiously or ludicrously phrased. Each answer qualifies the "catechumen" for some prestigious ecclesiastical, political, or military title. At the culmination of the examination, the most unlikely candidate—perhaps a fat girl of jolly spirits—is acclaimed as "Pope." [10] Such burlesque

[9] Gladys A. Reichard, *Navaho Religion,* Vol. II (New York: Pantheon, 1950), pp. 491–492.

[10] Alfred Metraux, "Voodoo in Haiti," Charles Leslie, ed., *Anthropology of Folk Religion* (New York: Random House, 1960), pp. 439–440.

borders on sacrilege, except that it is performed in a buoyant rather than malicious spirit for the common sport of all.

Of similar order were the three medieval festivals following Christmas: Holy Innocent's Day, the Feast of Fools, and the Feast of Asses.[11] On Holy Innocent's Day (*festum puerorum*), the gravity and grandeur of the holy office of bishop was suspended in the appointment of a boy bishop. For a day the awesome authority and responsibility of the church was returned to the playful innocence of childhood, with the boy bishop officiating at a service in which the ecclesiastical positions and functions were assumed by children, concluding later with his bestowal of the episcopal blessing from the residence of the archbishop. The Feast of Fools (*festum stultorum*) had less of the aura of innocence about it. In a period of revelling following Christmas, the inferior clergy burlesqued the offices and roles of their superiors. In many cases a Lord of Misrule was elected to supplant the holder of the *baculus* (wand of office), his installation occurring at Vespers during that portion of the *Magnificat* beginning with the words, "He hath put down the mighty from their seats, and exalted them of low degree" (Luke 1:52). In some instances this theme was elaborated to include also a Fool's Pope. The Feast of Asses (*festum asinorum*) became yet another vehicle for comic profanation. As a festival commemorating Mary's flight into Egypt, an ass was ridden into the sanctuary by a young girl carrying an infant boy. With the ass and its riders standing beside the altar, a mass was sung in dog-Latin rhyme, with priest and congregation braying the refrains: "Haw, Sir Ass, he-haw." The dangers of such festivities degenerating into outright sacrilege are evident in the many ecclesiastical critiques and attempts at suppression. And yet in their own bizarre ways they point to the necessity, not

[11] Cf. A. P. Rossiter, *English Drama from Early Times to the Elizabethans* (New York: Barnes & Noble, 1950), pp. 56–60.

only of permitting the periodic overturning of traditional hierarchies and structures, but, from the standpoint of both the religious celebrant and that which is celebrated, of comically profaning the sacred, and hence providing for both moments in the dialectic of holiness and humor. In fact, the double meaning of the words "celebration," "festival," and "holy day" (holiday) suggesting both solemnity and gaiety represents the historical actualization of this dialectic.

The same function has, of course, been fulfilled in all cultures, quite aside from seasonal festivities and carnivals, in the less formalized and more spontaneous indulgence in humor or invention and circulation of jokes. Whether in the repertoire of the "professional"—clown, comedian, minstrel, or jester—or in the momentary remark of the "layman," a perennial profusion of religious puns, anecdotes, and witticisms has always existed alongside sacred places, persons, beliefs, acts, and objects. They represent an inevitable, and essential, human response to the sacred. Some are completely innocuous, others quite risqué; some a profanation of the holy only in the sense of interspersing seriousness with humor, others more substantively in an overt caricature of religious and moral themes. Jokes are constantly being evoked by the sacred—not simply the responses of piety and devotion; and all attempts to suppress them are not only ineffectual but misguided. It has been the characteristic concern of despots and dogmatists alike to safeguard ideologies and dogmas from the disturbances of humor; yet comedy and laughter are at most only driven underground.

A most unusual instance of the juxtaposition of the sacred and the comic—and one that opens up further dimensions of the relationship—is to be found in the Holy Fool tradition, appearing as early as the sixth century in the Greek Orthodox Church, but reaching its fullest development in the Russian Orthodox Church between the fourteenth and the seventeenth centuries.[12] The role of the fool is here given a unique turn. Using the Pauline idea of the foolishness of Christian preaching, of the cross, and of God (I Cor. 1:18–31), and of Christian disciples as "fools for Christ's sake" (I Cor. 4:10), a type of sainthood developed in which the expression of piety was that of publicly making a fool of oneself. The monk manifested his sincerity not by projecting an atmosphere of intense seriousness and sanctity but by playing the part of the clown. He indicated his self-effacement by making himself ridiculous in his appearance and performance and thus becoming the object of mockery. He became, in effect, the court jester of the church. Through a holy madness, feigned or real, analogous to that often found among court fools, he abased himself either in a renunciation of spiritual pride or in a revelation of the folly of the people. He humbled himself, as it were, by a comic identification with the humiliation of Jesus —the Jesus that is not only a tragic but a comic hero who assumes the burdens of others as the butt of the joke, the carpenter who is hailed as king by being given a crown of thorns and a cross for a throne (a Fool's King), the scapegoat sent forth in mock regal robes who ironically saves others but cannot save himself.

The Religious Taboo Against Comedy

That proportionately little analysis in the field of religious studies has been devoted to the correlation of the sacred and the comic is itself a reflection of the defense mechanisms that commonly surround the experience of the holy. Within this experience, humor, at first sight, seems quite out of place. Even when the sacred is defined most broadly as anything or

[12] G. P. Fedotov, "The Holy Fools," *The Russian Religious Mind*, Vol. II (Cambridge: Harvard University Press, 1966), pp. 316–343.

any time that is set apart as having special importance and inviolability—as with the sacredness of one's person, property, rights, social role, etc.—humor suggests a disrespect for that particularity and importance. But especially when the sacred is defined in the profounder sense as the sphere of ultimate concern, or as the fundamental center and ground of meaning and value, does any expression of humor in relation to it appear to be simply reducible to a failure to take the sacred seriously and ultimately, perhaps even an outright rejection of its sacrality. The comic mood, therefore, gives the initial impression of standing in contradiction both to the sacredness of the sacred and to the more pious emotions and manifestations which it ordinarily evokes.

In a limited sense this sentiment is correct insofar as humor does in fact represent the refusal to take the sacred with unqualified seriousness, to absolutize the sacred, and is an act by which the sacred is momentarily and periodically profaned. There is justifiable and understandable anxiety from the side of the sacred in that humor does tend to negate the distance between the sacred and the profane, and to annul the distinction between the holy and the unholy. It is the special talent of the clown to return us to the paradise of innocence where there is neither good nor evil; and the revel and permissiveness of the carnival becomes a symbolic, if not actual, repetition of that primordial chaos prior to the creation of the sacred cosmos. Even when the distinctions between sacred and profane, or between good and evil, are kept in focus, the sphere of the comic is clearly not that of the rationality of *logos* or the legality of *nomos,* but of spontaneity, irrationality and absurdity (the basis of the comic twist). And, as the medieval church often insisted, there is a certain "pagan" aura that clings to comedy, and a demonic suggestiveness about the comic mask, if not a bit of the rogue Satan himself in the devilish gleam in the eyes of the harlequin. The sacred apart from the comic, however, is as close in its own way to the demonic as is the comic apart from the sacred.

Partly because of its "pagan" and profane connotations, and partly as a result of the taboo structure of the sacred as such, comedy within the sanctuary, or in the context of serious religious deliberation, is commonly considered quite out of keeping with the momentousness of faith and the hushed and sober mood of reverence. A certain hierarchy of emotions is viewed as appropriate to times of worship and devotion, or to earnest theological discourse, with laughter being excluded as alien to a profound spiritual sensitivity and expression. Humor is acceptable in the outer courts of the temple, perhaps in the vestibule, but hardly in the Holy of Holies. The sacred is only to be approached in fear and trembling, in aweful solemnity, in lowly obeisance and adoration, not in levity and gaiety. If there is "a time to laugh" and "a time to dance" (Eccl. 3:4) it is not at the altar but in the streets. Humor has no place therefore, it may be concluded, in matters of ultimate concern; it is out of place. Similarly, in relation to moral issues—the ethical dimension of the holy—the comic spirit suggests the opposite of that attitude of commitment and involvement so essential to moral rigor and responsible action. It seems appropriate neither to the ultimate reality of the sacred, nor to the deepest realities of the human situation. Thus, beyond a certain preliminary and largely incidental point, and apart from peripheral and miscellaneous concerns, faith it would appear excludes humor, holiness separates itself from laughter, and the sacred is lifted beyond the reaches of the profane.

Perhaps the most radical—yet by no means uncommon—declaration of this position is that made by the seventeenth-century Quaker, Robert Barclay, in his defense of strict moral and religious solemnity: "It is not lawful to use games, sports, plays, nor among other things comedies among Christians, under the notion of recreations, which do not agree with Christian silence, gravity, and sobriety; for laughing, sporting, gaming, mocking, jesting, vain talking, etc., is not Christian liberty, nor harmless mirth." [13] This type of attitude has been paid compliment by Harold Watts as "a by-product of that modesty which kept the comic writer strolling in the public square and which forbade him to have traffic with holy places, be they temples or churches, synagogues or chapels." [14] Yet, apart from the question whether this is not as much an expression of the perennial fear and suspicion the priest has of the clown and comedian as of pious constraint, the playfulness of humor, and the spontaneous irruptions of laughter, as well as the more serious forms of comedy, are in their own peculiar manner as legitimate responses to the sacred as any of the more devout posturings.

Humor lies on the frontier between the sacred and the profane. This is not to say what Niebuhr has said, that humor is "a 'no-man's land' between faith and despair." [15] The spirit and perspective of the comic stance has a more essential and intimate relation to faith and the sacred than this. To speak of humor as a profanation of the sacred is not to identify it simply with the sphere of the profane, nor with a weakening of faith, but to see in it an interlude, half-playful, half-serious, which takes place in a zone between the sacred and the profane, and which has its own validity within the religious encounter. Humor as profanation must be distinguished from humor as profanity. By profanation is not meant blasphemy or desecration. As a profanation of the sacred, humor may degenerate into outright profanity. If so, it has passed beyond

[13] *Apology for the True Christian Divinity* (1676), Defense of Proposition XV [*See Appendix*].

[14] "The Sense of Regain: A Theory of Comedy," *University of Kansas City Review,* Vol. XIII (Autumn, 1946), p. 20.

[15] *Discerning the Signs of the Times* (New York: Charles Scribner's Sons, 1946), p. 115. [See Chapter 8 below.]

the boundary between the sacred and the profane into the realm of the profane, of unfaith; it has become the raucous, hollow laughter that is outside of faith and in opposition to the sacred. It is no longer a matter of comic distance but of comic rejection. The comic mood alone is superficial and self-consuming; in this the warnings of pietists and moralists are right. If it represents merely an exchanging of the sacred for the profane, the reduction of all things to the dimensions of the farce, it is involved in a nihilation that would ultimately destroy humor as well. Seriousness is the prerequisite and ground of humor; it is the precondition apart from which humor would be reduced to cynical contempt. Especially is this true in the religious sphere where humor exists in the context of faith; if it ever dissolves this completely, it dissolves itself.

Humor as a profanation of the sacred, however, is to be differentiated from that which has no basis in the sacred, from that which is not grounded in faith. Religious expression functions within a delicate dialectic between faith and laughter. On the one side is the peril of idolatry; on the other side is the peril of cynicism. Faith without laughter leads to dogmatism, while laughter without faith leads to despair. In this sense, Niebuhr is correct in placing humor midway between faith and despair—though it is only a "no-man's land" when it ceases to be midway. There is the perennial danger that humor may slip into cynicism, that it may finally become only the last bitter guffaw of nihilism. This is the occupational hazard of the clown and the comedian, as is arrogance and pretension that of the prophet and priest. Cynicism is humor given over to despair, whereas humor itself is on the boundary between the sacred and the profane, the rational and the irrational, cosmos and chaos. In both directions lie those demonic possibilities that may be realized by eliminating either side of the dialectic of the sacred and the comic: in the one direction, absolutism and fanaticism; in the other, nihilism and absurdity.

As this suggests, the various taboos erected by the sacred against the comic are not without warrant. In particular is this true in a situation in which the sacred object or rite is not being taken seriously at all, when something is being parodied or ridiculed precisely because it is not seen as sacred. Unfortunately, the greater part of humor is of this sort. A clear distinction must therefore be drawn between inner-directed and outer-directed humor; between laughter with respect to those things that *we* cherish as sacred, and those things that *others*—in ways that may seem bizarre or foolish to us, and therefore funny—cherish as sacred. Laughter at the expense of the ideas and traditions holy to others is often but a technique of intolerance and aggression, a convenient instrument of ridicule and sport, or a means of avoiding laughter at ourselves, thereby only reinforcing our own beliefs and conventions. The comic profanation of the sacred with which we are presently concerned is not of this order, but a movement within an *inner* dialectic of the sacred and the comic. In this context the comic spirit is more than a keen wit, quick repartee, clever wordplay, or the wag's talent for making others laugh—all of which might take place completely outside the comic perspective in relation to oneself, as an examination of the biographies of certain well-known clowns and comedians would clearly reveal. An externalized sense of humor in no way guarantees its internalization. As in the case of the correlation of the comic and the tragic, there is a radical difference between comedy with respect to one's own tragedies and those of another. Laughter over the flaws and foibles of someone else, or in relation to the misfortunes that have justly or unjustly befallen another, is not only incongruous itself, but sadistic. This may, of course, be a means whereby we objectify our own circumstances, and therefore indirectly laugh at ourselves, or a pedagogical device for helping others gain sufficient perspective to be able to laugh at themselves—the inestimable value of a comic performance. But the outermost limits of laughter at another are reached in a context of justice, not injustice—e.g., when a haughty person is caught in a ridiculous pose—and even then only in a situation of relatively trifling significance. It would not, for example, be appropriate to laugh at a verdict of life imprisonment regardless of how just such a sentence might be. Aristotle called attention to this double-possibility of humor in his distinction between a "liberal" and an "illiberal" humor.[16] Like satire and irony, comedy can be used to devastate as well as temper, to deride as well as humble. It can be sarcastic, mocking, cruel, malicious, vulgar, and bitter. The laughter of the mob at the crucifixion of Jesus was of this baser sort: "He saved others, himself he cannot save." This, however, is humor outside of both innocence and faith; it is humor in the hands of pride, belligerence, and unbelief. Here it becomes a bad joke—in the most literal sense a "sick joke."

Even humor in relation to oneself can be a two-edged sword. On the one hand it can become a masochistic device for self-abasement and humiliation. On the other hand, and more commonly, it can become a means of avoiding, rather than moving toward, humility and contrition. It is possible to laugh at oneself as a way of excusing oneself, as a technique for not looking candidly at oneself, and of casually evading the deeper necessities of repentance, seeking forgiveness, and gaining restitution and change. Here humor, instead of being the servant of seriousness and objectivity, becomes the screen of irresponsibility. Instead of the harlequin's costume serving to unmask pretension, it may only mask it more effectively. Humor can become an easy path of escape from intellectual labor, moral accountability, and religious commitment. It

[16] *Nichomachean Ethics* viii.

can degenerate into a frivolous diversion from the tortuous and often intractable issues that confront mankind. It can become a substitute for all seriousness whatever. If it is to perform the task of leveling or tempering or amelioration, it requires a profounder setting than it could ever pretend to provide.

The comic, therefore, requires the sacred as much as does the sacred the comic. Obviously humor by itself is not enough; this is the limit of all comic profanation. It is not a substitute for rigorous thought and action. In itself it is powerless to solve the deepest problems of human existence. It is incapable singlehandedly of overcoming meaninglessness, of assuaging suffering, of redeeming sin and guilt, or of preventing the dissolution of itself in cynicism and despair.[17] Without faith, humor becomes superficial, empty, and helpless. Laughter turns into mockery, banter into blasphemy, comedy into tragedy. Humor passes over into despair if it has no groundedness in the sacred, if it is not essentially and inwardly related to holy things. But if it has this foundation, it can play its own peculiar role in the inner dialectic of the sacred and the comic.

[17] See Chapter 8.

The Humanity of Comedy

WILLIAM F. LYNCH

To our inquiry as to what comedy is, we get our first if superficial sense of an answer from its vocabulary. Its image of the finite is the most concrete, the most dense, of all the images created by the art of man. In terms, then, of its peculiar images, it is the most cognitive and least magical of the arts. If, as I believe, it proposes these images as a road into the infinite, it hides nothing, and reveals most, of the finite as such a path. Indeed, its whole function is to be a perpetual and funny, if disconcerting, reminder that it is the limited concrete which is the path to insight and salvation. Its whole art is to be an art of anamnesis, or memory, of the bloody human (in the sense in which the English use that adjective) as a path to God, or to any form of the great.

In *Hobson's Choice*, the cinematic art of comedy revolves around its center in the form of a brass ring which has originally tied the fortunes of Maggie and Willie together in the days of their hardships. In the days of the beginning of glory Willie wishes to supplant the brass with gold, but Maggie, with her comic memory, will have none of it and clings to the brass. Comedy is perpetually reminding the uprooted great man that in some important sense he was once, and still is, a bit of a monkey. Thus, in the Scotch film, *High and Dry,* the American great man cries out that "nobody's going to get away with trying to make a monkey out of me." But the Scotch peasants *do* make a monkey out of him, and do reduce the new, "god-like" American rhythms to the subjection of their own incredibly permanent rhythms. The same thing happens to Jacques Tati in *The Big Day.* As village postman, he too aspires one day to the dream rhythms and power of the American postman ("neither wind nor rain . . ."). But the fabulously old lady reminds him in the end that this is a brilliant task for little Victor the child, and there are other and more basic musical modes for the soul of a man. In the movie *Tight Little Island,* there are two comic visions which emerge for the metaphysics of the comic: 1. The brilliant power of the finite, the age-old power of the people, i.e., of man, comes forth in the endless resourcefulness of the islanders for the hiding of their whiskey from the "god-like" man of this particular situation; 2. The complete and funny reminding of the collapsibility of the divine man is demonstrated to the echo of the laughter of a whole people. This time the great refrain to be attacked had been: "Anybody who knows me knows that when I start a thing I push it all the way through."

The one offense, therefore, which comedy cannot endure is that a man should forget he is man, or should substitute a phony faith for faith in the power of the vulgar and limited finite. The key sentence which describes its art in terms of its opposite is the sentence of Prince Hal, in forgetful glory, to Falstaff: "I know thee not, old man." The comic hates all the forms of the man who cannot stand the sight of himself, and it would have understood the words of Christ to Judas who could not stand this sight, as Peter could after a sin as great. But this case of Judas is, of course, only the sinful and most serious form of the non-comic. Below it are a thousand other forms of the refusal to remember, ranging all the way from the forgetfulness of Falstaff's friend Justice Shallow ("I will devise matter enough out of this Shallow to keep Prince Harry in continual laughter . . . O, you shall see him laugh till his face be like a wet cloak ill laid up . . . this Shallow, now in glory, was for all the world like a forked radish, with a head fantastically carved upon it with a knife") to the classical example of the dignified man who is disturbed because he slips on a banana. We are not Judas but we are all guilty, in a little way, of the fear of being man.

There are different levels of comic remembrance and, even though we need not equate them, at least they are all somehow one in some kind of love of the human and some kind of refusal to be ashamed of human parentage. Sometimes the deliberate image of the ugly human actuality is only the image of wit, anything not to miss a point (cf. Falstaff's "I will turn diseases to commodity"). Again it may be only the sudden insertion, into the perfect, perfect Morris dance movement, of a crazy irregularity which simply cannot tolerate the perfect, univocal form. Or it may be the brass ring of Maggie. At the top of the heap of memory is the intense remembrance of the souls in glory in the *Paradiso* who long for the day when again they shall possess those bodies that had budded forth such glory and shall someday add to it. These present lines on comedy are written on the eve of Christmas, so that, finally, this writer cannot help but think of the liturgy's anamnesis, its recalling of the power of the earth in which the maggots and the Sybil work to bud forth a Saviour (*aperiatur terra et germinet Salvatorem*). These memories are profoundly one and profoundly different, one enough to make our point, different enough to save our reverence.

The Pseudo-Comic

Unfortunately, there are many kinds of remembrance. One presumes, even from the purely biological feeling in the stomach which springs out of the comic memory, that it involves funniness and a kind of joy; but not every recalling does this. Perhaps it is better, before analyzing the anamnesis which is proper to comedy, to eliminate all the forms of remembrance which are not at all comic.

1. Let us start with the "comedy" of the clown. I place the word in quotes because he may be entertaining, but I do not believe that he is really funny. He is basically sad, and perhaps the word *frightening* is not too strong a word for him. Indeed, he remembers the human condition, but is it not clear to all at times that he feels he is *trapped* in that situation, and really feels he is crucified? Charlie Chaplin is certainly an artist who sums up many comic strains; when he becomes rich and in the midst of it is driven by the comic instinct to pick up the precious cigarette butt from the gutter, the vision of the comic is there. But it is not altogether surprising, perhaps it is rooted in the deepest corners of the self-pitying spirituality of the clown, that Chaplin himself should have hated the role of Charlie ("I've finally gotten rid of the little bastard"). And it is hard for some of us to accept the final vision, no matter what our trap today, behind the clown art of Rouault. This may be an art that does not leave room, with its clown Christ, for the slightest sense of the Christus Victor (even on the Cross) who has been so indigenous to certain periods of Christian art. We shall have something to say later about this triumphant note in comedy itself, and we give only an example of it now, from *The Horse's Mouth*. Gulley Jimson discourses as follows about this remarkable strength of the truly comic figure:

I'm not a wild ass of the desert, I'm an old hoss. I know something. I've been ridden by the nobility and gentry. Millionaires have cut an important figure on my back. Hickson kept me in the stable for years and trotted me out for his visitors. His Gulley Jimson, his pride and his joy. My stomach has had two kicks a day for sixty years, one to put the saddle on and one to take it off. It can take anything. And eat its own hay. And organize its own kicks. And save up a bite that will take the bloody pants off the seat of government. If it likes.[1]

This is surely a kind of theme song of what we conceive to be the truest and the most accurate form of comedy and laughter: this song of indestructibility, the song of the indestructibility of the people. In preliminary theorizing on this subject I had long been tempted to think that the following was one of the basic lines of division between tragedy and comedy: in the first, we are in full unhidden contact with the real world and we suffer its consequences, whatever the consequences of being; in comedy it seemed that the suppositions were different. We were to hypothesize that the man does not really get hurt as he flies out the window or is hit by a pie. The assumption was the assumption of unreality, psychic distance with a vengeance. I now prefer to think that the comic chant is altogether different. It chants the fundamental indestructibility, the strength, of the human thing, of the finite with the vulgar interstices and smells, which lies below all categories. The chant is there. It is there, if you remember, in the five cars that come banging violently together to the sound of hé-hi-hé-hi-hó in *The Lavender Hill Mob*. Nobody gets hurt in this world because this is a region below all temporal status or manners or category where it is impossible that anybody be hurt. Rock bottom being cannot be hurt. It is not the world of the clown. There is no sadness or self-pity in it. Our only sad lot is that

[1] Joyce Cary, *The Horse's Mouth* (London: Michael Joseph, 1953), p. 114.

we have lost contact with it; we live in a world of categories where we are always threatened.

It is only on the level of truly popular being that we can find indestructibility, equality before any man, and freedom; but today it is a level not much in fashion. It is regarded with a squint and thought to be a pitiful thing which requires many defenses. Not so, though, with Sancho Panza. He has just been patronizingly asked to the table of Don Quixote, "that you may be even as I who am your master and natural lord, and eat from my plate and drink from where I drink; for of knight-erranting one may say the same as of love: that it makes all things equal"; to which Sancho replies:

Many thanks . . . but if it is all the same to your grace, provided there is enough to go around, I can eat just as well, or better, standing up and alone as I can seated beside an emperor. And if the truth must be told, I enjoy much more that which I eat in my own corner without any bowings and scrapings, even though it be only bread and onions, than I do a meal of roast turkey where I have to chew slowly, drink little, be always wiping my mouth, and can neither sneeze nor cough if I feel like it, nor do any of those things that you can when you are free and alone.[2]

Again there is no clownish sadness here, nor feeling of being trapped in the desperate predicament of being human. Rather there is a kind of native confidence, not in power, but in the power of rock bottom being. And it is just this confidence and vitality which this chapter proposes as a substantial clue to the mystery of comedy.

2. We turn next to the meticulous man. If ever there was a non-comic man, it is he. For he recalls whence he was born, but with a refined if not a violent distaste. He is a fastidious, prim and ritualistic man, not with a ritual that is the crown of

[2] Miguel de Cervantes, *Don Quixote*, p. 80.

religious passion and a true revelation, but with one that has a nice geometric movement safely separated from both. Here is the way *he* remembers the human (it is a pity to take these lines from a comedian of the stature of George Bernard Shaw, but he was indiscreet enough to have written them and thus for a moment to have revealed as much of his contempt for his trade as did Chaplin):

In Italy, for instance, churches are used in such a way that priceless pictures become smeared with filthy tallow-soot, and have sometimes to be rescued by the temporal power and placed in national galleries. But worse than this are the innumerable daily services which disturb the truly religious visitor. If these were decently and intelligently conducted by genuine mystics to whom the mass was no mere rite or miracle, but a real communion, the celebrants might reasonably claim a place in the church as their share of the common human right to its use. But the average Italian priest, personally uncleanly, and with chronic catarrh of the nose and throat, produced and maintained by sleeping and living in frowsy, ill-ventilated rooms, punctuating his gabbled Latin only by expectorative hawking, and making the decent guest sicken and shiver every time the horrible splash of spitten mucus echoes along the vaulting from the marble steps of the altar: this unseemly wretch should be seized and put out, bell, book, candle, and all, until he learns to behave himself.[3]

It would be hard to find another paragraph which images forth so perfectly the meticulosity of the new religious man. And this writer cannot but feel that there is a marked, if somewhat elliptic, parity between this Shavian distaste and the distaste with which the sophisticated instincts of every form of pure intellectualism, and every form of "pure" and invisible religion, confront the historicity of Christ and Christianity.

[3] Bernard Shaw, *An Essay on Going to Church* (Boston: John W. Luce & Co., 1905), pp. 50–51.

The sins of Rabelais and the guilty conscience of Chaucer are much less remote from the truth. If it were only a problem of belief, of an inability on the top of the head to believe in the actual, then the problem would be relatively light. But this non-comic sense, the lack of confidence in rock bottom being, has invaded every level of the human personality. Even with the people, it begins to lead to a tenuous and seductive culture which must lure them away from that true comedy which was the proud invention of their fathers' fathers.

Is not this, indeed, our greatest cultural crime, that we un-people the people and steal from them their comic sense of their own inward worth, which needs no cheap potions or irrelevant magics? But much of our present situation is the work of meticulous men who hardly dare to remember their parentage and who have accomplished the stunningly clever trick of telling us *ad nauseam* that this is what the people want, that those who wish rememberingly to defend the people are eggheads. In this whole matter of eggheads, we must alas realize there are two kinds: one who roosts among the intellectuals of the far Left and has scant regard for the tradition of the people, and another, a far more baleful threat, who is artificially concocting in his Hollywood and TV factories a new tradition of a cheap angelism for all the people, and is, unfortunately, totally accepted by them for the moment—as his alienated, nonconformist brother of the Left is not. Let us only hope that what Chesterton said of England ("The people of England have not spoken yet") is also true of this country. And hasten, O Lord, the day of speech.

3. We could at this stage spend a great deal of time on the genesis and the history of the idea of disgust. Jean-Paul Sartre and some of his colleagues have made a profession of the idea, but theirs is only a sleight-of-hand, a brilliantly dialectical summary of the wave of nausea that has plagued the poets since the latter part of the nineteenth century. However, to

trace history here is deceptive; what seems truer is to recognize that disgust is an indigenous, ever-cropping strain of the human spirit, very close to comedy but with a devil of a difference. Indeed, that is why it is essential to treat the subject here, in order to sort out the laughter of the disgusted man from the comic. There is such a thing as a love of disgust, a professional love of the monstrous, which is as far away from Falstaffian man as night is from day. One of the great technical (and theological!) questions, therefore, is: How far can you go in inventing interstices and smells for man before you are lodged in the disgusting, the monstrous, and (this is the point) the non-human? This is the critical problem of the difference between laughter at the human and the non-human.

There is a little section in the play within a play in *Midsummer-Night's Dream* which may be taken as a miniature essay on this problem of disgust. Its simple, total point is that in penetrating to the concrete human which is the subject of comedy one cannot pass beyond the point where the memory of the human has been transgressed or annihilated. Despite its length, I include it; only recollect how the playlet, in its wildest fantasy, is only dealing with Bottom the weaver and Snug the joiner.

BOTTOM: There are things in this comedy of Pyramus and Thisby that will never please. First, Pyramus must draw a sword to kill himself, which the ladies cannot abide. How answer you that?
SNOUT: By'r laking, a parlous fear.
STARVELING: I believe we must leave the killing out, when all is done.
BOTTOM: Not a whit: I have a device to make all well. Write me a prologue; and let the prologue seem to say, we will do no harm with our swords, and that Pyramus is not killed indeed; and, for the more better assurance, tell them that I Pyramus, am not

Pyramus, but Bottom the weaver, this will put them out of fear.
SNOUT: Will not the ladies be afeared of the lion?
STARVELING: I fear it, I promise you.
BOTTOM: Masters, you ought to consider with yourselves: to bring in, God shield us!—a lion among ladies, is a most dreadful thing; for there is not a more fearful wildfowl than your lion living, and we ought to look to it.
SNOUT: Therefore, another prologue must tell he is not a lion.
BOTTOM: Nay, you must name his name, and half his face must be seen through the lion's neck; and he himself must speak through, saying thus, or to the same defect, 'Ladies,' or 'Fair Ladies,' 'I would wish you,' or, 'I would request you,' or, 'I would entreat you, not to fear, not to tremble: my life for yours. If you think I come hither as a lion, it were pity of my life: no, I am no such thing: I am a man as other men are:' and there indeed let him name his name, and tell them plainly he is Snug the joiner.

Enter Puck. You may love him but he seems a dubious comic spirit: he is intent on transforming the human. Why are we frightened at his work?—because we are frightened at that which comes into our world as the strange, the totally non-human, the Other, the invader, man as *really* an ass. In the following scene, Bottom is no longer recognizable as Bottom.

QUINCE: O monstrous! O strange! we are haunted. Pray, masters! fly masters. Help!
PUCK: I'll follow you, I'll lead you about a round,
Through bog, through bush, through brake, through brier:
Sometime a horse I'll be, sometime a hound,
A hog, a headless bear, sometimes a fire:
And neigh, and bark, and grunt, and roar, and burn,
Like horse, hound, hog, bear, fire, at every turn.
BOTTOM: Why do they run away? this is a knavery of them to make me afeard.
SNOUT: O Bottom, thou art changed! what do I see on thee?

BOTTOM: What do you see? you see an ass-head of your own, do you?
QUINCE: Bless thee, Bottom! bless thee! thou art translated.
BOTTOM: I see their knavery: this is to make an ass of me; to fright me, if they could.

The variety of levels of Pucks in human history have been endless. They are never comic. In most cases they are harmless; in others their essentially non-human point becomes startlingly clear. In some periods there is an intellectual finesse about the abandonment of the human as a way into being (witness the story of the decadents in the nineteenth century); in others the professional interest in the monstrous is open, flagrant and public; you are protected from the fright because other fools are laughing with you; it is a public act of laughter. Let us go further:

Lampridius tells us that Alexander Severus could make no use of all the male and female dwarfs, fools, worthless chattering fellows, actors and pantomimes collected by his predecessor, Heliogabalus, so he gave them away to the people. Plutarch describes how in the market in Rome many purchasers would pay no attention to the most beautiful slave girls and boys who were exposed for sale and would seek out horrible freaks and monstrosities. Longinus tells us that children were deliberately stunted, and Quintilian observes that the greater the deformity the higher was the purchase price of these unfortunates. Imbecility, like deformity, had evidently a real pecuniary value: "He has been described as an idiot," says Martial indignantly, "I bought him for twenty thousand sesterces. Give me back my money, Gargilianus, he has his wits." [4]

This is indeed degenerate curiosity and the love of disgust, witless laughter at the witless. But we need not be too quick to judge. There is in our own air many a Puck and many a

[4] Enid Welsford, *The Fool, His Social and Literary History* (London: Faber & Faber, 1935), pp. 58–59.

Heliogabalus trying to turn us humans into asses and witless people, who will think as they do that their comedy, their songs, their rhythms, are funny.

4. We come at last to the laughter of hatred. The fundamental rationale behind this form of non-comic humor is that it hates the human and, desiring to wipe out the memory of it, desires to destroy the thing itself. In Adrian Leverkuhn, the hero of Thomas Mann's *Doctor Faustus,* we have the pure intellectual, the kind of brilliant student who lives off the very topmost part of his head, unmothered by the earth. It is always so hard to tell whether the laughter he moves toward is that of a child or a devil. Leverkuhn begins with uninterest:

Oddly enough, it was best at the grammar school, there I was pretty much in the right place, because in the upper forms they dealt out the greatest variety of things, one after the other, changing the subject from one five-and-forty minutes to the next— in other words there was still no progression. But even those five-and-forty minutes were too long, they bored one—and boredom is the coldest thing in the world.[5]

The genesis of diabolical laughter continues ("I am embarrassed at the insipidness which is the supporting structure of even the work of genius"). Nothing is serious, everything is a parody of itself, about to laugh at itself. It has to laugh, it was born laughing, it suddenly sees that the most divine beauty carved by man has a trick of matter or man behind it, stupid, produced, and grown out of mud or an onion. ("And I, abandoned wretch, I have to laugh, particularly at the grunting supporting notes of the bombardone, Bum, bum, bum, bang!") Can you imagine, O Beauty, O Angel, being born of a double bassoon? Can any good come out of Nazareth? "I have always had to laugh, most damnably, at the most mysterious and im-

[5] Thomas Mann, *Doctor Faustus* (New York: Alfred A. Knopf, 1948), p. 130.

pressive phenomena. I fled from this exaggerated sense of the comic into theology, in the hope that it would give relief to the tickling—only to find there too a perfect legion of ludicrous absurdities." [6]

There is the problem of the comic and theology in a nutshell. The scandal of the double bassoon and the earth and Christ and the hatred of the pure intelligence for all three. The permanent debate of our time is really between two forms of intellectualism, the forms which I will take the liberty of calling the analogical and the univocal intelligences. Much may be learned about the comic by observing how it aligns itself in this debate.

Comedy and the Univocal

The comic is par excellence the great enemy of the univocal mind. I call univocal that kind of mind which, having won through to all the legitimate unities and orderings of the logical and rational intelligence, insists, thereafter, on descending through the diversities, densities and maelstroms of reality in such a way as to give absolute shape to it through these unities and orderings. This mentality wishes to reduce and flatten everything to the terms of its own sameness, since it cannot abide the intractable differences, zigzags and surprises of the actual. It is, therefore, impatient, rigid, inflexible, intolerant, and even ruthless.

Here the rigid thinker and the classical dreamer are at one. Alcestes in *The Misanthrope* has simply made up his mind that his lawsuit is just, and therefore will not make a single contact with the realities of his legal situation ("I am in the wrong, or I am in the right"). There are moralists like that; Pascal thought the Jesuits impious because they polluted them-

[6] *Ibid.*, p. 134.

selves with the realities of moral cases. And what shall we say of the incredible purity from reality of Don Quixote; he rescues a young lad from a cruel switching by a country tyrant, and then tells the lad to go home with his master who will no more switch him ever ("It is sufficient for me to command, and he out of respect will obey"). Notice the hankering for divine power, free of the mud of detail or precaution. And notice how the human comic, aware of the absurd in reality, inverts the phrase ("I have but to say a word, and my dog does what he pleases").

On the surface, comedy, with its antipathy to the order of things, seems anarchic (and, indeed, it does have a propensity for thieves, villains, drunkards, fools, idiots, lawbreakers and other people like the reader and the writer). But it is not at all anarchic; it is only a defender of another and more human order (more muddy, more actual, more free). Metaphysically it is a defender of being against the pure concept or category. We have seen how in the perfect Morris dance it must introduce the note of irregularity for very sanity's sake. In *Tight Little Island* it is inveighing against a pharisaical order, upon all those who from the chair of Moses impose too great a burden upon the people. In the medieval Feast of Fools, it annually gave itself a bit of a foolish fling because of its little fear of the non-human in the sacred order. And it is significant that this comic intrusion into the liturgy began with the singing of the Magnificat at vespers, with the words "He hath put down the mighty from their seat and hath exalted the humble and meek."

Eliot has said that "human kind cannot bear very much reality." I am not so sure of that. The bigger truth is that they cannot stand very much unreality. At any rate, he might also have said, were he writing a comedy, that men cannot stand too much order. Observe the characters who are so classically non-comic: the heretic, who sees all reality as simple and reduces a multitudinous creed to a single, exacerbating, crusading formula; the scrupulous man who reduces the overflowing life of being and the mind to a worrisome pin point; the great conquerors, the men who have the universe under perfect control and have it forever fixed in an icy stare.

Comedy and Analogy

We must, then, look for a form of order that orders indeed, but leaves reality, every iota of yours and mine, intact— multitudinous, different and free, but together at last. This is what we call analogical order, and it is the home of the comic. What is it?

The medieval idea of the analogy of being is a fascinating doctrine. On the surface all it says is that being is the same and one everywhere, but everywhere profoundly different. Every difference this tremendous drive in the world creates is being and is one. Thus this unity cannot proceed one generative step without creating difference (the many) and without creating itself (the one). Therefore, it need not move out of itself to be enormously creative, open and free. But this is the most fundamental statement of comic remembrance: that a thing need not step out of the human to be all things, and to achieve the liberty of the children of God. The mud in man, the lowermost point in the subway, is nothing to be ashamed of. It can produce (St. Thomas would call it *potentia oboedientialis*) the face of God. *Aperiatur terra et germinet Salvatorem.*

What is funny? Things are funny, precisely because they can recall the relation between God and themselves. In tragedy the fact of the comic is concealed precisely because the inner logic of the action (a man moves from unawareness to awareness) is so extraordinarily logical, tied together and complete (as in the case of Oedipus). Nothing is omitted; step calls for step, emotion for emotion, word for word. Until we forget, for the logic, that "my end is my beginning." To recall this, to recall this incredible relation between mud and God, is, in its own distant, adumbrating way, the function of comedy.

This anamnesis is accomplished in either of two comic ways. By foreshortening the steps between the beginning and the end, or by multiplying them—far beyond the perfect logic of tragic action.

1. By foreshortening: the comic is sudden, and full of surprises and skippings of intervening steps; the man of dignity (he could be the saint) slips on the banana peel. The lion is Bottom. The Pope is dust. Let us not talk of incongruity as the secret clue to comedy, but of congruity, of the tie between the earth and Christ, with all the logic omitted. Why should we laugh or magnify the Lord? Because this is the way things are.

2. Or by multiplying the intervening steps. So that the bewildering vitality of the finite, within the analogical form, goes beyond the logic of tragedy and everything is seen as lively and extraordinarily bouncing. This is the method of Rube Goldberg. That this should lead to this! The buffoon exploits his own weaknesses. Falstaff says: "I shall turn diseases into commodity." Gulley Jimson says: "See what my mother became in the years of misery; a great human; a person in the grand style. Yes, by God, you need technique to make a good job out of life. All you can get. You need to take necessity and make her do what you want; get your feet on her old bones and build your mansions out of her rock." And St. Paul said: "I glory in my infirmities."

It is ridiculous, in a Catholic world, to be afraid of the irreverent in so many secret places. Therefore, the thoughts of the writer, as he thinks of the glory of the comic, turn to the Mother of God. In the office of the Feast of the Circumcision there are these words which think of her: *cum essem parvula, placui Altissimo, et de meis visceribus genui Deum et hominem. Beatam me dicent omnes generationes, quia ancillam humilem respexit Deus.*

Cum essem parvula. Though I was small, and very small, I was pleasing to the Most High. Does this not seem, we say it with reverence, to be the final clue to a theory of the comic which, if pitched below the theological level, would make stupid sense indeed? The sins of comedy are many, but not incarnadine. They are vulgar, but being blessedly vulgar— and completely literary in the most decent sense of the word— they pass far beyond that world where in the morning Walter Pater put in a comma and in the evening took it out. The sins of comedy have been many indeed; but they have never been in the direction of the fastidious or the aesthetic or the magical. Therefore, much will be forgiven it. Comedy, on its own modest level, has stood in the adumbrated presence of that Lady who was herself surprised that this could lead to that.

The abyss of the finite, tragedy stands, as it were, in the presence of God (abyss calls to abyss). Therefore it does not laugh. But comedy stands, with full, cognitive confrontation and remembrance, in the presence of man, down to the last inch of the little beastie. And seeing what can come of it, seeing how safe and strong a way it is, seeing, through its own ruses and techniques, what St. Thomas meant by being and *potentia oboedientialis,* it laughs indeed. For things *are* funny and a final theory of comedy must be as simple as that.

THREE

The Bias of Comedy and the Narrow Escape into Faith

NATHAN A. SCOTT, JR.

"Comedy," Aristotle tells us, "aims at representing men as worse, Tragedy as better than in actual life." But is this really so? It is true, of course, that tragedy and comedy represent men differently, but is the difference quite of the sort which Aristotle suggests?

Let us approach the matter in this way. We may say, I think, that true tragedy has always thrust us into those acute situations of crisis in which man's unhappy consciousness of the contradictions of human existence impels him to perform an act of radical self-transcendence. He is led to ask himself what it means to be a man, what it means to-be rather than not-to-be, and how dependable is the essentially human thing in himself. And when a man thus becomes a problem to himself, it is because in some critical moment life, in its fundamental axiological structure, has appeared to be at cross-purposes with itself, ultimately and irremediably. He discovers that what he believes to be most valid and authentic in himself is somehow radically contradicted or threatened by the objective order that constitutes the theatre of the human enterprise. So he begins to wonder how he can "choose" himself, or if perhaps, in a universe in which man, as such, is fundamentally defective, his having already "chosen" himself is not the cause of his present embarrassments. In this "boundary-situation," the tragic man is not simply a passive agonizer: he is committed to a course of action, and this is why it is proper to refer, as we do, to the great tragedies in literature as "tragic actions," for in them the central figure is one who not only suffers but who actively resists whatever it is that would destroy his dignity and bring to naught his highest purposes. What we see, in Richard Sewall's summary of the matter, is "man at the limits of his sovereignty—Job on the ash-heap, Prometheus on the crag, Oedipus in his moment of self-discovery, Lear on the heath, Ahab on his lonely quarter-deck." And here, "with all the protective covering ripped off," [1] the hero, facing into the utter insecurity of his situation, is led to muster all his resources in one great effort to transcend the fundamental limitations of his creaturehood. It is not, as Aristotle says, that he is better than we are: it is rather that he is, as Henry Myers puts it, more of an extremist than most of us are. "To reach his goal, whatever it may be, he is always willing to sacrifice everything else, including his life. Oedipus will press the search for the unknown murderer, although he is warned of the consequences; Hamlet will prove the King's guilt and attempt to execute perfect justice, whatever the cost may be to his mother, to Laertes, to Ophelia, and to himself; Ibsen's Solness will climb the tower he has built, at the

[1] Richard B. Sewall, *The Vision of Tragedy* (New Haven, Yale University Press, 1959), p. 5.

risk of falling into the quarry; Ahab will kill Moby Dick or die in the attempt." [2] It is precisely with this kind of intensity that the protagonists of the great tragic actions live in the world; and it is, therefore, not surprising that most of them die early and never enjoy the felicity of a long and complete life. For they soon exhaust themselves in the effort to gain release from the restrictions that are a consequence of their finitude: this is an essential part of what we are to include in the "tragic rhythm of action," which is the rhythm that man's life has when it is lived at the difficult and perilous limits of human capability.[3]

However, the systole and diastole of the "comic rhythm of action" are altogether different, and the best way of measuring the difference is to consider the personage who has always been the presiding genius of comedy—namely, the clown. The particular clown I want to recall is Charlie Chaplin, whose art places him, I believe, among the few great comic geniuses of the modern period. It is not, however, the Chaplin image of the late films—*Monsieur Verdoux,* or *Limelight,* or even *The Great Dictator*—that I have in mind, but rather the Tramp of the early and middle films, *The Kid* and *The Gold Rush* and *City Lights*: the little, downtrodden, but urbane and chivalrous man in big, baggy trousers and wrinkled, out-of-size shoes, who has an expression of amazement and alarm written into the innocence of his face. This is the Chaplin who has provided us with an image more memorable than any other in cinema history of the lonely, unprotected individual clinging to his humanity amid the horrible impersonality and dehumanization of the modern world. Charlie's Tramp represented the little man, the *homunculus,*

[2] Henry Alonzo Myers, *Tragedy: A View of Life* (Ithaca, Cornell University Press, 1956), p. 45.

[3] See Francis Fergusson, *The Idea of a Theatre* (Princeton, Princeton University Press, 1949), Ch. 1.

who, amid the dreary facelessness of men completely involved in the rituals of a money culture, insisted on behaving as though his fellow human beings were still human. And he was, of course, as a result, to them a scandal, an utterly absurd little scandal. But he was never regarded as a serious threat, for the society's dedication to its materialism was so complete that no one ever really took the trouble to consider his eccentricity for the profoundly subversive thing it was: in film after film he was simply regarded by the sober fools with whom he collided as a charming, though utterly irrelevant, little scapegrace.

Yet, erratic and unpredictable as the Tramp's behavior was, he was never ridiculous. One wants instead to say that he was touching, for everything that he did was so utterly human, even his pranks and his mischief. And when one occasionally sees these old films again in little art-cinema houses, one feels that here is a man, that here is a richly particularized and wonderfully eccentric human being living out his life—a little hobo whose every gesture somehow manages to redeem the human image by revealing how beautifully mysterious it would be were it unencumbered by the mechanical reflexes which it has learned in an unpropitious time. When, in *The Kid*, he dreams that all men are angels, when he topples over the bannisters in *His Favorite Pastime*, when he shares his last sausage with a bulldog in *The Champion*, when he sets out to walk to the horizon in *The Tramp*, we feel that here is the real human thing itself—clothed not in the unearthly magnificence of tragic heroism but in the awkward innocence of essential humanity.

A particularly memorable film is *City Lights*, in which Charlie strikes up a relation with a rich man on a drunken spree who, taking a fancy to him, domiciles him in his great mansion. But when his host recovers his sobriety, he is so repelled by the little man that he flings him out of the house.

And the fun of the movie arises out of the alternations that ensue between inebriate acceptance and sober rejection and that continue, to Charlie's utter bafflement. In the allegory of the film, the rich man is a representative of that bourgeois mentality which is completely captive to the materialistic ethic of "the skin game." When he is half intoxicated, he cannot resist the charming gaiety and insouciance of the little fellow who regards material affluence as too ephemeral and as requiring altogether too much trouble to make it worth scrambling after. One suspects that the rich man embraces Charlie in his drunkenness because the lackadaisical little tramp is in some way his own deeper self which he has submerged and repressed and for which he yearns. But in his moments of sobriety he rejects Charlie, expels him from his house. Again, one suspects that he does so because the tramp, with his languid, smiling irony, engenders in him the remembrance that to be a man and to be a great material success are not one and the same thing, and this is a fact which he has not the courage to face. So he finally drives the clown out of his life, since Charlie evokes memories with which he has not the spiritual resources to deal.[4]

Here we come upon what is perhaps the basic function of the comic man, and it is, I believe, simply to be a kind of icon of the human actuality. It is not, as Aristotle says, that the tragic man is better than we are: no, what differentiates him from the rest of us is that he is more of an extremist than most of us are; and, in the resistance he offers to whatever he feels ultimately to threaten the human enterprise, he is, by seeking to transcend the limitations that attach to our creatureliness, always in danger of forgetting that he is not an angel and only a man. Moreover, the comic man is not, as Aristotle says, worse than we are: on the contrary, it is his

[4] See Parker Tyler, *Magic and Myth of the Movies* (New York, Henry Holt, 1947), pp. 36–38.

function simply to be an example of the contingent, imperfect, earth-bound creatures that in truth we all really are, and it is also his function to awaken in us a lively recognition of what in fact our true status is. He asks us not to be afraid to acknowledge that we are only human and that our residence is not in the heavens. And he asks us to examine critically all the spurious stratagems we employ to evade a frank acceptance of our finitude, whether they be those of bourgeois worldliness or of philosophical and religious mysticism. What the comic man cannot abide is the man who will not consent to be simply a man, who cannot tolerate the thought of himself as an incomplete and conditioned creature of a particular time and a particular place.

The great difference between the tragic man and the comic man is something that arises out of their different ways of dealing with the burden of human finitude. For the tragic man it is a profound embarrassment and perhaps even a curse, for he would rather be pure intellect or pure will or pure something-or-other, and nothing wounds him more deeply than to be reminded that his life is a conditioned thing and that there is nothing absolute at all in the human stuff out of which he is made. But the comic man is unembarrassed by even the grossest expressions of his creatureliness: though the world may not be all dandy, he has no sense of being under any cruel condemnation; nor does he have any sense of desperate entrapment within a prison. He can say, without ironic bitterness, "I'm only human," in full recognition of the fact that making this admission is itself the condition of his life's being tolerable and of his being able to address to God an appropriate *Confiteor*. He does not insist upon life's conforming to his own special requirements but consents to take it on the terms of its own created actuality, and the art of comedy is devoted to an exhibition of his deep involvement in the world: so it shirks nothing—none of the irrelevant absurdities, none of the vexatious inconveniences that are the lot of such finite creatures as ourselves.

An incisive essay by Aldous Huxley, "Tragedy and the Whole Truth," begins by recalling that famous Twelfth Book of Homer's *Odyssey,* in which Odysseus and his men, in the course of their journey back to Ithaca, encounter the monster Scylla and the whirlpool Charybdis. And in this story, Odysseus relives that dreadful day and sadly remembers the poor, hapless souls whom Scylla had devoured. He again sees them being lifted, struggling, into the air: he hears their screams and the despairing cries for help. He recalls how he and the other survivors could only look helplessly on at the awful struggle, and adds that it was the most pitiable sight he had ever seen in all his "explorings of the passes of the sea." But, then, once the danger that night had been passed, Odysseus and his men went ashore to prepare their dinner on the Sicilian beach—and prepared it, Homer says, "expertly." The entire episode is concluded by the poet's telling us that "when they had satisfied their thirst and hunger, they thought of their dear companions and wept, and in the midst of their tears sleep came gently upon them."

Now this, Mr. Huxley tells us, is "the truth, the whole truth and nothing but the truth."

In any other poem but the *Odyssey,* what would the survivors have done? They would, of course, have wept, even as Homer made them weep. But would they previously have cooked their supper, and cooked it, what's more, in a masterly fashion? Would they previously have drunk and eaten to satiety? And after weeping, or actually while weeping, would they have dropped quietly off to sleep? No, they most certainly would not have done any of these things. They would simply have wept, lamenting their own misfortune and the horrible fate of their companions, and the canto would have ended tragically on their tears.

Homer, however, preferred to tell the Whole Truth. He knew

that even the most cruelly bereaved must eat; that hunger is stronger than sorrow and that its satisfaction takes precedence even of tears. He knew that experts continue to act expertly and to find satisfaction in their accomplishment, even when friends have just been eaten, even when the accomplishment is only cooking the supper. He knew that, when the belly is full (and only when the belly is full) men can afford to grieve, and that sorrow after supper is almost a luxury. And finally he knew that, even as hunger takes precedence of grief, so fatigue, supervening, cuts short its career and drowns it in a sleep all the sweeter for bringing forgetfulness of bereavement. In a word, Homer refused to treat the theme tragically. He preferred to tell the Whole Truth.[5]

Now Mr. Huxley does not go on to say that the Whole Truth is the truth of comedy, but this is a line that he might very well have taken. Indeed, if I may propose at this point another amendment of the Aristotelian formulation, I should say that the art of comedy is not an art that is dedicated to the ludicrous, but is rather an art that is dedicated to the telling of the Whole Truth: this is what it is that comedy "imitates"—not the ludicrous, but the Whole Truth. Surely Mr. Huxley is luminously right in finding Homer to be a poet of the Whole Truth, for Homer knew that, however grief-stricken men may be by the loss of dearly beloved companions, they will remember to weep only after they have satisfied their hunger, and that they will then forget their tears in slumber. In other words, the point made in the Scylla-Charybdis episode is that men are not pure sensibility, that they also have bodies which must be fed and which, when overcome by fatigue, must relax in sleep. And this is, in a way, the point that comedy is always making: we are not pure, disembodied essences; indeed, we are not pure anything-at-all, but we are

[5] Aldous Huxley, *Collected Essays* (New York, Bantam Books, 1960), p. 98.

men, and our health and happiness are contingent upon our facing into the fact that we are finite and conditioned, and therefore subject to all sorts of absurdities, interruptions, inconveniences, embarrassments—and weaknesses. This is, we might say, the courage that the comic vision requires of us.

But to turn from this poet of ancient Hellas to a modern novelist such as Virginia Woolf is immediately to have a splendid example in our own time of what the comic writer is most emphatically not like.

Indeed, what is most impressive in Mrs. Woolf's most characteristic novels—particularly in *Mrs. Dalloway, To the Lighthouse,* and *The Waves*—is the profound distaste for, and the deep fear of, the conditioned and limited world that is actually the scene of human life. Hers is an intelligence (and in this she is like so many of the artists of our time) which has neither the courage nor the patience to temporize with the concrete, substantial stuff that constitutes the occasion and the circumstance of man's actual career in time. It is an intelligence that cannot dive into the thick, coarse realities of the human condition, for these are not realities that are regarded as leading anywhere or as associable with what is Radically Significant in life. There is no deep faith or confidence in the realm of human finitude and in the possibility of its being a glass of vision into the ultimate. So an effort is made to flee into the safe and impregnable citadel of pure consciousness, and this is surely what accounts for the vulgarity that we may sometimes feel in the very refinement and delicacy and exquisiteness of sensibility that Mrs. Woolf's most ardent admirers like so much to praise. That is to say, we find vulgarity in the delicacy and the elegant sensitiveness, because it is all so bloodless and so far removed from the elemental things of human life. In her works there is so much impatience with the clumsy grossness of the human creature and with the rough, ragged edges of life, and there is so much in the daily round of human living that Mrs. Woolf will not deign to bring within her orbit that, paradoxically, we feel finally that a kind of dirt is being done on life. She will never allow us to wallow about in the rucky mire of our humanness, and no one in her books ever howls or moans or really laughs over the human fate. There is no passion because the characters in her novels have all been abstracted by her preciousness into fragile, gossamerlike states of mind: it seems that only in this way could the human reality become for her just barely tolerable.

The recoil into sensibility is but one of many detours away from the human actuality to be encountered in modern literature, and principal among the others is the recoil into disgust which is archetypally expressed in Jean-Paul Sartre's novel of 1938, *Nausea*. The hero, Antoine Roquentin, is a young intellectual who takes up residence in the provincial town of Bouville-sur-Mer to finish a biography of an obscure eighteenth-century nobleman, the Marquis de Rollebon. The novel is written in the form of his journal, which is devoted to the record that he keeps of his experience during his sojourn in this place. As he lives alone in his squalid roominghouse and works amid the dreariness of the town's public library, Roquentin's spirits are soon depressed to the point of utter distraction by the drabness and monotony of life in this little coastal village, and, after a time, his restlessness making sustained scholarly labor impossible, his thinking becomes solely a matter of introspection and self-analysis. What is borne in upon him ever more deeply in the vacant, joyless days that ensue is his own isolation and the unshakeable indifference of the world to the human spirit. So intense does this vision become that he is stricken by first one and then another attack of sheer physical wretchedness: he is positively sickened by the amorphous factuality of the phenomenal world, by the obscene stubbornness with which things persist in retaining a *thereness* that seems to have no link with his own existence and that seems, therefore, to that extent to oppose his own inward being. Indeed, his inner exacerbation becomes so acute that even the most commonplace objects in his environment at last prove capable of throwing him into a spasm of retching or into utter gloom—a pebble on the beach, a glass of beer, his own face in a mirror, the knob of a door. The whole of existence becomes for him simply one vast, obscene, bulging pile of junk, and his fundamental sensations come to be those of nausea and disgust. It is the very arbitrariness with which events occur and things exist that fills him with distress, for it deepens his sense of the contingency and finitude of his own being. Everything seems to be fragmentary and disheveled and messy—and the obscenity of it all makes him twitch with fury.

There is only one diversion that lights up the gray tedium of his days: it is to hear a gramophone record of a Negro song-stress singing the jazz melody "Some of These Days." At the end of the novel, after having given up his research and completed preparations for his departure, he sits in a dingy little cafe listening to the song and its saxophone accompaniment for the last time. Suddenly, what he has really wanted all his life dawns on him: it has been, he says, "to chase existence out of me, empty the moments of their fat, wring them out, dry them, purify myself, harden myself, so as to give out finally the clean, precise note of a saxophone."

It is clear that what fills Roquentin with horror is simply the sheer untidiness of existence: he is oppressed by the messiness of things, the bedragglement of the world; and his imagination is fixed upon images of *le visqueux,* because the opaqueness of things reveals to him how ultimate is the ontological discontinuity between himself as a discrete, finite creature and everything else that exists. Every object and every event he experiences seem, in the sheer arbitrariness and contingency of their reality, to imply that the kind of metaphysical order he craves is an impossibility. His sense of justice is outraged, and, in his consuming disgust, he desires to be disembodied into the purity of sound made by a blues-saxophonist: he would live the incorporeal life of the angels, being no longer a man but a mere breath of music.

This deep shudder of Sartre's hero before the phenomenal world presents us with an excellent example of the response that is made to existence by him who is the antithesis of the comic man. What Antoine Roquentin reveals in the violence of his distaste for the created order is precisely that profound distrust of creation which the comedian always calls into question, in effect, at least, if not by intention. For the comic man, characteristically, grapples with the thickness and the density of the concrete world of human experience, delighting in all its smells, sounds, sights, and tactilities. The comedian is not generally an aviator: he does not journey away from this familiar world of earth; he refuses the experiment of angelism; he will not forget that we are made out of dust; and, when his wrath is aroused, as it sometimes is, it is not because man is bound to the things of earth but rather because man sometimes foolishly supposes that he can simply fly away from them.

This is, indeed, always the lesson of comedy: we are creatures whose nature it is to form an earthly City and who become ridiculous when we commit ourselves to some abortive venture beyond the precincts within which alone we can hope to win some proper understanding of our true human stature. It is not, of course, the purpose of the comedian to enforce a simple Sunday school lesson: all he wants to do is to give his suffrage to the Whole Truth and, as Susanne Langer says, to "reincarnate for our perception . . . the motion and rhythm of living" in the world. "Real comedy," says Mrs. Langer, "sets up in the audience a sense of general exhilaration, because it presents the very image of 'livingness.' " [6] Because, we might add, it tells us what Homer tells us in the Twelfth Book of the *Odyssey,* what Shakespeare tells us through Falstaff in the *Henry IV* plays when he takes us to Gad's Hill or into Eastcheap, or what Charlie Chaplin in *City Lights* tells us. This means, of course, that, when men decide that they are pure mind or pure will or pure sensibility, it is natural for the comic imagination to take on a critical, even polemical, aspect. It is appropriate, for example, that the Socrates of *The Clouds,* in his contempt for the common world of human experience and in his consuming passion for the clear and distinct idea, lives ridiculously suspended in a basket high up in the air. It is further appropriate that Aristophanes brings this philosopher down from the clouds, does not allow him to get away with his pretense that he lives above the relativities of history, and makes him confront some of the elemental facts of life. Or, again, we feel the justice of comedy to be operative in Molière's *Le Misanthrope,* when the outrageous pharisaism of Alceste finally has the consequence of relegating him to an essentially private universe between which and the actual world there ceases to be any connection at all. And, had an Antoine Roquentin entered the orbit of so superb a modern comedian as Joyce Cary, he would have been reminded that he is not really a pure breath of music but a man who eats, sleeps, defecates, catches colds in winter when he doesn't wear his long drawers, and that he had better remember these undignified facts if he wants to retain any dignity as a man.

The major purpose of the comedian is to remind us of how deeply rooted we are in all the tangible things of this world; he is not, like Shelley or the author of *To the Lighthouse,*

[6] Susanne K. Langer, *Feeling and Form: A Theory of Art* (New York, Scribner's, 1953), pp. 344, 348.

a poet of an "unbodied joy." The motions of comedy, to be sure, finally lead to joy, but it is a joy that we win only after we have consented to journey through this familiar, actual world of earth which is our home and, by doing so, have had our faith in its stability and permanence restored. The joy of comedy is a great joy, but it is a joy that can sometimes come only after humiliation—the humiliation the arrogant millionaire suffers when, walking down the street fully concentrated on his dignity and importance, he suddenly slips on the banana peeling he had failed to notice, and is thus reminded that he is, after all, only a man and as much subject to the law of gravitation as the rest of humankind. The event may not at first bring joy to the man himself, if his capacity for self-transcendence has been so long unused that he cannot immediately regard with wry amusement the spectacle that he has created before the gaping schoolchildren. But, even if he is not the comic hero but rather merely the comic butt of the event, we who are also looking on grasp the meaning of what has occurred, and it brings us joy because it reminds us again how inescapable our humanity is, how established and permanent and indestructible it really is. To be sure, the man's backside is bruised as a result of the fall—yet what is really hurt in him is his pride. The essentially human thing in him is not bruised: indeed, it is the lesson of comedy that this does somehow manage, again and again, to remain intact. True, it is often challenged, and men sometimes become ashamed of it and tamper with it and even reject it, but this stuff that is constitutive of what is human in them does, nevertheless, prevail—and its reassertion of itself is the central moment of comedy.

The comic way, then, descends into the mundane, conditioned world of the human creature, moving confidently into all the diverse corners of man's habitation. The difference between this way and the tragic way is not that the latter leads into suffering and agony and the former into rollicking mirth and jollity, for the men and women of comedy sometimes suffer too. Indeed, one of the most heart-rending moments in all Shakespearean drama is that in *Henry IV*, Pt. II, V. 5, when Falstaff, hearing his beloved master, Prince Hal, declare, "I know thee not, old man," turns to Justice Shallow a moment later and says "Master Shallow, I owe you a thousand pound." In this moment, his anguish is hardly less than that of Lear when he moans, "How sharper than a serpent's tooth it is/To have a thankless child!" But the agonies of the comic protagonist never have the kind of distilled purity that belongs to the sufferings of the tragic hero: the comic man, when he becomes involved in real difficulty, is no more pure-suffering than he is pure-anything-else: Odysseus and his men, when they finally stumbled upon the Sicilian beach that night, first ate their supper before weeping for their lost comrades, and then, being exhausted, their tears ceased to flow, and they fell off to sleep.

So the art of comedy reminds us, however far we may venture into the strange corridors of the world or however high we may climb the treacherous mountains of the mind, that we are of the earth and earthy—that we are creatures whose finitude is ineluctable. Kafka, in one of his Parables, says:

[Man] is a free and secure citizen of the world, for he is fettered to a chain which is long enough to give him the freedom of all earthly space, and yet only so long that nothing can drag him past the frontiers of the world. But simultaneously he is a free and secure citizen of Heaven as well, for he is also fettered by a similarly designed heavenly chain. So that if he heads, say, for the earth, his heavenly collar throttles him, and if he heads for Heaven, his earthly one does the same.[7]

And though it may be the office of tragedy to be the heavenly collar that throttles us when we head for earth, it is certainly

[7] Franz Kafka, "Paradise" (trans. Willa and Edwin Muir), *Parables* (New York, Schocken Books, 1947), p. 27.

the office of comedy to be the collar that throttles us when we make up our minds to expatriate ourselves from the conditioned realm of historical existence. For what comedy never gives up insisting upon is that we are not angels and that we belong, therefore, not to any unhistorical heaven of pure essences but to the moving, restless, dynamic world of time and space.

Now, at last, a tentative definition of the comic may be proposed, and it will be a gloss on the definition offered by W. H. Auden a few years ago in his "Notes on the Comic," in which he said that it is "a contradiction in the relation of the individual or personal to the universal or impersonal which does not involve the spectator in suffering or pity." [8] I should, however, prefer to put the matter a little differently and to say that the comic is a contradiction in the relation of the human individual to the created orders of existence; this contradiction arises out of an over-specialization of some instinct or faculty of the self, or out of an inordinate inclination of the self in some special direction, to the neglect of the other avenues through which it ought also to gain expression. This predilection of the self to identify too completely with some special interest or project (cf. Aristophanes' Socrates or Jonson's Volpone or Molière's Tartuffe or Sterne's Walter Shandy or Shaw's Professor Higgins) blinds the self to the integral character of its humanity and thus throws it out of gear with the fundamental norms and orders of human existence. However, in the comic action, this contradiction in the individual's relation to the created orders of life does not involve the spectator in suffering or pity, for he is not led to identify with the protagonist who, indeed, in the course of the action becomes the butt of his laughter.

But, this definition of the comic is not yet complicated

[8] W. H. Auden, "Notes on the Comic," *Thought*, 27 (Spring 1952), 57.

enough, for it suggests what is not quite the case, namely, that the comic protagonist is always the butt of laughter, and of laughter that is untempered with love or sympathy. This is, of course, very often the case, but not always. It is most certainly not true of the figure who must centrally be taken into account in any theory of comedy—Sir John Falstaff. This "swoll'n parcel of dropsies," this "huge bombard of sack," this "stuff'd cloakbag of guts," is—let us admit it—a rogue and a cheat, a braggart and a sensualist. Yet he is the most lovable rogue in all literature. He is old and fat and broken-winded, and yet there is in him a kind of fresh, prelapsarian innocence that makes us think of him always as youthful and even boyish. Like many of the boys in American literature from Mark Twain's Huck Finn to J. D. Salinger's Holden Caulfield, Falstaff is a great liar—he lies, however, like Huck and Holden, in order to protect himself against the conventional dishonesty of other men. Falstaff has traveled throughout the world, has met all types of people, suffered all sorts of hard knocks, and pinched ladies' buttocks in every corner of England: yet there is in him no fatigue, no world-weariness, and he retains a remarkable zest and enthusiasm for adventure. Above all else, he has a great capacity for living intensely in the present moment: one might say that he is the original existentialist hero, if one means by "existentialist hero" not the fastidious and disgusted man of Sartre's *Nausea* but rather the man who is *engagé*, who is intensely committed to the present moment and the present task: indeed, in this latter sense, Falstaff is perhaps the prototype of the existentialist man. And this may be why he is so impatient with the restraints of conventional moral codes and laws, for, however relevant they may be to the general circumstances of life, he always finds them ineffective and irrelevant to the uniqueness and contingency of the immediate occasion. Yet, despite his outrageous improvisation in morality, it is his passionate commitment to the present moment and to concrete reality that makes Falstaff so wonderfully and richly human.

Sir John's great scenes are, of course, in the two parts of *Henry IV* (rather than in *The Merry Wives of Windsor*), and it is no wonder that here his role becomes finally that of victim. These are plays whose whole drama is stirred into being by the anarchy that has overtaken the English realm; and since, in the world of Shakespearean experience, civil anarchy in every form is most "unnatural," the drama of *Henry IV* must, therefore, move toward the recovery of order in the body politic. Prince Hal is the one destined to be the agent through whom order will be restored; and, since he finds in plump Jack a symbol of everything that would endanger or subvert decorum and order, he drives him off. And that is precisely what Falstaff stands for. In the boldness, enterprise, vivacity, and wit of this fat old rascal we have the most brilliant image that the literary tradition affords of that zest, spontaneity, and independence in the human creature that makes him an intractable nuisance for every order that defines itself so constrictively as to leave no room for a man to move about in and stretch himself. So, despite all his faults, there is greatness in Sir John. He has vices, it is true, but, as Mark Van Doren says, "they have not the sound of vices. None of them is an end in itself—that is their secret. . . . He does not live to drink or steal or lie or foin o'nights. He even does not live in order that he may be the cause of wit in other men." [9] He simply lives for the joy of the adventure itself—and we must say, I think, to the glory of God. There is in him nothing of the protestant (small *p*): he has no quarrel with life: he is not a romantic: he is engaged in no cosmic debate: he is content simply to be a man. And though he is not a very virtuous, not a very good man, though

[9] Mark Van Doren, *Shakespeare* (Garden City, Doubleday Anchor, 1953), p. 114.

he is a rascal and a scalawag, he *is* a man, always and intensely human—and this, I take it, is why he is the great saint of Western comedy. We laugh at old Jack, but we also admire him and love him; and, when we laugh at him, it is simply because he is so different from the rest of us—different because he is so deeply rooted in the human condition that he restores our confidence in its resilience, in its essential stoutness and vitality. This is simply to say that he is the archetypal instance of the comic *hero*.

And now I am able to widen my definition of comedy to the extent of providing for two types of protagonist. That is to say, he may, on the one hand, like Volpone or Tartuffe or Dostoievski's "Underground" man, be the target of a fundamentally unsympathetic laughter because of his deviation from some accepted human norm. Or, on the other hand, like Don Quixote or Falstaff or Joyce Cary's Gulley Jimson, he may be a figure of heroic proportions whom we laugh at and yet admire. And the presence in a given action of the one or the other type determines the character of the resulting katharsis.

The comic katharsis does, I think, essentially involve such a restoration of our confidence in the realm of finitude as enables us to see the daily occasions of our earth-bound career as being not irrelevant inconveniences but as possible roads into what is ultimately significant in life. This restoration of our confidence in the conditioned realities of historical existence may be managed by the comic author in either of two ways, depending on which type of protagonist he has placed at the center of his action. If his central personage is one whose eccentricity arises out of some willfully maintained imbalance of character which is not of the sort that excites pity or fear, our awareness of the validity of the human norm from which he has deviated will be renewed and deepened as we see him rendered incompetent by this eccentricity. The Socrates of Aristophanes' *The Clouds* is an example of this kind of comic figure. But if the protagonist is, like Falstaff, a man whose eccentricity is a consequence not of his deviateness but of the very depth of his rootedness in our common humanity, then the experience of katharsis grows out of the joy we take in the discovery of how stout and gamy the human creature really is. And this is, of course, the discovery that the comic hero enables us to make. He is, Mrs. Langer says,

> the indomitable living creature fending for itself, tumbling and stumbling . . . from one situation into another, getting into scrape after scrape and getting out again, with or without a thrashing. He is the personified *élan vital;* his chance adventures and misadventures, without much plot, though often with bizarre complications, his absurd expectations and disappointments, in fact his whole improvised existence has the rhythm of primitive . . . life coping with a world that is forever taking new uncalculated turns, frustrating, but exciting. He is . . . now triumphant, now worsted and rueful, but in his ruefulness and dismay he is funny, because his energy is really unimpaired and each failure prepares the situation for a new fantastic move.[10]

This is the comic man *par excellence,* and this is the rhythm of action that, in its greatest moments, his life exemplifies.

Now it seems that the great sympathy which the Christian imagination may feel for the testimony of the comedian is, in large part, a consequence of the extent to which it is governed by the same robust materialism in which comedy is so deeply rooted. This is a characteristic of Christianity that, among its recent interpreters, the late Archbishop Temple often liked to remark: indeed, one of the most striking sentences in his Gifford Lectures asserts that, "One ground for the hope of Christianity that it may make good its claim to be the true

[10] Langer, *Feeling and Form,* p. 342.

faith lies in the fact that it is the most avowedly materialist of all the great religions." [11] I assume that when Temple spoke of the materialistic character of Christianity he meant that the Christian belief in the Creation and the Incarnation makes for a profound respect for nature and time and history which is not easily to be found elsewhere in the history of religion. And this means that the Christian imagination is enabled to rejoice in the quiddities and haecceities of existence in a way that accords very closely with the path taken by the comic vision.

That which first guarantees the Christian's confidence in the realm of the finite is his belief in the doctrine of Creation. This is not, of course, a doctrine that purports to be a scientifically accurate account of a dateable beginning of the cosmic process. It is, rather, a mytho-religious way of asserting that, though man and his world are in all respects enmeshed in relativity and contingency, creation is neither illusory nor evil nor a mere concretion of some universal World Spirit. To say, as the Bible does, that God created the world out of nothing is to assert that He is the sole Ground and Source of everything that exists, and it is to assert the utter dependence of the world upon Him; but it is also, against all the various forms of Idealism and Gnosticism, to emphasize the genuine reality of finite existence: for it was *made* by God. And though this world of ours has been injured by man's sin, it is, despite its distinctness from God, *essentially* good, because it proceeds from Him and exists by His design. Nor can the doctrine of Creation be reconciled to any form of Pantheism, for in effect this doctrine denies both that the world is identical with God and that it is in some way an emanation of the "World Soul": it says that "every creature in [the world] possesses a true self which, however much perfected," "is never swallowed up or lost in God. Therefore, all God's creatures are images of Him in the same way, and to the same limited extent, as a work of

[11] William Temple, *Nature, Man and God*, p. 478.

art is an image of its maker—his, yet in a manner distinct from him." [12]

The crucial Biblical word here is a very simple word: it falls at the very beginning of the story, in the great first chapter of Genesis—"And God saw everything that he had made, and behold, it was very good." And upon what is implicit in this single sentence rests the whole Biblical interpretation of life and history: a view fundamentally premised upon the assumption that the world of finite and contingent existence is not essentially defective simply by reason of its finiteness. Indeed, when the Christian faith has been true to itself, it has never quite forgotten that its genius in large part consists in its understanding that the finitude and particularization of created existence are not in themselves evil, since they are a part of God's plan for the world.

There are, of course, many passages in Biblical literature that dwell upon the discrepancy between the Creator and the created world. "All flesh is grass and all the goodliness thereof is as the flower of the field; The grass withereth, the flower fadeth: . . . but the word of our God shall stand forever." "Thou, Lord, in the beginning hast laid the foundation of the earth; and the heavens are the work of thy hands: They shall perish; but Thou remainest; and they all shall wax old as doth a garment; and as a vesture shalt thou fold them up, and they shall be changed: but Thou art the same, and thy years shall not fail." "Behold, the nations are as a drop of a bucket, and are counted as the small dust of the balance: . . . all nations before him are as nothing; and they are counted to him less than nothing." One could go on to cite many other passages which point to the incommensurability between the created world and its Creator, but what is significant is that this kind of testimony never has as its purpose to suggest that the

[12] Dorothy L. Sayers, *Further Papers on Dante* (New York, Harper, 1957), p. 187.

transiency and fragmentariness are in themselves evil. On the contrary, as Reinhold Niebuhr remarks in his Gifford Lectures:

The fragmentary character of human life is not regarded as evil in Biblical faith because it is seen from the perspective of a centre of life and meaning in which each fragment is related to the plan of the whole, to the will of God. The evil arises when the fragment seeks by its own wisdom to comprehend the whole or attempts by its own power to realize it.[13]

There is in the Biblical doctrine of Creation a sober realism and sanity that prompts the Hebraic imagination simply to accept the insufficiency and the incompleteness of human life as a part of God's design. And when the transiency and finiteness of human existence are dwelt upon in Biblical literature, they are stressed only in contrast to and as proof of the glory and majesty of God, and there is no suggestion that this discrepancy bears any moral connotation. On the contrary, what is robustly affirmed is that the created world is good, because it is the work of God.

The finiteness of the human condition is, of course, never minimized; our human nature remains creatural, even in the highest reaches of its freedom and self-transcendence, and we never cease to be involved in the relativities of historical existence. But always in Christian history, when the full implications of the doctrine of Creation have been understood, the Biblical insights into the essential goodness of finite existence have been preserved. "And God saw everything that he had made, and behold, it was very good."

Perhaps an even more crucial doctrine for the Christian estimate of the essential character of finitude is the doctrine of

---

[13] Reinhold Niebuhr, *The Nature and Destiny of Man*, 1 (New York, Scribner's, 1943), p. 168.

the Incarnation, wherein it is declared that the glory of God Himself dwelt in our mortal flesh and became manifest to the eyes of men. Even the distinguished Protestant theologian Karl Barth, who is closely associated with the contemporary reaction against the "Jesus of history" movement of nineteenth-century Liberalism, insists in his *Church Dogmatics* that the central passage of the New Testament is John 1:14, "The word became flesh and dwelt among us." And the Christian community has from time immemorial perceived that what is of the essence in the Gospel is a divine act of Condescension to our low estate—whereby, as the Nicene Creed puts it, "God the Father Almighty, Maker of heaven and earth . . . for us men and for our salvation came down from heaven, And was incarnate by the Holy Ghost of the Virgin Mary, And was made man." This is unquestionably the heart of the Gospel and the central miracle of Christian experience.

Now when, in its worship, the Church recites these words, its intention is to assert that "in the fullness of time" God did really become man without ceasing to be God. It does not merely assert that through the life of Jesus the carpenter of Galilee we may come to discern what God is like: it says, rather, that Jesus Christ *is* God Himself incarnate. We have not in Christ merely a religious genius or hero of some sort; nor are we dealing in the New Testament with a God who, like the gods of pagan Greece, merely disguised Himself as a man. On the contrary, as Langmead Casserley robustly puts it:

His was a real babyhood and youth, a real growth in mind and stature, a desperately human hunger, an exquisitely human pain, an agonizingly human death. In His thirty years of incarnate existence, God was touched and harrowed by all that is most menacing in the lot of man—physical pain, economic insecurity, subtle temptation, a tragic death foreseen and awaited, the frustration of noble purposes, intellectual misunderstanding, the wearisome, disillusioning absence of sympathy, slander, unpopularity, injustice, persecution, rejected love. All that most easily overcomes the spirit of man He faced without defeat, all that is most prone to embitter and distort the human character He absorbed without bitterness or spiritual loss, smiled kindly through the endless frustrations which so often cynicize and disillusion romantic and idealistic men, loved unwearyingly through the rejection of love with a love which not even hatred could remould in its own image, confronted temptation with an invincible perfection of character and purpose against which the hitherto victorious powers of evil were powerless, and finally placed in the hands of death a life so intense and concentrated on its destiny that death's age-old mastery over life was revealed as a broken thing.[14]

It is the Christian faith that a tremendous phenomenon occurred in this astonishing series of events, that in the unique segment of history that is constituted by our Lord's earthly career we were, in effect, "delivered from the woe of being alive," as Denis de Rougemont says in *Passion and Society*. And I assume this is in part what Paul Tillich meant when he spoke, as he so often did, of Christ as "the center" of history, the center round which the entire human story arranges itself. For, in the event of Jesus Christ, the whole of human existence, contaminated though it had been by the poisons of sin, was made valid and put right again, when God Himself entered the sphere of our life and brought grace and truth into our very midst.

Emil Brunner is, of course, altogether right in contending in his little book, *The Divine-Human Encounter*, that the ultimate significance of the Incarnation is misunderstood if it is supposed that Jesus Christ came merely to come. No, says Dr.

[14] J. V. Langmead Casserley, *No Faith of My Own* (New York, Longmans Green, 1952), pp. 35–36.

Brunner, He "did not come merely to come, but He came to redeem. To be sure, only the Incarnate Lord—very God, very man—can be the Redeemer. But the Bible guides us to ponder less the secret of the Person of Jesus than the mystery of His work." [15] And I do not myself want to suggest here that the full significance of the doctrine of the Incarnation is properly construed in terms merely of the *Person* of Christ or in terms of how it illumines the true relation of the finite and the infinite. But, at the same time, I am eager to avoid the imbalance that so much of Protestant theology often represents today, of interpreting the Incarnation in such a way that, as the Lutheran theologian Joseph Sittler has noticed, it receives "only that light which can be reflected backward upon it from Calvary. While, to be sure, these events cannot be separated without the impoverishment of the majesty of the history of redemption, it is nevertheless proper to suggest," says Dr. Sittler, "that our theological tendency to declare them only in their concerted meaning *at the point of fusion* tends to disqualify us to listen to the ontological-revelational overtones of the Incarnation." [16] And surely it is not to do violence to the true import of Biblical faith to insist that God's having condescended to "tabernacle amongst us," to assume a human body, a human mind, a human soul, and to submit Himself to all the conditions of our life in the natural order—surely it is not improper to insist that His having deigned to do this has the effect of giving a new value to all the finite vehicles and instrumentalities which He thus employed. And the consequence is that the Christian's fundamental attitude toward existence must always be profoundly affirmative: the particularity and fragmentariness of existence can never be, for

[15] Emil Brunner, *The Divine-Human Encounter* (Philadelphia, Westminster Press, 1943), p. 142.

[16] Joseph Sittler, "A Theology for Earth," *The Christian Scholar*, 37 (1954), 374.

him, the offense that they are to more fastidious men: nor can he ever in any way impugn the validity of the natural and the temporal order, since for approximately thirty years this was the home of God Himself.

This, then, is what I assume Temple had in mind when he spoke of the materialism of Christianity—the attitude of respect, of esteem, of love even, for the actual, specific, concrete things of this world which belong to the order created by God and which formed an adequate theatre for the drama in which His Son took the leading part. The Christian imagination does not shrink from the tangibility and gross concreteness of our life in time, and it is not afraid to face the limited, conditioned nature of human existence. It is, indeed, affirmative—radically affirmative—in its attitude toward nature and time and history. It does not spend its time looking about for an elevator that will whisk it up out of the world into eternity, for it is committed to the world, and it wants the world to confront itself, not to run away from itself. It believes that God's way of dealing with us is by and through the things and creatures of this world, and that He is Himself to be met not *in* Himself but in His works and in His gifts. And it believes that in the Incarnation God Himself affirmed the world, affirmed the realm of finitude, the realms of nature and history. Therefore, the religion which finds its main fulcrum in the Incarnational event is one which does not take us out of this world: it takes us, rather, deeper and deeper into it. This is to say that, unlike the kind of modern imagination represented by Virginia Woolf, the Christian mind has no desire to be an angel, but, rather, to the scandalization of idealists and angelists, it persists in wallowing about in all the temporal, creatural stuff of human life, for it was in this stuff that God Himself became Incarnate.

I earlier contended that the function of comedy is to enliven our sense of human actuality, to put us in touch with the

Whole Truth, particularly when, in pursuit of some false and abstract image of ourselves, we have become embarrassed by the limitations of our creatureliness and undertaken to bring our life in history to an end, either by some violently conclusive action or by some disillusioned flight into the realm of pure idea. Forsaking all the meretricious forms of eschatology, comedy moves toward the actual: it asks us to be content with our human limitations and possibilities, and to accept our life in this world without the sentimentality either of smugness or of cynicism. And when we wish to be pure discarnate spirit or pure discarnate intellect, the comedian asks us to remember the objective, material conditions of life with which we must make our peace if we are to retain our sanity and survive. He will not let us forget that we are men, that we are finite and conditioned creatures—not angels. In its deeply affirmative attitude toward the created orders of existence, in the profound materialism of its outlook, the comic imagination, it seems to me, summarizes an important part of the Christian testimony about the meaning of human life.

Indeed, this profoundly affirmative quality in the comic vision makes the appreciation of it involve, in our time, a very strenuous effort of the moral imagination. For the kind of vision which has the most direct appeal for us is one which, in offering some radical and extremist conception of ourselves, promises to increase the psyche's temperature. The great heroes of our cultural life, as Lionel Trilling remarked in *The Opposing Self,* are "the tigers of wrath"—the Kafkas and the Sartres and the Becketts—and they are cherished as examples of a charismatic power, which we covet for ourselves, of being able to endure the stigmata of our Alienation with such fierceness and valor that the inconveniences and disadvantages of history might be left behind, and the spirit liberated from the conditioned character of our mundane existence. We are, in fact, as a people always on the verge of electing to bring our life in history to an end.

[We] are discontented with the nature rather than with the use of the human faculty; deep in our assumption lies the hope and the belief that humanity will end its career by developing virtues which will be admirable exactly because we cannot now conceive them. The past has been a weary failure, the present cannot matter, for it is but a step forward to the final judgment; we look to the future when the best of the works of man will seem but the futile and slightly disgusting twitchings of primeval creatures.[17]

So the way of comedy which attempts to lead us into that special sort of truth which Aldous Huxley calls the Whole Truth is one of the most difficult ways which the modern imagination can be asked to take. Yet, if this way be taken, it may be a *preparatio* that will permit us once more to be brought to the point of being able, with both laughter and reverence in our hearts, to say with the Psalmist, "The earth is the Lord's and the fulness thereof, the world and those who dwell therein." This, I suspect, is a large part of what Christopher Fry means, when he tells us that "comedy is an escape, not from truth but from despair: a narrow escape into faith." It is, he suggests, the "angle of experience where the dark is distilled into light. . . . It says, in effect, that, groaning as we may be, we move in the figure of a dance, and, so moving, we trace the outline of the mystery." [18]

Fr. William Lynch tells us that "it would be unfair to tragedy to think that it is only to the tragic that comedy is

[17] Lionel Trilling, *E. M. Forster* (New York, New Directions, 1943), p. 22.

[18] Christopher Fry, "Comedy," *Tulane Drama Review, 4* (March 1960), 77.

addressing itself as semantic challenger, vocabulary against vocabulary." [19] And Mr. Fry says that he is always on "the verge of saying that comedy is greater than tragedy." But, he says, "On the verge I stand and go no further." Nor have I wanted to put comedy into the kind of competition with tragedy that would necessitate our opting for one against the other: so to pose the issues would, of course, entail an impossibly narrow kind of scholasticism, since, as Mr. Fry has reminded us, "we find ourselves in [comedy or tragedy] by the turn of a thought," [20] and the man who is unqualified for tragedy is also unqualified for comedy. But I have wanted to suggest that comedy affords the Christian student of modern literature a high and promising ground from within literature itself for a radical critique of the various Gnosticized forms of tragedy that constitute our period style. And, obversely, I have also wanted to suggest something of the kind of constructive theological insight (heretical as this may be within the forums of post-Arnoldian criticism) that the literary imagination itself, in its comic phase, proposes to the Christian intelligence—that, as Fr. Lynch states (and in all this he has been, as his readers will recognize, my fundamental guide):

a thing need not step out of the human to be all things, and to achieve the liberty of the children of God. The mud in man, the lowermost point in the subway, is nothing to be ashamed of. It can produce . . . the face of God. . . . To recall this, to recall this incredible relation between mud and God, is, in its own distant, adumbrating way, the function of comedy.[21]

[19] Lynch, *Christ and Apollo,* p. 95.
[20] Fry, p. 78.
[21] Lynch, p. 109.

FOUR

The Clown as the Lord of Disorder

Wolfgang M. Zucker

The center of Aristotle's theory of the theater is taken by the hero. The dramatic plot, not invented by the playwright, but taken over from mythological tradition, is only an occasion for demonstrating the virtue and the "flaw" of the super-human hero, his ascent to an exalted height where he dares to challenge the gods, and his downfall into a depth where the consolations of common humanity are no longer relevant. Aristotle's problem was primarily neither esthetical nor ethical, but what, for lack of a better term, we may call "existential." He tried to answer the question about the significance of tragic theater for a middle-class audience whose experiential reality was far removed from heroic action and passion.

This essay, dealing with the clown, the counter-figure of the hero, asks an analogous question. Numerous books and essays have explained the image and character of the clown in political, sociological, psychoanalytical, and anthropological terms. We have learned to see in the clown a universal stock character of the stage, and to relate him to cultic practices of prehistorical times. However, all these skillful and learned "explanations" remain somehow unsatisfactory, because they reduce, by genetic derivations, an enormously complex phenomenon to one or another function of human society or of the human mind which are taken as simply assumed. In other words, the clown remains a curious spectacle of the stage or of the circus ring, somewhere outside the concrete existence of the audience. What we attempt here, in a most preliminary and incomplete manner, is an existential analysis of the self-understanding of the audience that interacts with the clown. Such an approach may be called "ontological" or "theological," because in it the distinction of object and subject is transcended and both are understood as manifestations of Being itself.

I

We begin with the concrete appearance: the clown of the circus arena. The official stage of our age, the theater of the educated middle class, has rediscovered the clown only in the last twenty years, after he had been banned from it in the age of enlightenment that had no appreciation for his irrational playfulness, his unedifying pranks, and his disreputable attire. It is still too early to decide whether his re-emergence in "the theater of the absurd" is really the continuation of an age-old tradition, or merely one manifestation of the fact that the bourgeois middle-class has lost its self-assuredness. The circus and the puppet show of the country fair had given refuge to the theatrical stock characters of the past, and precisely because these forms of unsophisticated entertainment had been contemptuously excluded from the moral and educational reforms of the nineteenth century, it was there that the clown could survive with all his complexity and self-contradiction.

Self-contradiction, indeed, is the clown's most significant feature. Whatever predicate we use to describe him, the opposite can also be said, and with equal right. He is a type whom everybody in the audience immediately recognizes when he stumbles, jumps, rolls through the sawdust of the arena from which athletic acrobats and trained animals are just withdrawing—and yet every single clown is an individual. He is crude and mean, but also gentle and magnanimous; clumsy and inept, but, simultaneously, incredibly agile and endowed with astonishing skills; ugly and repulsive, yet not without elegance and attractive charm. His chalk-white face, in which the eyes almost disappear while the mouth is enlarged to a ghoulish bigness, looks like the mask of death; but the children in the audience greet him with laughter and delight as a well-known friend. On everybody in the arena he plays his malicious tricks, on the professional performers, on the attendants, and even on the spectators near the ringside, but, in the end, it is he who is kicked around, beaten up, and chased out with contempt. His ill-fitting rags, his baggy sagging pants, loose waistcoats, and battered hats, mark him as a bum and disorderly person; his gestures are unashamedly obscene, his behavior is undignified, unreasonable, and sometimes even idiotic, yet he is considered good fun for the whole family. By all counts he is a misfit, a social outcast, a person who would not be allowed to show himself on the street outside, but in the arena he is applauded for being what he is, and for not being what he mockingly pretends to be.

Certainly it is possible to trace back his various forms of appearance to different types, masks, impersonations in the history of the theater and of religious cults. Learned investigations can relate him to the characters of the *Commedia del'Arte* and to tribal dances, to Orphean animal impersonations and to phallic symbolizations, to the Minus of the

Roman stage and to the Etruscan "Fescennines," to the masks of the Morris dancer and to fertility cults all over the world. But the unsophisticated audience of the circus is hardly aware of such historical derivations and of the speculations of learned antiquarians. It accepts the clown as he is, a paradoxical figure without logic or consistency; and it is right. The self-contradictory nature of the clown is not the incidental result of a complicated syncretism or fusion of divergent elements, but an expression of the absurdity and paradox of human existence, revolting against the confinement and definedness of the conditions into which it finds itself thrown.

II

The clown is not simply a pauper who clothes himself with the worn-out garments cast away by more fortunate members of society. Neither is he the victim of social injustice or deprivation of status. On the contrary, his incongruent dress is deliberately chosen with a kind of laughing contempt for all status. When he adds to his attire some foppish accessory, as a stiff top hat, a useless flexible cane, or the attaché case of an office clerk, he does it not in a futile attempt to improve his appearance. Rather he demonstrates with such additions his disregard for all status symbols. To see in him an underprivileged member of society means to misunderstand him fundamentally. He stands outside of rank and order, because he debunks both. He is undignified, because he has no regard for the insignia of a socially assigned and carefully sustained dignity. Holding himself outside of the social stratification, he arbitrarily mixes and confuses the symbols of status by which the special order, the "nomos" of society, simultaneously manifests and reinforces itself. The art of debunking, practiced by the clown with superb skill, is not a weapon of the person who is excluded from the higher ranks, as long as he is still within the nomos. Only the one who stands outside of all order can make the symbols of order ridiculous.

Rhetoric, whether it appears as verbal oratory or as the parading of nonverbal insignia, is the attempt to defend a specific nomos against erosion by doubt and lawlessness. It is a dead-serious undertaking for all insiders, and hilariously funny for all outsiders. Like Socrates, the philosophical clown and clowning philosopher, the circus clown is anti-rhetorical. He seldom speaks, but when he does, he uses the rhetoric of the insiders with such exaggeration and such empty formalism that it turns against language itself. In *Waiting for Godot,* Lucky gives a magnificent example of such speech directed against all language, and when he is finally brought down by force, he reverts to his beast-like speechlessness. Usually the clown refrains from speaking. He does not argue, because since he does not recognize any binding nomos, he also has no logos. Aristotle's definition of man being the animal that has logos, does not apply to him.

Therefore it is erroneous to interpret the clown as the protagonist of a lower class protest against rulers and their arrogance. He is not a revolutionary, but a rebel; not a reformer and promoter of a new and better social order, but a despiser and destroyer of any nomos. His audience, belonging mostly to the underprivileged strata of society, is quite aware of this fact; as much as the spectators laugh at his impudent jokes and his disorderly behavior, they never identify with them. When the later Chaplin in his feature-length movies posed as a comical revolutionary with a message, he lost his original audience. The same people who had applauded him in all his transmutations, as pious pilgrim or as policeman, as prospector and as hobo, felt bewildered when he explicitly took up the fight against "modern times." With a clearer instinct than the reform-minded critics of esthetical journals, they noticed that Chaplin began to abandon the role of the clown when he carried the flag of revolution.

This lack of identification is most significant. The one who stands outside of all accepted values, whose jokes and pranks demonstrate a playful disregard for every nomos, is seen neither as a victorious leader in action nor as a brother in suffering. When he is mistreated and beaten up by the other characters of the stage as punishment for his own mean tricks, the audience laughs with the same pleasure with which it before received his many disruptions of order. It does not show pity or compassion when he cries and complains bitterly about his miserable fate. Nobody listens to Rigoletto when he asks for help. The clown does not find sympathy because he really is not a sympathetic figure. The melancholic harlequin of the sentimental Roacoco was an invention of the same century that had relegated him from the official stage. Watteau and Fragonard, Cezanne and Picasso painted the clown as a human figure in grotesque disguise, but in the circus where the old clown lived on for the cruel enjoyment of the lower classes he remained subhuman. The attitude of the circus audience is, and always has been, one of amused rejection, basically not different from the attitude displayed toward the village idiot, the deformed cripple, the dancing bear, and the uniformed monkey. There is no feeling of solidarity, but only one of contemptuous hostility. It offers satisfaction to witness the destruction of the destroyer of all accepted values. When in 1696 Louis XIV drove the Italian clowns from the stage, because they had dared to ridicule Madame de Maintenon, it was an act of vengeance for an attack on his authority. When in the circus the clown is kicked out of the arena, it is not even vengeance but merely an entertaining interlude of disorderly events.

The clown does not belong to human society with its ranks and its symbols. These symbols of attire, of speech, gesture, and behavior are the criteria by which every society decides whom it acknowledges as a human being. To be human is not the same as being the member of a zoological species. Thus the Christian society of the sixteenth and seventeenth century was capable of feeling—in spite of all social distinction—a vague solidarity even with the lowest rank of the brute peasant at home; but it sincerely doubted whether the so-called "savages" of the newly discovered territories really belonged to the human race. In the illustrations of that time they were represented like feathered monkeys, similar to human beings, and yet so strange that sympathetic identification with them was possible only with unusual philosophical effort. Precisely because they had outward similarity with humans, their ways of dressing and eating, of fighting and of love-making, to say nothing of their speech, were held to be decidedly "out of order." In the eighteenth century this hostility gave way to a new cult of the "noble savage," a glorification of a way of life outside of civilization. But this display of sympathy, contemporary with the psychological humanization of the clown, was confined to the philosophically educated members of the middle class and, most probably, an indication of the beginning deep erosion of the ruling nomos. The lower classes were hardly affected by such sophisticated humanism, as the fate of the American Indians in the nineteenth century proves.

III

The clown then is an impostor, arrogating human dignity and status; but since he really is not human, that which is funny and ridiculous is, at the same time, frightening and obscene. The apes in the zoo are cute when they sit at a table or drink out of a cup, but when, to the embarrassment of their keepers, they revert to uninhibited sex play, they are an insult to social norms, the more so because they resemble human beings. The reaction of the audience, both in the zoo and in the circus, is a peculiar mixture of laughter and indignation. Laughter, disorderly amusement, is provoked by a sense of relief, for the violation of the social taboo is not followed by an immediate destruction and annihilation of the violator. It is possible, at least for a time, to disregard the sacred order. The clown, a human-like being, may dare to challenge the nomos of the gods as did the hero in Greek tragedy; by this he demonstrates that a release from the restrictions of order is, at least, within the possible scope of human existence. Aristotle's remarks on catharsis, the purging of the soul from its antinomial tendencies, apply also to the clown. But, like the hero of tragedy, he must not eventually get away with such freedom. While the hero suffers his catastrophe in grand style, the clown, the German Hanswurst, the Italian Brighell, the Spanish Rustico, is chased around the ring before an applauding audience, humiliated, covered with dirt, trampled upon, indecent even when he is suffering. What a spectacle, what a twofold pleasure, to experience vicariously the assault on order and to witness simultaneously the reduction to nothingness of the transgressor!

The clown is the actor who has accepted the twofold role of breaking all taboos and receiving all the punishments for it. He has agreed to make himself so utterly grotesque that the people in the audience can despise him, insult him, and torment him to their heart's delight. He assumes the role of the scapegoat and receives the punishment for their half-hearted attempts at stepping outside of the common order; he shocks them pleasantly with his insolence and his obscenities. They call him "clown," a name of uncertain origin derived probably from the same root as words such as "clod," "clumsy," "club," "cluster." Prospero's half-human servant is called "Caliban"; in appearance and name he is the mythologized clown. Clowns and Calibans offer themselves as a butt for all the hostilities of the audience, and their art is considered the greater the more resolutely and the more shamelessly they give up their dignity. Of course, only a marginal person, a person "without honor," a person totally outside of the hierarchy of social rank, will accept such a role. The clown belongs to such vagrant people as jugglers, mountebanks, and peddlers, people who have no status and are therefore suspect to rich and poor alike. Consequently people from within the social order cannot "clown around" too long without losing face. "Clowning around" means behaving without dignity, without regard for what a specific status demands; eventually it will make the undignified person marginal.

IV

But marginality as a social role, accepting rejection and rejecting acceptance, does not fully elucidate the figure of the clown. In his image there are features that have their roots both in the religious foundations of human order and in the archetypal structure of the person. As a deliberately disorderly character, the clown stands outside not only of order but also outside of censure. His disorderliness is not just misbehavior, a lapse or a lack of discipline; rather it is the expression of a contempt for, and a principal opposition to, all order. It is as though the clown stands in the service of a power that is the declared enemy of organized society. He has no house, no home within the enclosure of the town; as an outsider he lives in a gypsy wagon that halts today in this field, tomorrow in another. Neither is he bound by the spiritual authorities of the city enclosure, of the "gorod"—the garden, the *hortus clausus,* that is both the symbol and the manifestation of the divine order. He is neither a child nor a servant of God. His lord is the "Lord of Disorder," as the devil was called in medieval literature. By his make-up he himself resembles the devil.

Harlequin is thought to be a magician, a practitioner of the art of the devil; his name may have been derived from the Germanic word *hellekin,* a dweller of hell. Such interpretation is well supported by the strange custom of the "Feast of

Fools" that was celebrated, in defiance of many prohibitions, from the twelfth to the seventeenth century in many cathedral churches of northwestern Europe. The feast started, significantly enough for Freudians, on the Day of the Circumcision, January first, at the moment when the liturgy of the day prescribed the singing of the Magnificat. The words "He has put down the mighty from their seat and has exalted the humble and the meek" were the signal for the younger members of the clergy to jump up and drive the bishop and his assistants from the church. Hereafter the young men put on masks, brought out wine and food, converted the altar into a banquet table, and shouted an obscene parody of the Holy Mass. Sometimes a braying ass was brought in and worshipped as an incarnation of the Lord of Disorder. Thus the celebrants, now dressed like clowns, performed a devil's mass; and it certainly was not incidental that the season for this perversion of all sacred order was the time of the Saturnalia and of the Twelve Nights of Christmas. A study of the documents deploring these outrageous acts leaves us with the impression that they were ritualized outbreaks of anarchy, temporary suspensions of all distinctions of rank and status, comparable perhaps to the freedom of the fools of Mardi Gras and the celebration of the Carnival in western and southern Europe.

Of course, the Feast of Fools, like the *Maskenfreiheit* (the liberty under the protection of the mask) of the European pre-lenten season, was limited in time. Carnival ends with the first minute of Ash Wednesday; the reign of the Lord of Disorder ceased with the Day of Epiphany. Yet the phenomenon of toleration of disorderliness, for even the shortest period, provides us with some insight into the ontological ambiguity of all order. In other words, the clown-hellekin, the little representative of the devil in the midst of our worldly order, has a genuine function. He makes us aware of the ambivalence of order. The clown and the "Feast of Fools" are only especially expressive forms of pressure release which as institutionalized festivals exist in every culture.

V

The essence of all festivals is the interruption and suspension of the rules of everyday. Whatever the special form of celebration is, it represents something extraordinary, something outside of, and contrary to, the usual nomos of life. In this sense it is socially sanctioned and formalized disorder.

At the Roman Saturnalia the difference between masters and slaves was temporarily abolished; in a similar manner social distinctions are obliterated by the masks and costumes worn at the Mardi Gras. The considerable sexual license tolerated during the last three days before Lent in the southern German *Fasching* sometimes disregards even the vows of marital fidelity. On Christmas day in England many grownups put on colored paper hats in the shape of foolscaps. Yet, the same people that "fool around" and behave like clowns on the day or days of the festival will insist on strict observance of social custom as soon as the festival has come to its end. Only the professional jester is expected to continue in his foolishness which is always an attack on the system that upholds the security and restricts the liberty of everyone in society. Thus the clown makes manifest the ontological paradox of order itself.

Order, the nomos of the social group, defines the role of every individual belonging to it. It creates, maintains, and protects the social structure in which man is at home, where he knows his way about and where he is, more or less, safeguarded against the shocking experience of otherness. But whatever defines also sets limits. The nomos not only protects the individual but also deprives him of freedom. Like a firm wall the nomos conveys to those who adhere to it the certainty of having a proper place inside of the sacred reality; but the same wall also cuts them off from the infinite possibilities of the outside. Every order calls itself "sacred" and denounces the outside as inferior, sinful, unclean, and despicable. The temple, as the etymology of the word signifies, is that spatial region which has been cut off from all that is impure; it is the "fanum" from which profanities are strictly banned. But there is something that no order can ban, regardless of all restrictions and protestations: the awareness that there exists an outside, an unprotected, insecure, untested otherness which by its very existence makes it impossible to maintain the absolute and infinite validity of the accepted order. Every nomos is finite, not because it is not sacred enough, but because it necessarily implies that there is something outside of its reach. Every order claims to be from God, but it is never possible to uphold this claim in an absolute sense, because, after all, God allows something to exist outside of this order. The Tower of Babel is a mythical attempt to build an unbroken ladder and connecting road between the finite human order, where all speech must be of one accord, and God's own reality. The failure of this construction makes all order limited. People from different orders always speak different languages.

VI

The clown, then, plays the role of the outsider, the one who is outlandish in costume, mores, and manners. But he is not a stranger committed to another nomos. On the contrary, his challenge to the ruling nomos is specifically aggressive, because he is fully acquainted with it and yet ridicules it. Chaplin was not simply a hobo, but the caricature of the society dandy. Marcel Marceau's top hat once crowned the head of a solid dignitary of the Republic. The Hanswurst of the German low comedy and puppet show imitates the magical skills of the learned Doctor Faustus. The dress of the Stupid Augustine in every circus performance consists of the typical garments of the bourgeois wardrobe of the past, shirts with detachable collars and cuffs, innumerable waistcoats and overcoats. The clown does not attack the nomos with open hostility, but, on the contrary, he maliciously imitates all its symbols out of context. Behaving like a self-confident hero, the clown debunks heroism; with emphasized haughtiness he ridicules the mannerisms of those who are used to command others; his overdone sadness and his excessive weeping persiflages all sentimentality. He imitates the stunts of the real acrobats and displays the fearlessness of the lion tamer. For the short time that he appears on the stage, he mockingly plays all social roles while his audience laughs at all of them even though it consists of people who in everyday life play the same roles in all seriousness.

About whom do they laugh? About the clown or about themselves? About the failure of the clown to live up to the nomos, or about the nomos itself? About the ruling order's arrogant claim to be the only possible one, or about the person who defies this claim? Who laughs? Is it the clown, the marginal outsider, or is it the audience when it is taken to and beyond the limits of its own restricting order? Or still another possibility: is not the clown perhaps himself the laughter of the Infinite about the Finite when it pretends to be absolute? The laughter of God: for the insiders of the nomos the very possibility of God laughing is already blasphemy. But that God should laugh about the order which its inventors, maintainers, and utilizers attribute to his holy will, this is worse than blasphemy. It is the beginning of the rule of the Lord of Disorder, the threatening end of all cohesion. This is the reason why a suppression of the clown will be attempted again and again. But it will never succeed. If the complete ban of this unruly, ungodly character is not possible, then, at least, he can be restricted to the entertainment of the lower classes, to low comedy and the puppet show. There he need not be taken seriously. There he can make his jokes and jests, a sub-human being for the amusement of people who do not count.

Yet the challenge persists. And the strange fact remains that the clown, always suspected of being the emissary of the devil, really challenges the lords of this world not in the name of a mythical and unreal Lord of Disorder, but in the name of that Power before whom all human nomos becomes like nothing. Precisely because he wears the mask of the devil, precisely because he plays the role of the mischievous unruly counterpart, he knows something that his frightened, laughing audience does not know: that there is no Lord of Disorder. Inspired by this freedom he pretends to be the opponent of all that society calls sacred.

An old German name for the devil is *der Widersacher*, the representative of the opposite cause, the counter-advocate. But can the one and only God have a counter-power? *Nemo contra Deum nisi Deus ipse,* wrote Leibniz (nobody can oppose God except God himself). Thus, eventually, this *advocatus diaboli,* the clown, testifies to the uncontested majesty of the only Lord by reducing *ad absurdum* all presumptuous claims that any human nomos can ever be absolute.

FIVE

The Clown
in Contemporary Art

SAMUEL H. MILLER

The mystery which concerns us is the mystery of the changing metaphor—the way metaphors are born and die, the way they serve an age and are exhausted, the way they lapse from the dynamic to the static. What excites and satisfies one epoch is utterly lifeless to another; what arouses intense reaction in one age may not have power enough in another to cause a person to raise an eyebrow in passing. A metaphor may indeed be something like revelation, disclosing an unsuspected unity of relationship, or it may be a mere cliché, worn out by custom and no longer capable of surprise.

I do not know when I first began to notice it, but it was a long time ago. It took time, like a seed in the dark soil, to germinate and become visible, a form or an idea, perhaps only an intimation. But once its suggestion was in the air, I wondered why I had not seen it earlier or more clearly. It seemed so self-evident. Yet it still was not without its mysterious distances, somewhat hazy, vague, and indistinct. Even when

I am sure about it, there are breaks in it, where it does not fall together perfectly, but only with a kind of tantalizing sense that it would, if I were more perceptive and knew more about it.

What I am talking about is the prevalence of clowns, of one sort or another, in the arts of our time. In poetry, drama, novel, painting, they stand all around us, a varied but ubiquitous company with faces marked with an extreme seriousness of whatever it is they are trying to tell us. There are Picasso's Harlequins, his company of acrobats, derived from Rilke's poem; there are Rouault's powerful visages of the clown in stained glass starkness like crude Gothic saints; there is Charlie Chaplin himself; there are the poems by Hart Crane through which his art was celebrated; there are the clowns of Genet and Henry Miller and Heinrich Böll and Archibald MacLeish, of Mallarmé, of Eliot, and of Joyce. They are symbols, living symbols of something which crowds the pages of our literature and presses its face against the windows of our imagination on all sides. What is this grease-paint, this "sacre"? What does it denote of the human condition, the mystery of being man? Why does the clown fascinate the imagination of our age, preempt the mind of the novelist, the vision of the artist, the lines of the poet? Where does he take his place in what Wallace Stevens calls "the mythology of the self"? He is more than the small change of casual entertainment. What kind of coin in the commerce of passion and tears is he, and what do we buy with him?

I

The clown, by his excessive exaggeration and gross simplicity, touches the hem of the metaphysical, that realm which tends to be smothered in ages proud of their pragmatic and utilitarian efficiency. Eric Heller, in *The Disinherited Mind*, tells of the Munich clown whom he characterizes as "one of the greatest of the rare race of metaphysical clowns," measuring everything within reach with a small ruler and then in turn measuring the ruler with another. He recounts how he once enacted the following scene: the curtain goes up and reveals darkness; and in this darkness is a solitary circle of light thrown by a street-lamp. Vallentin, with his long-drawn and deeply worried face, walks round and round this circle of light, desperately looking for something. "What have you lost?" a policeman asks who has entered the scene. "The key to my house." Upon which the policeman joins him in his search; they find nothing; and after a while he inquires: "Are you sure you lost it here?" "No," says Vallentin, and pointing to a dark corner of the stage: "Over there." "Then why on earth are you looking for it here?" "There is no light over there," says Vallentin. Here laughter cannot dispel the profoundly disturbing meaning which hovers over the event, just out of sight. The humor is human, but the meaning is transcendent. The beyond speaks to something hidden within.

So it is with Emmet Kelly. Out of outrageous rags and tatters, he contrives a costume of great self-importance, or he acknowledges proudly the moment of triumph only to lose his trousers, or he earnestly and patiently does his utmost to sweep the spotlight from the ground into a dustpan. These actions, simpler than language, push beyond the limits of language to a reality much more whole and stubbornly beyond our control.

Undoubtedly one of the great clown figures of all time was Cervantes' Don Quixote. Of profound and seemingly inexhaustible implications, the don exhibits all the absurdities of the human situation. His illusions and heroism, his credulity and chivalry, are bound together in a way which touches the quick of our own contradictions and embarrassments. He is the "picaro and the pilgrim," caught in the most outlandish absurdities, but everywhere transcending the bitter by the

sweetness of himself, acting from a cosmic or transcendent
source which enables him to triumph even in failure. He is
a fool, to be sure, but in being fool, he is Everyman, and by
being himself, he is everybody. Eric Auerbach has written of
him very perceptively (*Mimesis,* Princeton University Press,
1953, pp. 305, 307–8):

> Don Quixote is not only ridiculous. He is not like the bragging
> soldier or the comic old man or the pedantic and ignorant doctor
> . . . with all his madness, Don Quixote preserves a natural dig-
> nity and superiority which his many miserable failures cannot
> harm. . . . He even develops, and grows kinder and wiser as
> his madness persists. . . . There are levels of tone represented
> here (in Don Quixote) which one is not accustomed to finding
> in purely comic contexts. A fool is a fool. But what are we to
> say of a fool who is at the same time wise, with that wisdom which
> seems the least compatible with folly, that is, the wisdom of
> intelligent moderation. This very fact, this combination of in-
> telligent moderation with absurd excesses results in a multiplicity,
> which cannot be made to accord altogether with the purely comic.
> But that is not all. It is on the very wings of his madness that his
> wisdom soars upward, that it roams the world and becomes richer
> there . . . the levels of gaiety are multiplied as never before.

He acts out of a reservoir of resource beyond the banal
routine of facile conformity. In him, various worlds collide,
and instead of thunder one hears laughter, which is a kind
of explicit recognition that both worlds are necessary. Indeed,
as Geoffrey Clive points out, Schubert's celebrated song, *Der
Doppelgänger*, particularly with its unresolved ending, might
well be *the* song of our times.

It is a very interesting question which rises from the work of
Albert Camus, whose basic philosophical vision of the "absurd"
determines the moral climate of his essays and fiction, why this
does not eventuate in the creation of a clown in the numerous

personae of his novels and plays. One might have presumed that the imbalance, the incongruity between man's dreams and aspirations and the cosmic necessities, would have quite naturally produced the clown figure. Not that one does not see many touches of it—in the diffidence of Meurseault, in the exaggerations of Caligula, in the ironies of Jean Baptiste, in the not quite closed interstices of the little stories and the longings and the failures of understanding between people. Is it that the sublime and the transcendent realities from which it was derived in the Middle Ages have become exhausted in the modern age? Has the situation, in the colder light of reason which burgeons throughout the world like a hard noonday sun, allowed no place for illusions and the softer fantasy of the human heart? Has the horror and the terror of the last years, of Dachau and Hiroshima, and the sickening shame of it all, left us without recourse to the ritual of laughter, by which we might be cleansed? Has life been so flattened out by the industrial juggernaut of senseless speed and cluttered claptrap that men can utter only one note, like a mechanical toy, and the complex music of humor, that rare blend of the solemn and the foolish, of the tender and the cruel, cannot be voiced? One can scarcely say what the answers are to these questions, except that they are disturbing and urge us to continue our attention to the subtler factors of our contemporary culture.

II

We may be able to disentangle some of the strands in this phenomenon by beginning with a rather simple novel, called *Doubting Thomas*, by Winston Brebner. It is not a great work in any sense of the term, but it does illustrate the place and function of the Clown—with a capital C. The story occurs in a city-state, where society has been "computerized"—all actions have been routinized, all irregularities eliminated, all human concerns efficiently fitted into a pattern. The system is maintained by a central agency of machines. No mistakes, no embarrassments, are permitted. The system is perfect, and the highest degree of conformity is the only civic virtue.

In this situation, somewhat reminiscent of the first chapter of Dostoevski's *Letters from the Underground,* Thomas, a magistrate in the bureaucracy which runs the agency, manages once a year during the State Holiday, which has replaced all traditional holidays, to escape from routine by telling his family he has been asked to visit a neighboring city by the authorities. Instead, he goes to a nearby hotel, disguises himself as a clown, and mixes gaily with the crowds. In the course of ten years, he becomes not only famous but is held in great public affection. He is *the* clown, their clown, and his advent is looked forward to with excited expectation. In describing him, the author says, "his costume was human frailty, human helplessness, and his lot was the human lot of one disaster after another. His comedy was misfortune, and his enduring grace the patience and dignity with which he survived an existence of interlinked catastrophes." One of his admirers says, "You have a special gift, Mr. Clown . . . for making us laugh at ourselves, at our weaknesses, our foolish suspicions, our pretensions. . . ." He is spoken of as "hilariously crucified." The closing paragraph contains the following: "Clown stood up. Facing the impassive glass countenance of Mr. Bixby's office, he bowed with exaggerated gravity, then turned and shuffled slowly toward the exit, a frail, ridiculous man whose sloping shoulders bore the burden of every human embarrassment and indignity, an absurd little man whose face wore the mask of unreasonable persecution, a man who would survive and endure because he was frail, because he was ridiculous and persecuted—and because he was loved."

The gist of this simple story is that humankind is redeemed from its false pretensions by the enactment of its true humanity, its very frailty. The false perfections which make life an impossible burden are swept away by the gestures and mimicry of all the blundering embarrassments of our all too human condition. The Clown reminds them, dramatically, visually, in ways beyond debate or denial, of their essential humanity— and they are saved. He is the Clown with a capital C—the source of their salvation.

The plot thickens, however, as we step from this simple story to one told by Henry Miller, called "The Smile at the Foot of the Ladder." Here a clown by the name of Auguste, sitting at the foot of a ladder which reached to a moon fastened to the roof of the tent, would sit in contemplation, with an extraordinary smile on his face, a smile which "expressed the ineffable." This simulation of ecstasy which he had brought to perfection, always impressed the audience as incongruous. "Never had the buffoon thought to depict the miracle of ascension."

As Henry Miller describes him, "Each evening as he applied the maquillage, Auguste would hold a debate with himself. The seals, no matter what they were obliged to do, always remained seals. The horse remained a horse, the table a table. Whereas Auguste, while remaining a man, had to become something more: he had to assume the powers of a very special being with a very special gift . . . he wanted to endow his spectators with a joy which would prove imperishable."

After playing this part, so extreme that the usual laughter turned to jeers, Auguste fled from the circus, remembering the most important moment in his life, what he called "a revelation" in himself. He finally makes his way back to the circus and shares in the menial drudgery with great satisfaction. But when a clown is taken ill, he takes his place, explaining, "It's droll, what! A little grease paint, a bladder, a funny costume —how little it takes to make oneself into a nobody! That's what we are, nobodies. And everybody at the same time. It's not us they applaud, it's they themselves."

A tragedy ensues, partly because of Auguste's effort to help, and once again he is thrust into pondering the mystery of his being a clown. "His real tragedy, he began to perceive, lay in the fact that he was unable to communicate his knowledge of another world, a world beyond ignorance and frailty, beyond laughter and tears. It was this barrier that kept him a clown, God's very own clown, for truly there was no one to whom he could make clear his dilemma."

"And then and there it came to him—how simple it was! that to be nobody or anybody or everybody did not prevent him from being himself. If he were really a clown, then he should be one through and through, from the time he got up in the morning until he closed his eyes. He should be a clown in season and out. . . ."

As Miller says in his very moving epilogue, "A clown is a poet in action. . . . It is the same story over and over— adoration, devotion, crucifixion."

This is the story of a reality seldom perceived, of another world, another world not separated from this one but perceived through it and in it. The metaphor by which it is indicated is a ladder, an imperishable smile, and a moon dangling from the tent roof. And it is a world of such magic and mystery that everybody becomes nobody, and the nobodies everybody. It is a world from which no one is excluded except the man who refuses to enter it. Through it, sustaining and supporting it, is the mystery of the transcendent, out of which the "imperishable joy" comes.

One begins to see the complex symbolization involved in the clown or in the medieval fool. As R. W. B. Lewis points out, using William Empson's formula, "Since in the medieval view all men were fools in the eyes of God, so the type of fool was exactly 'Everyman in the presence of God.' " The human fool, so ridiculous and even contemptible to human eyes, was just the way any man, Everyman, looked when inspected by the Creator. As motleyed jester, as invented figure in poetry and drama, in impromptu festivals, the fool was a device for commenting on power, wealth, and intellect in an other-worldly perspective—from which perspective the comment could sound not only like good precautionary sense but a humbling echo of the wisdom of God. He was at the same time a device for acknowledging and celebrating those nonrational and antinomian aspects of human nature that it is always perilous for a culture to suppress or to undervalue.

III

A third step which we are about to take leads us into the realm of the poets, whose metaphors act like mirrors in which we catch obliquely glimpses of a reality we would otherwise miss in our direct vision. The two poems I want to use at this juncture of our investigation are Wallace Stevens' "The Comedian as the letter C" and Hart Crane's "Chaplinesque."

Let us look at the first. Here man is described as the "sovereign ghost," "the Socrates of snails," "musician of pears," "nincompated pedagogue"—in short, Crispin, the ancient clown whose changing relations with the universe constitute his mortal pilgrimage in the course of which, like Auguste, he learns to strip himself down to his essential self. Early in the venture, the "mythology of self, blotched out beyond unblotching" in his confrontation with the sea, "washed away by magnitude," cuts him down from the figure of the swaggering valet to a "skinny sailor peering in the sea-glass," until nothing of himself remained except some "starker, barer self in a starker, barer world."

Bereft of a flamboyant romanticism, he then turns to an

introspective voyage of exotic and grandiose color until he finds a "new reality in parrot squawks." Disillusioned in the last "distortion of romance," he becomes a "searcher for the fecund minimum," a "sinewy nakedness," "the essential prose as being." Finally, he comes to reckon with the hard, involuble lump of life, and "dropped the chuckling down his craw, without grace or grumble."

> Hence it was,
> Preferring text to globes, he humbly served
> Grotesque apprenticeship to chance event,
> A clown, perhaps, but an aspiring clown.

"The Comedian" was written in 1923; later, in 1937, he wrote "The Man with the Blue Guitar," a poem about the same problem, namely, man's relationship with the world. The Man, in this case, is not a clown, although there are passages that suggest it, as

> He held the world upon his nose
> And this-a-way he gave a fling.

> His robes and symbols, ei-yi-yi-
> And that-a-way he twirled the thing.

But here again rises that strange meeting of two worlds, as in "The Comedian":

> The man bent over his guitar,
> A shearsman of sorts. The day was green.

> They said, "You have a blue guitar,
> You do not play things as they are."

> The man replied, "Things as they are
> Are changed upon the blue guitar."

Or, later,

> Throw away the lights, the definitions,
> And say of what you see in the dark
>
> That it is this or that it is that,
> But do not use the rotted names.

Here is "the wrangling of the two dreams," the dream within reality, the reality within dream. The hotel is better than the church, but the sacred light burns there, a "time beyond us as we are," "the blue guitar and I are one," "the missal found in the mud." Here all the tangled contradictions of what Camus calls "the absurd" are repeated in the bright enamelled colors of Stevens' poetry; here is the laughter that rises from the sad embarrassment of humanity as he twists grotesquely in his rags to reach dignity.

With Hart Crane's poem, we come to a less brilliantly colored and sparkling portrait of the clown, but one which actually speaks more poignantly, as if the clown himself were speaking, or better still, as if a man had identified himself with the clown and knew in himself the stuff of dreams and disillusionment which are the very substance of clown reality. The poem was written after Hart Crane had seen Charles Chaplin in *The Kid*. This man, who has proved to be one of the great clowns of the world, holding in the rather tipsy humor of his mimicry the passion and heartache of the world, had profoundly impressed Crane, whose own dreams and failures opened his heart wide with natural understanding. Remembering that figure with its dapper mustache, the baggy trousers, and the twirling flimsy cane, one catches the overtone of that large and comic absurdity that lies beneath the flip gestures of the lonely one.

> We make our meek adjustments
> Contented with such random consolations
> As the wind deposits
> In slithered and too ample pockets.
>
> For we can still love the world, who find
> A famished kitten on the step, and know
> Recesses for it from the fury of the street
> Or warm torn elbow coverts.

As Hart Crane moves on past the doom that always pursues the clown in the shape of the dour policeman, he rises at last in the last quatrain and says:

> The game enforces smirks; but we have seen
> The moon in lonely alleys make
> A grail of laughter of an empty ash-can
> And through all sounds of gaiety and quest
> Have heard a kitten in the wilderness.

Even the simplest clown manages by gesture and incident to explore the mythology of the self. He, too, like the saint, extends the dimension of consciousness beyond its normal limits. His ritual has its own sanctity as it elicits from us all the subtler dramas of our destiny.

IV

The clown recovers for us the nature of our humanity. In him, in his ludicrous contradictions of dignity and embarrassment, of pomp and rags, of assurance and collapse, of sentiment and sadness, of innocence and guile, we learn to see ourselves. We follow in his bold bluff, and crumple in his public disasters. We are, in short, restored to our humanity, delivered of all the unreal bombast, the pretence of invulnerability, the emperor complex of being beyond it all. The smirks, the traps, the sudden descent, the shattering realization of reaching beyond ourselves, the startling disclosure of our absurd weakness, our naked self uncovered in its ludicrous contradictoriness—all this is part of salvation. It is the tilted tipsy halo, half broken, that crowns the Clown with a capital C.

But the amazing second fact, seemingly in open denial of the first, is that the clown lives by his illusions. His dreams are the engines which drive him beyond all his temporary shames; they pick him up after each dismal collapse; they repair his dignity and clothe his outraged countenance with an equally outrageous smile. His longings have no limit; his heart is invincible. However deep the failure, or shocking the sudden storm of embarrassment, or bewildering the descent of judgment, his tenderness is inviolable. He begins over again, whatever invisible burden his heart holds. There is a world beyond him, within him, a world of inexhaustible hope, of infinite patience, of undeniable good will. He is indeed the *Doppelgänger,* the man with two shadows, two worlds, one in the dust, crumpled, embarrassed, shattered, the fool, the failure—the other in the sky, incredibly gay, utterly impossible but never unbelievable, where the bright banners of his lonely dreams and shy hopes fly in the heroic winds of a very human heaven.

Indeed, I suspect the authentic clown is only possible in the world of the imagination, where there is a very solid and sustaining belief to sustain the double vision. Humor, warm, kind, openhearted, hospitable, a humor in which we can all share and be one in a burst of laughter, this humor disappears in a one-level world, a so-called realistic world, from which dreams have fled in the face of condescension or derision. Such a world has but one reaction to embarrassment or human frailty, namely, violence. And our world, especially the world of entertainment, is filled with it. Much more violence of gangsterism than, let us say, the invisible gaiety of the clown.

Would one be treading on too holy ground, would one be speaking offensively, if he were to suggest that the reason there is so little space for a *Doppelgänger,* a clown, may be the same reason for there being so little space for a Christ? He, too, was incognito, disguised in the flesh, of no reputation, despised and rejected, a man acquainted with sorrow and grief, of such a countenance that no one thought him comely, the drama of his crucifixion played against the pretensions of power.

SIX

The Rhetoric
of Christian Comedy

BARRY ULANOV

In the second scene of the first act of *A Midsummer Night's Dream* six of the most delightful fellows ever called together by Shakespeare make themselves a company to perform "The Most Lamentable Comedy and Most Cruel Death of Pyramus and Thisby." The occasion is the wedding feast of Theseus, Duke of Athens, and Hippolyta, Queen of the Amazons. The actors, as far removed in station as possible from the nobility of the bride and bridegroom, are a carpenter, Peter Quince, a weaver, Nick Bottom, a bellows-mender, Francis Flute, a tinker, Tom Snout, a tailor, Robin Starveling, and a joiner, one Snug. Thus, quickly, is the classical definition of comedy served:

As for Comedy, it is (as has been observed) an imitation of men worse than the average; worse, however, not as regards any and every sort of fault, but only as regards one particular kind, the Ridiculous, which is a species of the Ugly. The Ridiculous may be defined as a mistake or deformity not productive of pain or harm to others; the mask, for instance, that excites laughter, is something ugly and distorted without causing pain.[1]

Men intrinsically worse than the average? Well, not exactly; Aristotle draws his estimation of character from caste, and so does Shakespeare. These are plebeians. They are also suited by every other means to offer a dramatic imitation of the ridiculous. Peter Quince identifies his cast:

Here is the scroll of every man's name which is thought fit, through all Athens, to play in our interlude before the Duke and Duchess on his wedding-day at night.

And "fit" the names are, that is, ridiculous: Quince, Bottom, Flute, Snug, Snout, Starveling. And fit the men as well, especially Bottom, who would like to play a lover—one who kills himself for love—

If I do it, let the audience look to their eyes; I will move storms; I will condole in some measure.

Bottom, who would like to play not only lover, but beloved—

An I may hide my face, let me play Thisby too. I'll speak in a monstrous little voice.

Bottom, who would like to play every part—

Let me play the lion too. I will roar that I will do any man's heart good to hear me; I will roar that I will make the Duke say, 'Let him roar again, let him roar again.'

(MND, I, ii)

[1] Aristotle, *Poetics*, 5, trans. Ingram Bywater, in *The Basic Works of Aristotle,* ed. Richard McKeon (New York, 1941), p. 1459.

Bottom, who would like to play all, ultimately plays the one
part for which he has not cast himself. By a small masterpiece
of preternatural mischief, he is assified, provided with a don-
key's head. In return for his itching pains and scratchy sounds
he is suffered to make a kind of love to Titania, Queen of the
Fairies, and to be loved by her. "Methinks," he says, "I am
marvellous hairy about the face; and I am such a tender ass, if
my hair do but tickle me, I must scratch." "Methought," she
says, "I was enamour'd of an ass." (IV, i)

A *Midsummer Night's Dream* is a comedy of enchantments
and disenchantments, entanglements and disentanglements.
Every romantic type is encountered in the play. There are
young lovers and old lovers, triangles and quadrangles, fideli-
ties and betrayals, hostilities and tranquilities. But what is
most betrayed, what is most hostile and least faithful, is love
itself. In a fairyland that is monstrously perverse, love is
mimicked, love is mocked, love is everything but sweet and
tender and true. Love can be summoned or dismissed by the
sprinkling of the juice of an herb called love-in-idleness.

> The juice of it on sleeping eyelids laid
> Will make or man or woman madly dote
> Upon the next live creature that it sees. . . .
>
> Be it on lion, bear, or wolf, or bull,
> On meddling monkey, or on busy ape . . .   (II, i)

Love in idleness, we may possibly conclude, is not the most
delicate of sentiments.

What saves a warm summer dream from turning into a
wintry nightmare is our easy acceptance of a constant irony of
situation and a corollary rhetoric. Texture, tone, and type are
all consistent. Everything is turned upside down. The four
points of a compass of couples are convincingly interchanged:

north is south and east is west; love is crossed and double-crossed. That is the nature of this comedy of inversion. An ass's head really belongs atop Bottom.

Shakespeare's inversions were apparently an old English custom, at least old enough in 1578 to draw scorn from George Whetstone as something that had been too long with his people. Whetstone, who will always have a lien on posterity for having provided Shakespeare with the plot of *Measure for Measure* in his own unperformed comedy *Promos and Cassandra,* the plot of which he in turn took from Giraldi Cinthio, offers in the dedication to *Promos* a "rehearsall of the use and abuse of Commedies," to the end, at "least that I Checke that in others which I cannot amend in my selfe." In that dedication he arraigns, in order of lasciviousness, Italians, Frenchmen, and Spaniards: "the Germaine is too holye, for he presents on everye common Stage what Preachers should pronounce in Pulpets." But most startling of all is the Englishman, as a playwright "most vaine, indiscreete, and out of order." He is indecorous. He is unreasonable.

he fyrst groundes his worke on impossibilities; then in three howers ronnes he throwe the worlde, marryes, gets Children, makes Children men, men to conquer kingdomes, murder Monsters, and bringeth Gods from Heaven, and fetchetch Divels from Hel. And (that which is worst) their ground is not so unperfect as their workinge indiscreete: not waying, so the people laugh, though they laugh them (for their follyes) to scorne. Manye times (to make mirthe) they make a Clowne companion with a Kinge; in theyr grave Counsels they allow the advise of fooles; yea, they use one order of speech for all persons: a grose *Indecorum,* for a Crowe wyll yll counterfet the Nightingale's sweete voice; even so affected speeche doth misbecome a Clowne. For, to worke a Commedie kindly, grave olde men should instruct, yonge men should showe the imperfections of youth, Strumpets should be lascivious, Boyes unhappy, and Clownes should speake disorderlye: entermingling all these actions in such sorte as the grave matter may instruct and the pleasant delight. . . .[2]

Irony was too acute in the English, however, at least in those of talent, to permit such simple-minded characterization. Kindly, grave old men could offer sententious advice that was a good deal less than instructive, except, by a double irony, for getting on in the world. Witness Polonius. And certainly playwrights could, no matter how indecorous it might seem to some, put sage advice in the mouths of fools and make a clown a fit companion for a King. Witness Feste and Speed and Launcelot Gobbo and Lear's Fool. Especially in comedy would they not scruple to be "indiscreete" or to ground their work "on impossibilities." What better way to express their scorn for men's follies? The typology of comedy of this sort was one of foolish men doing foolish things, either because of their state of life or in spite of it. For the writers of such works, there was no melodrama, no warfare between illustrious houses, no tempests, no exotic scenes,

> But deedes, and language, such as man doe use,
> And persons, such as *Comoedie* would chuse,
> When she would shew an Image of the times,
> And sport with humane follies, not with crimes,
> Except we make 'hem such, by loving still
> Our popular errors, when we know th'are ill.
> I mean such errors as you'll all confesse,
> By laughing at them, they deserve no lesse:
> Which when you heartily doe, there's hope left then,
> You, that have so grac'd monsters, may like men.

The prescription is Ben Jonson's in the Prologue to *Every Man in His Humour,* written either in the same year as *A Midsummer Night's Dream,* 1596, or at most two years later.

---

[2] George Whetstone, Dedication to *Promos and Cassandra,* in *Elizabethan Critical Essays,* ed. G. G. Smith (Oxford, 1904), I, pp. 59–60.

The moral purpose of comedy thus understood is clear enough: "altogither to the good amendment of man by discipline and example," as George Puttenham said in 1589; "to make the vice scorned and not embraced," as Sir John Harington explained in 1591; "an imitation of the common errors of our life, which he [the playwright] representeth in the most ridiculous and scornful sort that may be; so as it is impossible that any beholder can be content to be such a one," as Sir Philip Sidney explained in 1583.[3] But the range of meditation that accompanied such moralizing was wider than these definitions suggest. It went beyond trope and examplum to the anagoge in its rhetoric, beyond discipline and illustration to the elevation of the spirit.

At the end of *A Midsummer Night's Dream*, Oberon, King of the Fairies, brings the pageant to a happy conclusion and a holy one.

> Now, until the break of day,
> Through this house each fairy stray.
> To the best bride-bed will we,
> Which by us shall blessed be;
> And the issue there create
> Ever shall be fortunate.
> So shall all the couples three
> Ever true in loving be;
> And the blots of Nature's hand
> Shall not in their issue stand;
> Never mole, hare-lip, nor scar,
> Nor mark prodigious, such as are
> Despised in nativity,
> Shall upon their children be.

[3] George Puttenham, *The Arte of English Poesie,* Chap. XIV, in Smith, *op. cit.,* p. 33. Sir John Harington, Preface to the translation of *Orlando Furioso,* in Smith, II, p. 209. Sir Philip Sidney, *An Apologie for Poetrie,* in Smith, I, pp. 176–177.

With this field-dew consecrate,
Every fairy take his gait,
And each several chamber bless,
Through this palace, with sweet peace;
And the owner of it blest
Ever shall in safety rest.

(MND, V, i)

Not even Puck's easy excuse to those who may have found
the theatrical indignities offensive—

Think but this, and all is mended,
That you have but slumb'red here
While these visions did appear.

—can altogether dissipate the effect of Oberon's beneficence.
To "all the couples three" has been restored nothing less than
their preternature. They shall never again lose themselves in
hostility or infidelity. They have found themselves in virtue.
And the virtues of the fathers shall be visited upon the sons:
"the blots of Nature's hand Shall not in their issue stand."
This is not the conventional happy ending, which so many,
such as Dante, had learned from the comedies of Terence.
Dante's vision was, of course, a little larger than the Roman
playwright's, his understanding of the end of comedy a little
loftier: "it is clear why the present work [the *Commedia*] is
called a comedy. For if we examine the theme, in the beginning it is frightening and foul, because it is hell; at the end,
fortunate, desirable, and joyful, because it is paradise." [4] And
so it is with the *Dream*, even if its extremes are not quite so
obvious and its view into eternity not quite so clear. It is unmistakably hellish when the plot spins around the juices of
love-in-idleness and unmistakably heavenly when the ben-
ediction is accomplished with consecrated field-dew, as holy

[4] Dante Alighieri, *Epistolae,* X, 10.

a water as a love-game comedy has ever made accessible to its contestants. And so at the end, we are summoned, gently, as befitting the texture of the comedy, to contemplate the terrors instinct in "the blots of Nature's hand" and the joys potential in all who will "Ever true in loving be."

Christian comedy inevitably finds its identifying rhetoric in this antithesis. That rhetoric is not, however, a simple series of dualisms, with hell always hanging fire at one end of the dialectical exchange and heaven always oozing honey at the other. It is rare that the comedy is reduced to terms so naive. Even when heaven and hell can be discovered open to the eye, as in Dante's *Commedia* in the early fourteenth century, or the *Suenos* (the *Visions* or *Dreams*) of Francisco de Quevedo, in the early seventeenth century, there is very much more to both states than meets the eye. In *Los Suenos,* for example, Quevedo's visions usually turn upon a bitter dismissal of this world. Hell is not the next world; it is this one— or rather, to be exact, it is Quevedo's seventeenth-century Spain. In one of the *Visions,* there is a general revolt in hell. The damned attack the devils and come very close to taking over hell. A spokesman for the damned—"a monstrous talker" —convinces Lucifer that his devils are a lazy lot, with no sense of responsibility, no fundamental concern for hellish affairs, and little loyalty to Satan. They are not organization men. Another shows him that he is very close to losing his crown: there are lawyers and doctors and a lay apostle (a "mongrel priest," Quevedo calls him, "a kind of lay elder") plotting to replace him. Lucifer puts down the revolt with a handsomely constructed legal document, which is frightening simply because of the sheer weight of its oppressive legal language. But it is the last item of this solemn decree that really terrorizes all hell, damned and devils alike. Lucifer promises to unleash duennas—a positive rain of old chaperons—in his dominions.

"Ah! cursed Lucifer," cried everyone to himself, "stow them anywhere, so they come not near me." And with that, they all clapped their tails between their legs, and drew in their horns, for fear of this new torment. Lucifer, finding how the dread of old women wrought upon the devils, contented himself, at the present, to let it pass only *in terrorem;* but withal he swore, by the honour of his imperial crown, and as he hoped to be saved, that what devil, devil's dam, or reprobate soever, should in time to come be found wanting to his duty and in the least degree disobedient to his laws and ordinances, all and every the said devil or devils, their dams and reprobates so offending, should be delivered up to the torture of the Duenna, and tied muzzle to muzzle; so to remain *in saecula saeculorum* without relief or appeal, or any law, statute, or usage to the contrary notwithstanding. "But in the meantime, cast them into that dry ditch," says he, "that they may be ready for use upon any occasion." [5]

That does it. The revolution is over.

The point of Quevedo's comedy is never heavily shrouded. It is at its clearest in the middle of the last of the *Suenos* when the advisability of returning to earth is being debated—with covert, if not open, apologies to Giovanni Pontano, Leon Battista Alberti and all the other renaissance worthies who followed Lucian's lead in developing this noble example of infernal argumentation. A brainy fellow, who has "entered very gravely upon the debate," lists all the miseries of life on earth, the physical discomforts, the psychological torments, and especially the terrifying example of an old man in love "put to gallant it against a company of young gamesters." But enough of that! Let us turn to happy events—"the comforts of life, the humours and manners." What happens then? The passage should be read with full diapason.

[5] Francisco de Quevedo, *The Visions,* trans. Sir Roger L'Estrange (1667), in *Quevedo: The Choice Humorous and Satirical Works,* ed. Charles Duff (London, 1926), pp. 290–291.

"He that would be rich must play the thief or the cheat; he that would rise in the world must turn parasite, informer, or projector. He that marries ventures fair for the horn, either before or after. There is no valour without swearing, quarrelling, or hectoring. If you are poor, nobody owns ye. If rich, you'll know nobody. If you die young, 'What pity it was,' they'll say, 'that he should be cut off thus in his prime.' If old, 'He was e'en past his best; there's no great miss of him.' If you are religious, and frequent the church and the sacrament, you're an hypocrite; and without this, you're an atheist or an heretic. If you are gay and pleasant, you pass presently for a buffoon; and if pensive and reserved, you are taken to be sour and censorious. Courtesy is called colloguing and currying of favour; downright honesty and plain-dealing is interpreted to be pride and ill manners. This is the world; and for all that's in it I would not have it to go over again. If any of ye, my masters," said he to his comrades, "be of another opinion hold up your hands." "No, no," they cried all unanimously, "no more generation-work I beseech ye; better the devil than the midwives." [6]

Here are a hundred comedies or more, all the plays of Molière, all the works, from Plautus to Dickens, in which humbug, hypocrisy, chicanery and doubledealing of any kind have been exposed, and all with at least an air of that special kind of melancholia that goes by the name of misanthropy, that not quite sonorous lament which expresses a vote of no confidence in man.

Christian comedy does hold out some hope. Hell is just around the corner, in a lawyer's chambers, a doctor's surgery, an ample lounge chair filled with a duenna. But so is paradise. Even Lucifer, Quevedo tells us wryly, and very much in passing, hopes to be saved. By so doing, he tells us our case is almost as stubborn; we have about as much chance of being saved as the devil. In the hell we have made on earth, we have

[6] *Ibid.*, p. 275.

almost cast ourselves off from God's mercy. That is why, perhaps, *Los Suenos* ends just after Lucifer has made his threat
to visit hell with a pestilence of chaperons. The clouds disappear from the usually murky regions. The crowds disperse
in the face of the menace. At this point a voice emerges from
the clouds, like that of an angel, with the last word: "He that
rightly comprehends the morality of this discourse shall never
repent the reading of it." [7] The statement is ambiguous only to
those to whom the terms of Christian comedy or of salvation
are ambiguous.

The terms of Christian comedy must include hope. It is the
theological virtue best served by comedy of any kind. But in
the Christian genre, hope is not necessarily as neatly tied to
the curtain lines as William Webbe tells us it always is in
classical comedy. There, no matter how doubtful the begin-
nings, or how embroiled the plottings, the ending "by some
lucky chance" is always in "the joy and appeasement of all
parties." [8] In a Christian work, a sense of truth generally
precludes any such facile conclusion. What is merely a final
touch of fantasy in a play that has not strained at any kind
of distortion in order to amuse audiences or to express scorn,
in a Christian comedy would be intolerable. It would make
the whole drama seem synthetic. It would suggest a machinery
of providence quite out of keeping with Christian theology and
would impose symmetries on dramatic action at variance with
both theology and life. The effect would be as crude as a bit
of Aesopian moralizing at the end of a complex narrative of
many involutions. No, hope must be expressed more subtly in
Christian comedy and in sense will be clear only to him
"that rightly comprehends the morality" of the discourse.
Irony is the logical tone of Christian comedy. Its rhetoric is

[7] *Ibid.*, p. 291.
[8] William Webbe, *A Discourse of English Poetrie*, in Smith, *op. cit.*, I, p.
249.

customarily oblique, its figures frequently very difficult to understand. Hope is as much veiled in Christian comedy as it is in Christian life.[9]

Distance necessarily adds to the obscurity of the rhetoric, sometimes rather more than one would have expected. The robust sense of humor of the Christian mind of the middle

[9] Irony of this sort has high sanction. Christ uses this method of teaching, veiling truth in parables of an ironic texture, as for example when He compares the kingdom of heaven to a penny lost by a careless housewife, who then turns her house upside down in a frenzied effort to find it, or when He shows the efficacy of prayer by describing a beggar who makes such an uproar in the middle of a night that a man who wants to sleep must yield to the beggar or forego sleep entirely, or when He praises virtue by urging people to imitate an unjust steward and makes friends of the mammon of iniquity. It is to this august precedent that Giovanni Boccaccio appeals in the fourteenth century, in defending the right and a need of Christian poets for oblique figurative language and veiled fiction. See his *Genealogia Deorum Gentilium,* XIV and XV, passim, and especially chapters IX, X, XIII, and XIV of Book XIV. Charles Osgood's graceful translation of Books XIV and XV is called *Boccaccio on Poetry* (Princeton, 1930; now available in the Library of Liberal Arts).

The delights of this method were not lost on any of the great Christian wits. St. Thomas More teaches a serious truth by means of a humorous irony that unfortunately many people seem to miss when he suggests that the only place a perfect natural society can be found is Nowhere, in *Utopia.* Erasmus spreads wisdom by praising Folly. Jonathan Swift makes his most impassioned defense of faith by means of AN ARGUMENT *To prove that the Abolishing of CHRISTIANITY IN ENGLAND, may as Things now stand, be attended with some Inconveniences, and perhaps not produce those many good Effects proposed thereby.* Courageously, he insists, "though I were sure, an Order were issued out for my immediate Prosecution by the Attorney-General, I should still confess that in the present Posture of our Affairs at home or abroad, I do not yet see the absolute Necessity of extirpating the Christian Religion from among us." And so he continues in that teasing tone until he concludes, "Whatever some may think of the great Advantages to Trade by this favourite Scheme, I do very much apprehend, that in Six Months time after the Act is past for the Extirpation of the Gospel, the Bank, and *East-India* Stock, may fall at least One *per cent.* And since that is Fifty times more than ever the Wisdom of our Age thought fit to venture for the Preservation of Christianity, there is no Reason we should be at so great a Loss merely for the sake of destroying it."

ages and of the renaissance has regularly been misunderstood, though its rhetoric is not exactly devious and the veils on its figures are really no more difficult to see through than those of any other form of burlesque. It almost always works out that way, however. The concupiscence which the medieval mind sees so well and in so many places, and which it labors so heavily to censure, is found by later commentators, chiefly of the scholarly kind, to be served by the very works which seek to excoriate it. Or what is worse, the caustic ironies burn the wrong way. The exposure of the craft, the guile, the multiple rationalizations with which man covers up his susceptibilities and his indulgences is regarded by the humorless as a documentation of the quaint customs of the middle ages. Thus for example Andreas Capellanus's *De amore* becomes *The Art of Courtly Love* and all the elaborate ironies of that twelfth-century attack on cupidity become a hearty endorsement of passionate love. Andrew the Chaplain is metamorphosed into a kind of very early predecessor of Sigmund Freud and the columnists who give advice to the lovelorn, presiding in his bluff and friendly way over the revels at court, preferring, one gathers, pure love to mixed love, but not averse really to either.[10] Pure love? Let a man of the higher nobility speak:

This kind consists in the contemplation of the mind and the affection of the heart; it goes as far as the kiss and the embrace and the modest contact with the nude lover, omitting the final solace, for that is not permitted to those who wish to love purely. This is the kind that anyone who is intent upon love ought to embrace with all his might, for this love goes on increasing without end, and we know that no one ever regretted practicing it, and the more of it one has the more one wants. This love is distinguished by

[10] For a discussion that places Andreas and his ironies clearly in the context of his own time, see D. W. Robertson, Jr., "The Subject of the *De Amore* of Andreas Capellanus," *Modern Philology*, L (1951), 145–161.

being of such virtue that from it arises all excellence of character, and no injury comes from it, and God sees very little offense in it. No maiden can ever be corrupted by such a love, nor can a widow or a wife receive any harm or suffer any injury to her reputation. This love I cherish, this I follow and ever adore and never cease urgently to demand of you.

What about mixed love? Let the same learned representative of the revels speak forth:

that is called mixed love which gets its effect from every delight of the flesh and culminates in the final act of Venus. What sort of love this is you may clearly see from what I have already said, for this kind quickly fails, and one often regrets having practiced it; by it one's neighbor is injured, the Heavenly King is offended, and from it come very grave dangers. But I do not say this as though I meant to condemn mixed love, I merely wish to show which of the two is preferable. But mixed love, too, is real love, and it is praiseworthy, and we say that it is the source of all good things, although from it grave dangers threaten, too. Therefore I approve of both pure love and mixed love, but I prefer to practice pure love.[11]

Freud might have had some compunctions about the truncated expression which is "pure" love, or would he have called it sublimation?

Andreas's book is packed with ironies. One wonders how they can be missed. In the preface he says to the friend to whom he is outlining the art of love:

You tell me that you are a new recruit of Love, and, having recently been wounded by an arrow of his, you do not know how to manage your horse's reins properly and you cannot find any cure for yourself. How serious this is and how it troubles

[11] Andreas Capellanus, *The Art of Courtly Love,* Book I, Chapter VI, Eighth Dialogue, trans. J. J. Parry (New York, 1941), pp. 122–123.

my soul no words of mine can make clear to you. For I know, having learned from experience, that it does not do the man who owes obedience to Venus's service any good to give careful thought to anything except how he may always be doing something that will entangle him more firmly in his chains. . . .[12]

Andreas hopes to make his "reverend friend Walter" more cautious, more prudent. He will show him the way step by step. He delineates the sensitive distinctions among classes, which dictate some eight different vocabularies for wooing. Every class has its defenses; every defense can sooner or later be overcome. Peasants require almost no effort: "if you should, by some chance, fall in love with some of their women, be careful to puff them up with lots of praise and then, when you find a convenient place, do not hesitate to take what you seek and to embrace them by force." [13] The inference fairly obviously to be drawn from this chapter in the gamesmanship of love is that there is not much pleasure for the love games-man in that sort of forced labor.

The principles enunciated by Andreas are all inversions of the virtues. Everything should be a matter of stealth: there is no joy in open courting. Thus everybody realizes that there can be no love between husband and wife. Love requires plotting, an atmosphere of the clandestine, most of all, jealousy, "the nurse of love." Jealousy is certain to make love increase. If it is not really felt by one of the lovers, it can at least be feigned. Competition helps too to intensify one's love, Andreas counsels Walter: "I will go further and say that even though you know perfectly well that some other man is enjoying the embraces of your beloved, this will make you begin to value her solaces all the more. . . ." A certain amount of planned separation is valuable, too; and not only

---

[12] *Ibid.*, p. 27.
[13] *Ibid.*, I, XII, p. 150.

does separation increase love, but just the process of parting
—as Romeo and Juliet were later to testify. Scoldings by
parents are particularly useful, and so are their whippings.
A scolding has an additional purpose: it "gives a perfect
reason for beginning a love affair that has not yet begun." [14]

Andreas's final summation of this kind of love is a set of
thirty-one rules. They are inscribed on a parchment which
an adventuring Briton wins for himself after a series of con-
quests that read like a somewhat blurred parody of Arthurian
romance. The rules themselves are of the sort that Polonius
would have been proud to offer his son; in fact, allowing for
the change of scene and a few variations in vocabulary, this
is exactly the kind of advice that that master of worldliness
gives to Laertes. Andreas's canons are made up of ironies,
understatements, overstatements, and reiterations of the obvious.

Marriage is no real excuse for not loving.
He who is not jealous cannot love.
Boys do not love until they arrive at the age of maturity.
It is not proper to love any woman whom one should be ashamed
　　to seek to marry.
When made public love rarely endures.
The easy attainment of love makes it of little value; difficulty of
　　attainment makes it prized.
When a lover suddenly catches sight of his beloved his heart
　　palpitates.
A new love puts to flight an old one.
Jealousy, and therefore love, are increased when one suspects
　　his beloved.
A slight presumption causes a lover to suspect his beloved.
Nothing forbids one woman being loved by two men or one man
　　by two women. [15]

[14] *Ibid.,* II, II, p. 154.
[15] *Ibid.,* II, VIII, pp. 184–186.

Shall we call those innocent who are taken in by this sort of irony or would concupiscent be a better word? Do such persons know too little or too much? For the truly innocent, Andreas offers a palinode or recantation of the substance of his *De amore* in a concluding book, the third of three, called *De reprobatione amoris,* On the Repudiation of Love. Here, in a straightforward sermon, he explains the point of what he himself calls his double lesson.[16] The lesson was designed to demonstrate that when the delights of the flesh are enjoyed "in fullest measure" one at the same time invariably deprives oneself of "the grace of God, the companionship of the good, and the friendship of praiseworthy men. . . ." But it may be, Andreas muses, "we can do you good against your will." Thus does he express his hope, or perhaps it would be better to say his love. For that is surely the motivation and the purpose of this kind of comedy—a higher love, not a lower one. It is attained, *if* it is attained, by inversion, subversion, and irony, and against the will—the perverted will—of the person to whom it is addressed.

This is the procedure of Christian comedy in the middle ages; this is its rhetoric. Its masters continued to work at it for several centuries after Andreas. Chaucer poked enormous fun at every level of society, at every enormity of society. He did not offer nostrums; he presented a fair view of man to himself. Every distortion, every exaggeration, every pretension of which man is capable is duly noted by the poet, and especially the idiotic games man plays with himself in praise and pursuit of Venus. At the end of the proemium that opens the third book of *Troilus and Criseyde,* Chaucer appeals to the muse of epic poetry, having already invoked Venus, Jove, and Mars:

[16] Professor Parry's translation of Andreas's words in this passage in Book III makes confusing English of pellucid Latin. See Robertson, *loc. cit.,* p. 145.

Caliope, thy vois be now present,
For now is nede; sestow not my destresse,
How I mot telle anon-right the gladnesse
Of Troilus, to Venus herynge?
To which gladnes, who nede hath, god him bringe!

Chaucer's distress is in part ironic. It is the tone he has adopted for the telling of the pathetic tale of this love, mixed love, in the categories of Andreas. But we read too quickly if we see only the lightness on the surface and miss all the weight below. The overtone of the lines with which Pandarus, that very model of a modern lovebroker, produces Criseyde should not be left unheard:

III, 62

"See, who is here you comen to visyte;
Lo, here is she that is your deeth to wyte."

Criseyde is really a fatal attraction to Troilus. He is doomed to double-dealing and to death when he is dealt to her by his heart. But, says Chaucer at the end of his tale,

V, 1748

Swich is this world; who-so it can biholde,
In eche estat is litel hertes reste;
God leve us for to take it for the beste!

We take it for the best of possible earths; we do not make it into heaven, except at the risk of losing heaven. When Troilus achieves the "armonye With sownes fulle of hevenish melodye," and looks down on "This litel spot of erthe," his impulse is to "despyse This wrecched world" and to hold

V, 1817　　　　　　　　al vanitee
To respect of the pleyn felicitee
That is in hevene above . . .

He laughs to himself at the misery of those who bemoan the brevity of life and has only contempt for

V, 1824

> The blinde lust, the which that may not laste,
> And sholden al our herte on hevene caste.

Writers of Christian comedy do not laugh to themselves. They share the laughter. But their weeping is silent, buried beneath great caterwauls of amusement. Fallen man, they keep telling us, is as much a comic as a tragic spectacle. All his vain attempts to wrest some dignity from his low estate only make him a better butt for ridicule, like the poor fellow who slips on the banana peel and then standing high on his self-esteem does not see that the offending skin of the fruit is still where it was—and falls all over again. Thus the many agonies and the bower of delights of Boccaccio's *Decameron* and of Rabelais's tales of his humanistic giants, Gargantua and Pantagruel, and his moral dwarf, Panurge. Thus all the tales of swollen appetites and shrunken spirits—Shakespeare's, Henry Fielding's, Laurence Sterne's and all the others produced by writers that see man in this perspective. The list, it is true, has not been much added to in recent years.[17] As early as the eighteenth century, as Sterne reminds us in *Tristram Shandy*, the world was "ashamed of being virtuous." By the twentieth century the excesses inspired by concupiscence, those that Rabelais inflated to gigantic size to make them easier to see and thus to ridicule, were being taken seriously. Three-quarters of the novels and dramas of our time deal with these excesses as if they were love itself. Andreas's *Art of Love* is now by many thought to be a useful guide to the subject and by most a genuine history of twelfth-century behavior. For our own behavior is such that we may some-

[17] C. S. Lewis's *Screwtape Letters* is an honorable exception.

times find it hard to laugh at "The Most Lamentable Comedy and Most Cruel Death of Pyramus and Thisby" as played by Bottom and his friends. That ass's head on Bottom looks too familiar.

SEVEN

Christian Faith and the Social Comedy

PETER L. BERGER

The essence of the comic is discrepancy. This is well expressed in what are probably the most famous theories concerning the comic among recent thinkers, that is the theories of Freud [1] and Bergson.[2] In Freud's theory the discrepancy is between the exorbitant demands of the superego as against the world of the libido underlying it. Freud places strong emphasis on what he himself calls the "unmasking" character of wit. In Bergson's theory the discrepancy is between the living organism and the mechanical world. One is moved to laughter when something living acts like a machine. This laughter reveals the distinctive, unique quality of life as against all other phenomena in the world. This essay is not the place to discuss fully these theories or other interpretations of the

[1] Sigmund Freud, "Wit and Its Relations to the Unconscious," in A. A. Brill (ed.), *The Basic Writings of Sigmund Freud* (New York, Modern Library, Inc., 1938).

[2] Henri Bergson, "Laughter," in W. Sypher (ed.), *Comedy* (Garden City, N.Y., Doubleday & Company, Inc., 1956).

comic.[3] It seems to this writer that Freud's theory, indeed, tells us much about the psychology of laughter but little about the phenomenon of the comic itself. Bergson's theory, on the other hand, does penetrate into the phenomenon itself, but its identification of the comic discrepancy with that between the biological and the mechanical would seem to be too broad. It hardly seems possible for a plant to be comic. As to animals, they appear as comic in the degree to which it is possible to look at them in anthropomorphic terms. In other words, this writer would suggest that the comic is a specifically and exclusively *human* phenomenon. He would suggest further that the essence of the comic discrepancy is not that between life and matter but between spirit and world, as that latter discrepancy is revealed in the human condition. Man exists as a conscious being in an unconscious and apparently unconscionable world. It is in this basically human discrepancy that the clue to the comic is to be sought.

However, whether this interpretation may seem fanciful or not, or whatever one's conception of the comic may be, there can be little doubt about the sharp light which the comic perspective throws on crucial aspects of the human condition. We might quote Bergson at this point: "A situation is invariably comic when it belongs simultaneously to two altogether independent series of events and is capable of being interpreted in two entirely different meanings at the same time." [4] Bergson is speaking here of the comic in general, but the words he uses to describe the comic situation are deeply appropriate not only to the phenomenon we have called "alternation" but to the human condition in general. The aspect of spirit and the aspect of world, as interpretations of human situations, always constitute "independent series of events."

[3] Cf. Francis Jeanson, *Signification humaine du rire* (Paris, Editions du Seuil, 1950).

[4] Bergson, *loc. cit.,* p. 123.

When the worldly aspect is suddenly perceived as coexisting with the spiritual one, there takes place the "unmasking" of which Freud speaks. Thus we find out that the philosopher has haemorrhoids. Or we laugh because he turns out to be an anxious miser or an inveterate seducer. The comic source here is this discrepancy between spirit and all that which is not. No doubt this is why sexuality has been a source of comedy from immemorial times. It reveals most sharply the discrepancy between spiritual aspiration and bodily bondage, as Montaigne has commented upon. Sexuality then "unmasks" the pretensions of the spirit, as Freud has illustrated comically enough in his theory of everyday slips of the tongue, mistakes, and misnomers. And the comic in death, also an age-old theme, has the same source. Death, like sex, is the ultimate debunking of spirit by body. The pretensions of intelligence and will are "unmasked" in the facts proclaimed by a body oblivious of spirit. In the same way, the social drama takes on the character of a comic farce when looked at under the aspects of sex and death. Men engage in grandiose undertakings on the stage of society, involving the most complicated acts of deception, manipulation, and violence. But during all this time their libido keeps churning away within them, wanting one thing and one thing only, a thing ridiculously irrelevant to the empire-building being undertaken by the man to whom this libido belongs. And eventually everybody involved in the plot dies. Under the aspects of sex and death it is difficult to take social ambitions very seriously.

The declaration that the social drama is a comedy may well raise eyebrows and elicit the comment that one can only say this by being inhumanly blind to the tragic aspects of social existence. We would not accept this objection. The tragic and the comic perspectives are not mutually incompatible. The same human condition which provides materials for tragedy also and at the same time produces the stuff of which comedy is made. And to see the comic even in the midst of events that powerfully rouse our "tragic sense of life" (Unamuno) does not at all imply some sort of callousness toward human suffering. One may recall here a remark made somewhere by David Rousset, a Frenchman who has written about Nazi concentration camps as a former inmate. Rousset remarked that one of the new insights of his imprisonment was the realization that the comic is an objective element of reality, persisting and capable of being recognized no matter how wretched one may be subjectively. In other words, the comic has a status in reality beyond the observer's psychology. It is not just an element of certain types of human consciousness, but an essential ingredient of the human condition as such. Thus the Nazis were, indeed, the monsters of a nightmarish horror show, but at the same time they were inexorably ridiculous, appearing as figures of a surrealistic farce (Rousset uses the term *"ubuesque"* to describe this aspect, after Alfred Jarry's surrealistic play *King Ubu*). One might add that the art of Charlie Chaplin (and not only in *The Great Dictator*) is based on the same principle—as, indeed, is any comedy with a deep compassion for the vicissitudes of human existence.

Both tragedy and comedy place the social drama into the perspective of human finitude. Both a tragic and a comic mood allow us to perceive the failure of pretensions, ambitions, and aspirations before the hard facts of man's finite situation. The tragic hero finds his will and his virtue dashing against the walls of fate. The world, perhaps even his own body as a part of this world, defeats him. The comic hero enacts before us the same destiny, but in a different key, as it were. Both tragedy and comedy proclaim to us that pride is foolish, remind us of our humanity and hence of our imprisonment. But in tragedy what is put in question is man. In comedy not only is man questioned and not taken at face value, but there is also a question about the imprisonment. One can put this differently as well. Tragedy accepts the walls of the prison and perceives the human situation in terms of this acceptance. Comedy gives the impression that the walls too are not as grim as they look. Tragedy is perception of the human situation only under the aspect of immanence. Comedy is a signal, an intimation, of transcendence. It is here that its Christian significance is to be found.

The transcending direction of comedy is probably best expressed in the art of the clown. The clown is the living defiance of the laws of nature and the laws of man. He defies gravity and the resistance of matter. He waves his wand and the walls of our prison collapse. He walks into the presence of kings and laughs in their face. Not only are the social limitations of our existence thus denied, but finitude as such, finitude as the mode of human existence in the world, is transcended in the magic of the comic moment. We laugh and for one moment the walls are really gone. The comic catharsis is thus a very different one from the tragic one. Tragic catharsis makes us look upon the greatness man is capable of even within his finitude and thus prepares us to accept the human condition. Comic catharsis presents us with a fleeting image of man transcending his finitude and, if only for a brief moment, gives us the exhilarating idea that perhaps it will be man after all who will be the victor in his struggle with a universe bent on crushing him. In other words, tragedy gives us a sense of human courage, comedy a sense of wild, irrational hope. As Enid Welsford has pointed out in her discussion of the clown as a figure in Western literature, it depends on our general conception of human destiny how we shall look at the clown. If death is the last fact about man, then the art of the clown is a pathetic piece of emotional relief, a passing moment of benign illusion, doomed to the tragic finale of all things human. If, on the other hand, the universe is not a mindless machine destroying all within it, if death should turn out to be not the ultimate reality of the human phenomenon, then the clown's magic takes on a strange new dignity. The comic transformation now may suddenly appear as a promise of a reality yet to come. If we are now to put this in Christian terms, we obtain a somewhat startling perspective on the relative importance of tragedy and comedy. This bears looking into a little further.

A Christian understanding of human existence would reverse the common belief that tragedy is more profound than comedy. On the contrary, this Christian understanding would say it is comedy that gives us the more significant insights into the human condition. Tragedy can never go beyond immanence (this, incidentally, is why a Christian tragedy is a contradiction in terms). Comedy can. More than that, in a way strangely parallel to that of the Christian faith, comedy overcomes the tragic perspective. From the Christian point of view one can say that comedy, unlike tragedy, bears within it a great secret. This secret is the promise of redemption. For redemption promises in eternity what comedy gives us in its few moments of precarious liberation—the collapse of the walls of our imprisonment. It would not be surprising if, to the blessed, redemption appears after the terrors of the world as a form of comic relief. But there can be no doubt about one thing. There will be no tragedy in heaven—by definition, as it were. But man will remain funny for ever. If nothing else there will be material for endless comedies in his relations with the angels! The tragic thus shows us man in time, but the comic may well give us an intimation of what man is and always will be, even in eternity.

But our concern in this essay is not with heaven, so it is probably high time that we return to our theme, which is not the angelic but the social comedy. We would now suggest that such a Christian understanding of the comic has direct applicability to the perception of society. One can, obviously, conceive of society as essentially a tragic drama. Society then is seen as part of that inane world which bears down upon us and which will inevitably succeed in destroying us. But if society is conceived of as a comic drama, our social perception partakes of the secret referred to above. That is, in all our debunking of the cardboard structures of the social world there is a faint hint of redemption.

This sense of comedy may be illustrated by the difference between a Christian and a revolutionary challenge to the pretensions of the *status quo*. The revolutionary is almost always a thoroughly humorless type. He sees people as part of structures, either those he wishes to tear down or those he hopes to erect. Those who defend the *status quo* appear to him as fools or scoundrels. Revolution is an earnest undertaking. The revolutionary takes it and himself too with very great seriousness. There is little room for any comic perspective. The Christian challenge to the *status quo* begins by not taking it as seriously as it takes itself. It refuses to see individual human beings as incarnations of social symbols and principles. As we have tried to show before, the Christian challenge to society lies above all in its radical humanizing of all social problems. This process of humanization carries with it a comic perspective. It "unmasks" human pretensions very much in the sense meant by Freud in his discussion of wit: Finally, because it lives in confrontation with God, this Christian challenge cannot take itself ultimately seriously either. Only God is ultimately to be taken seriously. Everything human remains less than serious by comparison. Needless to say, this does not mean that the Christian challenge to injustice or cruelty will be less than serious in the sense of detached amusement, comfortable readiness to forgive everything, or lazy lack of commitment. Yet it will be less than serious in the sense that it will know that its own actions are caught in the comic ambiguities of all human endeavor and also in that it will never lose sight of the pathetic humanity that also is a quality of one's worst enemy.

Thus at the bottom of any debunking job undertaken in a Christian spirit is not a nihilistic guffaw but a redeeming smile. The "unmasking" of society is undertaken on behalf of an affirmation of man. This is done without the frantic hopes of the revolutionary utopian and without the misanthropic cynicism of the uncommitted observer. Debunking which is really the underside of Christian prophecy may sometimes be very sharp indeed, but it is not likely to become real bitterness. There is always an awareness that this particular colossus staring us in the face at the moment, like all the colossi of this world, is swallowed up in Christ's victory and will be swept away when this victory is consummated. Nothing human is ultimately dangerous, not even the most determined stupidity. Thus nothing human can ultimately keep us from the liberation of laughter.

The Christian faith bids us love our enemies. We would suggest that an essential part of this humanly unthinkable undertaking is to view these enemies under the aspect of the comic. In other words, the humanizing perspective of the Christian faith takes the enemy less seriously than he takes himself, addresses him as a human being instead of as the representative of awesome social forces, and thus may unexpectedly open the way for simple human communication. The following passage from a report on Christians in the Communist zone of Germany, published in a Swiss newspaper, illustrates this possibility:

And then we experienced that here and there a few of us began to talk to half and full Marxists with love. With love—that means undiplomatically, in all frankness and freedom, yet not self-righteously or moralistically. And almost everywhere where that happened, we saw that the evil spirits stole away and the sea became still. In the place of their dialectically grounded desire to liquidate us (for the moment only rhetorically) came human respect, then the assurance that they wouldn't do us any harm because we were 'good honest people' whom one protects and defends. Then, here and there, something quite different occurred. Suddenly the mask which looks so deceivingly like the real face fell, and revealed a helpless man who sinks under his load of sin and guilt, and who clings to the Christian who has treated him with a bit of love, who hasn't lied to him like the others.[5]

It goes without saying that this attitude will not always lead to these results in the situation of facing Communist functionaries. But its very possibility is a direct outcome of the humanizing quality of the Christian challenge developed above, a quality which includes in a very profound way the comic perspective on the social drama. As little men put on their terrifying masks and headgears and war rattles, and march into the arena with solemn chants, there is always some old lady who smiles at them, not unkindly, and suggests that the boys go play elsewhere where they cannot hurt anybody. We know all too well that even unimpressed grandmothers can be killed in the great war games of society. But there is also a possibility that men may discover their own humanity. This possibility is the important nexus between the comic perspective and Christian ethics.

To be ultimately serious about society means *ipso facto* to be caught within it. Thus even the revolutionary, who seeks to overthrow society and build a new one on the ruins of the old, is ultimately serious about his social involvements. Only a conception of man which transcends society can take social involvements with a grain of salt—or with tongue in cheek. Certainly the Christian faith is not the only such conception.

[5] Charles C. West, *Communism and the Theologians* (London, S. C. M. Press, 1958), p. 385.

But in the Christian understanding of man and of the nature of redemption lies an unusually fertile opportunity of gaining distance from the social problems pressing on one at the moment. Thus the refusal of taking society as ultimately serious (which means refusing to take it at the face value it usually puts on itself) not only is an experience of personal liberation but also has relevance to the effort to grasp society intellectually. To return to the general argument of this essay, we would now say that, insofar as the Christian faith contains within it a specific type of comic perspective and a specific interpretation of comedy, to that extent too does the Christian faith contribute to a clear perception of society. It is a commonplace observation, but still an important one, that a measure of distance allows one to see more clearly. The Christian faith, when it is true to itself and really is "in the world but not of it," provides distance from society and thus creates opportunities for perception. Thus the Christian faith relates to the enterprise of the social sciences not only because of its radical challenge to social delusions and alibis. In a more benign way, as it were, it relates to the "sociological imagination" (Mills) by way of the comic perspective on the social carnival. The Christian sees man as having a destiny over and beyond society, man straddling two worlds, those two worlds that Simone Weil called those of gravity and grace. In thus transcending society, the Christian faith at the same time makes it possible to see society more clearly.

Dietrich Bonhoeffer made the important distinction between "ultimate" and "penultimate" concerns in his *Ethics*. The entire domain of social and political action, however serious its involvements may often be, will always be "penultimate" in the Christian economy. Thus the Christian will engage himself in action passionately, but he will not allow his commitment to blind him to the comic aspects of his situation. He will deal with men without forgetting that they were children not so long ago. He will protest against injustice, but he will not absolutize this protest or make it the basis of his existence. He will build for the future, but he will do so in full awareness of the precariousness of all human construction on the quicksands of history. Above all, he will remember that the central message of the Christian faith is not a call to struggle but a call to joy.

We quite miss the point if we only laugh at Don Quixote because he rides against windmills. The point is that, in the magic of the Quixotic universe, the windmills really cease to be windmills and are metamorphosed into a promise of glory. Of course, we know that "in this aeon," as the New Testament puts it, the ride of Don Quixote ends in a sad return to what we take for granted as reality. But the Christian faith means looking toward the aeon that is to come. The magic moment of comedy foreshadows this aeon, when redemption becomes the one overpowering reality of the universe. Christian faith, just because it strives for clear perception, cannot look at Don Quixote through the eyes of Sancho Panza. The windmills of the Quixotic attack are the battlements of the New Jerusalem, as yet dimly seen on the horizon. But it is toward this horizon that the human caravan is moving. Don Quixote rides toward the dawn of Easter morning.

EIGHT

Humour and Faith

REINHOLD NIEBUHR

He that sitteth in the heavens shall laugh:
the Lord shall have them in derision.

Ps. 2:4

This word of the Second Psalm is one of three instances in the Bible in which laughter is attributed to God. God is not frequently thought of as possessing a sense of humour, though that quality would have to be attributed to perfect personality. There are critics of religion who regard it as deficient in the sense of humour, and they can point to the fact that there is little laughter in the Bible. Why is it that Scriptural literature, though filled with rejoicings and songs of praise, is not particularly distinguished for the expression of laughter? There are many sayings of Jesus which betray a touch of ironic humour; but on the whole one must agree with the critics who do not find much humour or laughter in the Bible.

This supposed defect will, however, appear less remarkable if the relation of humour to faith is understood. Humour is, in fact, a prelude to faith; and laughter is the beginning of prayer. Laughter must be heard in the outer courts of religion; and the echoes of it should resound in the sanctuary; but there is no laughter in the holy of holies. There laughter is swallowed up in prayer and humour is fulfilled by faith.

The intimate relation between humour and faith is derived from the fact that both deal with the incongruities of our existence. Humour is concerned with the immediate incongruities of life and faith with the ultimate ones. Both humour and faith are expressions of the freedom of the human spirit, of its capacity to stand outside of life, and itself, and view the whole scene. But any view of the whole immediately creates the problem of how the incongruities of life are to be dealt with; for the effort to understand the life, and our place in it, confronts us with inconsistencies and incongruities which do not fit into any neat picture of the whole. Laughter is our reaction to immediate incongruities and those which do not affect us essentially. Faith is the only possible response to the ultimate incongruities of existence which threaten the very meaning of our life.

We laugh at what? At the sight of a fool upon the throne of the king; or the proud man suffering from some indignity; or the child introducing its irrelevancies into the conversation of the mature. We laugh at the juxtaposition of things which do not fit together. A boy slipping on the ice is not funny. Slipping on the ice is funny only if it happens to one whose dignity is upset. A favorite device of dramatists, who have no other resources of humour, is to introduce some irrelevant interest into the central theme of the drama by way of the conversation of maid or butler. If this irrelevance is to be really funny, however, it must have some more profound relation to the theme than the conversor intended. This is to say that humour manages to resolve incongruities by the discovery of another level of congruity. We laugh at the proud man slipping on the ice, not merely because the contrast between his dignity and his undignified plight strikes us as funny; but because we feel that his discomfiture is a poetically just rebuke of his dignity. Thus we deal with immediate incongruities, in which we are not too seriously involved and which open no gap in the coherence of life in such a way as to threaten us essentially. But there are profound incongruities which contain such a threat. Man's very position in the universe is incongruous. That is the problem of faith, and not of humour. Man is so great and yet so small, so significant and yet so insignificant. "On the one hand," says Edward Bellamy, in *The Religion of Solidarity*, "is the personal life of man, an atom, a grain of sand on a boundless shore, a bubble of a foam flecked ocean, a life bearing a proportion to the mass of past, present and future, so infinitesimal as to defy the imagination. On the other hand is a certain other life, as it were a spark of the universal life, insatiable in aspiration, greedy of infinity, asserting solidarity with all things and all existence, even while subject to the limitations of space and time." That is the contrast.

When man surveys the world he seems to be the very center of it; and his mind appears to be the unifying power which makes sense out of the whole. But this same man, reduced to the limits of his animal existence, is a little animalcule, preserving a precarious moment of existence within the vastness of space and time. There is a profound incongruity between the "inner" and the "outer" world, or between the world as viewed from man's perspective, and the man in the world as viewed from a more ultimate perspective. The incongruity becomes even more profound when it is considered that it is the same man who assumes the ultimate perspective from which he finds himself so insignificant.

Philosophers seek to overcome this basic incongruity by reducing one world to the dimension of the other; or raising one perspective to the height of the other. But neither a purely naturalistic nor a consistently idealistic system of philosophy is ever completely plausible. There are ultimate incongruities of life which can be resolved by faith but not by reason. Reason can look at them only from one standpoint or another, thereby denying the incongruities which it seeks to solve. They are also too profound to be resolved or dealt with by laughter. If laughter seeks to deal with the ultimate issues of life it turns into a bitter humour. This means that it has been overwhelmed by the incongruity. Laughter is thus not merely a vestibule to faith but also a "no-man's land" between faith and despair. We laugh cheerfully at the incongruities on the surface of life; but if we have no other resource but humour to deal with those which reach below the surface, our laughter becomes an expression of our sense of the meaninglessness of life.

II

Laughter is a sane and healthful response to the innocent foibles of men; and even to some which are not innocent. All men betray moods and affectations, conceits and idiosyncrasies, which could become the source of great annoyance to us if we took them too seriously. It is better to laugh at them. A sense of humour is indispensable to men of affairs who have the duty of organizing their fellowmen in common endeavors. It reduces the frictions of life and makes the foibles of men tolerable. There is, in the laughter with which we observe and greet the foibles of others, a nice mixture of mercy and judgment, of censure and forbearance. We would not laugh if we regarded these foibles as altogether fitting and proper. There is judgment, therefore, in our laughter. But we also prove by the laughter that we do not take the annoyance too seriously. However, if our fellows commit a serious offense against the common good, laughter no longer avails. If we continue to indulge in it, the element of forbearance is completely eliminated from it. Laughter against real evil is bitter. Such bitter laughter of derision has its uses as an instrument of condemnation. But there is no power in it to deter the evil against which it is directed.

There were those who thought that we could laugh Mussolini and Hitler out of court. Laughter has sometimes contributed to the loss of prestige of dying oligarchies and social systems. Thus Cervantes' *Don Quixote* contributed to the decline of feudalism, and Boccaccio's *Decameron* helped to signal the decay of medieval asceticism. But laughter alone never destroys a great seat of power and authority in history. Its efficacy is limited to preserving the self-respect of the slave against the master. It does not extend to the destruction of slavery. Thus all the victims of tyranny availed themselves of the weapon of wit to preserve their sense of personal self-respect. Laughter provided them with a little private world in which they could transvalue the values of the tyrant, and reduce his pompous power to the level of the ridiculous. Yet there is evidence that the most insufferable forms of tyranny (as in the concentration camps, for instance) could not be ameliorated by laughter.

Laughter may turn to bitterness when it faces serious evil, partly because it senses its impotence. But, in any case, serious evil must be seriously dealt with. The bitterness of derision is serious enough; but where is the resource of forgiveness to come from? It was present in the original forbearance of laughter; but it can not be brought back into the bitterness of derision. The contradiction between judgment and mercy can not be resolved by humour but only by vicarious pain.

Thus we laugh at our children when they betray the jealous conceits of childhood. These are the first buds of sin which grow in the soil of the original sin of our common humanity. But when sin has conceived and brought forth its full fruit, our laughter is too ambiguous to deal with the child's offense; or if it is not ambiguous it becomes too bitter.

If we retain the original forbearance of laughter in our judgment it turns into harmful indulgence. Parental judgment is always confronted with the necessity of relating rigorous judgment creatively to the goodness of mercy. That relation can be achieved only as the parent himself suffers under the judgments which are exacted. Not humour but the cross is the meeting point of justice and mercy, once both judgment and mercy have become explicit. Laughter can express both together, when neither is fully defined. But, when it becomes necessary to define each explicitly, laughter can no longer contain them both. Mercy is expelled and only bitterness remains.

What is true of our judgments of each other is true of the judgment of God. In the word of our text God is pictured laughing at man and having him in derision because of the vanity of man's imagination and pretensions. There is no suggestion of a provisional geniality in this divine laughter. Derisiveness is pure judgment) It is not possible to resolve the contradiction between mercy and judgment, on the level of the divine, through humour; because the divine judgment is ultimate judgment. That contradiction, which remains an unsolved mystery in the Old Testament, is resolved only as God is revealed in Christ. There is no humour but suffering in that revelation. There is, as we have observed, a good deal of ironic humour in the sayings of Christ. But there is no humour in the scene of Christ upon the Cross. The only humour on Calvary is the derisive laughter of those who cried, "He saved others; himself he can not save. . . . If he be the son of God let him come down from the cross"; and the ironic inscription on the cross, ordered by Pilate: "The King of the Jews." These ironic and derisive observations were the natural reactions of common sense to dimensions of revelation which transcend common sense. Since they could not be comprehended by faith, they prompted ironic laughter.

There is no humour in the cross because the justice and

the mercy of God are fully revealed in it. In that revelation God's justice is made the more terrible because the sin of man is disclosed in its full dimension. It is a rebellion against God from which God Himself suffers. God can not remit the consequences of sin; yet He does show mercy by taking the consequences upon and into Himself. This is the main burden of the disclosure of God in Christ. This is the final clue to the mystery of the divine character. Mercy and justice are provisionally contained in laughter; and the contradiction between them is tentatively resolved in the sense of humour. But the final resolution of justice, fully developed, and of mercy, fully matured, is possible only when the sharp edge of justice is turned upon the executor of judgment without being blunted. This painful experience of vicarious suffering is far removed from laughter. Only an echo of the sense of humour remains in it. The echo is the recognition in the sense of humour that judgment and mercy belong together, even though they seem to be contradictory. But there is no knowledge in the sense of humour of how the two are related to each other and how the contradiction between them is to be resolved.

III

The sense of humour is even more important provisionally in dealing with our own sins than in dealing with the sins of others. Humour is a proof of the capacity of the self to gain a vantage point from which it is able to look at itself. The sense of humour is thus a by-product of self-transcendence. People with a sense of humour do not take themselves too seriously. They are able to "stand off" from themselves, see themselves in perspective, and recognize the ludicrous and absurd aspects of their pretensions. All of us ought to be ready to laugh at ourselves because all of us are a little funny in our foibles, conceits and pretensions. What is funny about us is precisely that we take ourselves too seriously. We are rather insignificant little bundles of energy and vitality in a vast organization of life. But we pretend that we are the very center of this organization. This pretension is ludicrous; and its absurdity increases with our lack of awareness of it. The less we are able to laugh at ourselves the more it becomes necessary and inevitable that others laugh at us.

It is significant that little children are really very sober though they freely indulge in a laughter which expresses a pure animal joy of existence. But they do not develop the capacity of real humour until the fifth or sixth year, at which time they may be able to laugh at themselves and at others. At about this age their intense preoccupation with self and with an immediate task at hand is partly mitigated. The sense of humour grows, in other words, with the capacity of self-transcendence. If we can gain some perspective upon our own self we are bound to find the self's pretensions a little funny.

This means that the ability to laugh at oneself is the prelude to the sense of contrition. Laughter is a vestibule to the temple of confession. But laughter is not able to deal with the problem of the sins of the self in any ultimate way. If we become fully conscious of the tragedy of sin we recognize that our preoccupation with self, our exorbitant demands upon life, our insistence that we receive more attention than our needs deserve, effect our neighbors harmfully and defraud them of their rightful due. If we recognize the real evil of sin, laughter can not deal with the problem. If we continue to laugh after having recognized the depth of evil, our laughter becomes the instrument of irresponsibility. Laughter is thus not only the vestibule of the temple of confession but the no-man's land between cynicism and contrition. Laughter may express a mood which takes neither the self nor life seriously. If we take life seriously but ourselves not too seriously, we cease to laugh. The contradiction in man between "the good that he would and does not do, and the evil that he would not do, and does" is no laughing matter.

There is furthermore another dimension in genuine contrition which laughter does not contain. It is the awareness of being judged from beyond ourselves. There is something more than self-judgment in genuine contrition. "For me it is a small thing to be judged of men," declares St. Paul, "neither judge I myself; for I know nothing against myself; he who judges me is the Lord." In an ultimate sense the self never knows anything against itself. The self of today may judge the self's action of yesterday as evil. But that means that the self of today is the good self. We are to judge our actions through self-judgment. But we do not become aware of the deep root of evil actions in such judgments. We may judge our sins but we do not judge ourselves as sinners. The knowledge that we are sinners, and that inordinate desires spring from a heart inordinately devoted to itself, is a religious knowledge which, in a sense, is never achieved except in prayer. Then we experience with St. Paul that "he who judges us is the Lord." There is no laughter in that experience. There is only pain. The genuine joy of reconciliation with God, which is possible only as the fruit of genuine repentance, is a joy which stands beyond laughter though it need not completely exclude laughter.

To suggest that the sense of humour is the beginning, but not the end, of a proper humility does not mean that the final fruit of true contrition destroys all vestiges of the seed from which it sprang. The saintliest men frequently have a humourous glint in their eyes. They retain the capacity to laugh at both themselves and at others. They do not laugh in their prayers because it is a solemn experience to be judged of God and to stand under the scrutiny of Him from whom no secrets are hid. But the absence of laughter in the most ultimate experience of life does not preclude the presence of laughter as a suffused element in all experience. There is indeed proper laughter on the other side of the experience of repentance. It is the laughter of those who have been released both from the tyranny of the law and from the slavery of pretending to be better than they are. To know oneself a sinner, to have no illusions about the self, and no inclination to appear better than we are, either in the sight of man or of God, and to know oneself forgiven and released from sin, is the occasion for a new joy. This joy expresses itself in an exuberance of which laughter is not the only, but is certainly one, expression.

IV

We have dealt thus far with humour as a reaction to the incongruities in the character of self and its neighbors. We have discovered it to be a healthy, but an ultimately unavailing, method of dealing with the evils of human nature. But men face other incongruities than those which human foibles and weaknesses present. Human existence itself is filled with incongruities. Life does not make sense as easily as those philosophers, who think they have charted and comprehended everything in a nice system of rationality, would have us believe. Man's life is really based upon a vast incongruity.

Man is a creature who shares all the weaknesses of the other creatures of the world. Yet he is a sublime creature who holds the ages within his memory and touches the fringes of the eternal in his imagination. When he looks into the world within, he finds depths within depths of mystery which are never completely fathomed. Man is a spirit; and among the qualities of his spirit are the capacity to regard himself and the world; and to speculate on the meaning of the whole. This man is, when he is the observer, the very center of the universe. Yet the same man "brings his years to an end like a tale that is told." This man groweth up like grass in the morning which in the evening is cut down and withereth. The brevity of human existence is the most vivid expression and climax of human weakness.

The incongruity of man's greatness and weakness, of his mortality and immortality, is the source of his temptation to evil. Some men seek to escape from their greatness to their weakness; they try to deny the freedom of their spirit in order to achieve the serenity of nature. Some men seek to escape from their weakness to their greatness. But these simple methods of escape are unavailing. The effort to escape into the weakness of nature leads not to the desired serenity but to sensuality. The effort to escape from weakness to greatness leads not to the security but to the evils of greed and lust for power, or to the opposite evils of a spirituality which denies the creaturely limitations of human existence.

The philosophies of the ages have sought to bridge the chasm between the inner and the outer world, between the world of thought in which man is so great and the world of physical extension in which man is so small and impotent. But philosophy can not bridge the chasm. It can only pretend to do so by reducing one world to the dimensions of the other. Thus naturalists, materialists, mechanists, and all philosophers, who view the world as primarily a system of physical relationships, construct a universe of meaning from which man in the full dimension of spirit can find no home. The idealistic philosophers, on the other hand, construct a world of rational coherence in which mind is the very stuff of order, the very foundation of existence. But their systems do not do justice to the large areas of chaos in the world; and they fail to give an adequate account of man himself, who is something less, as well as something more, than mind.

The sense of humour is, in many respects, a more adequate resource for the incongruities of life than the spirit of philosophy. If we are able to laugh at the curious quirks of fortune in which the system of order and meaning which each life constructs within and around itself is invaded, we at least do not make the mistake of prematurely reducing the irrational to a nice system. Things "happen" to us. We make our plans for a career, and sickness frustrates us. We plan our life, and war reduces all plans to chaos. The storms and furies of the world of nature, which can so easily reduce our private schemes to confusion, do of course have their own laws. They "happen" according to a discernible system of causality. There is no question about the fact that there are systems of order in the world. But it is not so easy to discern a total system of order and meaning which will comprehend the various levels of existence in an orderly whole.

To meet the disappointments and frustrations of life, the irrationalities and contingencies with laughter, is a high form of wisdom. Such laughter does not obscure or defy the dark irrationality. It merely yields to it without too much emotion and friction. A humorous acceptance of fate is really the expression of a high form of self-detachment. If men do not take themselves too seriously, if they have some sense of the precarious nature of the human enterprise, they prove that they are looking at the whole drama of life not merely from the circumscribed point of their own interests but from some further and higher vantage point. One thinks for instance of the profound wisdom which underlies the capacity of laughter in the Negro people. Confronted with the cruelties of slavery, and socially too impotent to throw off the yoke, they learned to make their unpalatable situation more sufferable by laughter. There was of course a deep pathos mixed with the humour, a proof of the fact that laughter had reached its very limit.

There is indeed a limit to laughter in dealing with life's frustrations. We can laugh at all of life's surface irrationalities.

We preserve our sanity the more surely if we do not try to reduce the whole crazy-quilt of events in which we move to a premature and illusory order. But the ultimate incongruities of human existence can not be "laughed off." We can not laugh at death. We do try of course.

A war era is particularly fruitful of *Galgenhumor* (gallows humour). Soldiers are known on occasion to engage in hysterical laughter when nerves are tense before the battle. They speak facetiously of the possible dire fate which might befall this or that man of the company. "Sergeant," a soldier is reported to have said before a recent battle, "don't let this little fellow go into battle before me. He isn't big enough to stop the bullet meant for me." The joke was received with uproarious good humour by the assembled comrades. But when the "little fellow" died in battle the next day, everyone felt a little ashamed of the joke. At any rate it was quite inadequate to deal with the depth and breadth of the problem of death.

If we persist in laughter when dealing with the final problem of human existence, when we turn life into a comedy we also reduce it to meaninglessness. That is why laughter, when pressed to solve the ultimate issue, turns into a vehicle of bitterness rather than joy. To laugh at life in the ultimate sense means to scorn it. There is a note of derision in that laughter and an element of despair in that derision.

Just as laughter is the "no-man's land" between cynicism and contrition when we deal with the incongruous element of evil in our own soul, so is it also the area between despair and faith when dealing with evil and incongruity in the world about us. Our provisional amusement with the irrational and unpredictable fortunes which invade the order and purpose of our life must move either toward bitterness or faith, when we consider not this or that frustration and this or that contingent event, but when we are forced to face the issue of the basic incongruity of death.

Either we have a faith from the standpoint of which we

are able to say, "I am persuaded, that neither death, nor life
. . . shall be able to separate us from the love of God, which
is in Christ Jesus our Lord" (Rom. 8:38–39), or we are
overwhelmed by the incongruity of death and are forced to
say with Ecclesiastes: "I said in mine heart concerning the
estate of the sons of men . . . that they might see that they
themselves are beasts. For that which befalleth the sons of
men befalleth beasts; . . . as the one dieth, so dieth the
other; yea they all have one breath; so that a man hath no
preeminence above a beast; for all is vanity" (Eccles. 3:18–
19).

The final problem of human existence is derived from the
fact that in one context and from one perspective man has no
preeminence above the beast; and yet from another perspective his preeminence is very great. No beast comes to the
melancholy conclusion that "all is vanity"; for the purposes
of its life do not outrun its power, and death does not therefore invade its life as an irrelevance. Furthermore it has no
prevision of its own end and is therefore not tempted to
melancholy. Man's melancholy over the prospect of death
is the proof of his partial transcendence over the natural
process which ends in death. But this is only a partial transcendence and man's power is not great enough to secure his
own immortality.

This problem of man, so perfectly and finally symbolized
in the fact of death, can be solved neither by proving that
he has no preeminence above the beast, nor yet proving that
his preeminence is a guarantee that death has no final dominion over him. Man is both great and small, both strong
and weak, both involved in and free of the limits of nature;
and he is a unity of strength and weakness of spirit and
creatureliness. There is therefore no possibility of man extri-
cating himself by his own power from the predicament of
his amphibious state.

The Christian faith declares that the ultimate order and

meaning of the world lies in the power and wisdom of God who is both Lord of the whole world of creation and the Father of human spirits. It believes that the incongruities of human existence are finally overcome by the power and the love of God, and that the love which Christ revealed is finally sufficient to overcome the contradiction of death.

This faith is not some vestigial remnant of a credulous and pre-scientific age with which "scientific" generations may dispense. There is no power in any science or philosophy, whether in a pre- or post-scientific age, to leap the chasm of incongruity by pure thought. Thought which begins on one side of the chasm can do no more than deny the reality on the other side. It seeks either to prove that death is no reality because spirit is eternal, or that spirit is not eternal because death is a reality. But the real situation is that man, as a part of the natural world, brings his years to an end like a tale that is told; and that man as a free spirit finds the brevity of his years incongruous and death an irrationality; and that man as a unity of body and spirit can neither by taking thought reduce the dimension of his life to the limit of nature, nor yet raise it to the dimension of pure spirit. Either his incomplete and frustrated life is completed by a power greater than his own, or it is not completed.

Faith is therefore the final triumph over incongruity, the final assertion of the meaningfulness of existence. There is no other triumph and will be none, no matter how much human knowledge is enlarged. Faith is the final assertion of the freedom of the human spirit, but also the final acceptance of the weakness of man and the final solution for the problem of life through the disavowal of any final solutions in the power of man.

Insofar as the sense of humour is a recognition of incongruity, it is more profound than any philosophy which seeks to devour incongruity in reason. But the sense of humour remains healthy only when it deals with immediate issues and faces the obvious and surface irrationalities. It must move toward faith or sink into despair when the ultimate issues are raised.

That is why there is laughter in the vestibule of the temple, the echo of laughter in the temple itself, but only faith and prayer, and no laughter, in the holy of holies.

NINE

The Traditional Roots of Jewish Humor

Israel Knox

There seems to be a fresh interest in Jewish humor, as evidenced by the numerous collections and anthologies that have been published in the past several years. The prevailing tendency has been to treat Jewish humor as though it were of recent origin only and dealt chiefly with the effect of the external environment upon Jewish life. The principal themes of Jewish humor, according to this view, would appear to be: first, the reaction to anti-Semitism in all its varieties and manifestations, with its implications for the position of the Jew in modern society; second, the marginal aspects of Jewish existence, insofar as it has not yet been fully integrated into the main currents of the dominant culture and has not yet acquired solid status; third, the ambiguity and, to an extent, the irrelevance of traditional values—inherited from the pre-Emancipation era—in the present age of change and transition.

These themes are, of course, grist for the mills of Jewish

humor. And it is true that the humor which we encounter is mostly of recent origin. In general, comedy that arises from the issues and events which are in the forefront of public attention and concern has a special appeal and exercises a more direct impact than comedy that is devoid of "a name and a local habitation."

But if there is some kind of continuity in Jewish history, then yesterday has a bearing on today; and therefore Jewish humor, although an expression of the current scene with its social relationships, can be understood only against a background of Jewish history and "destiny." Jewish humor is not merely a reaction or response to circumstances and environment but a product of Jewish experience, and is almost as old as the Jewish people itself.

There is perhaps no better illustration of the Jewish role in history and of Jewish "culture," including humor, than the *Book of Esther*. Mordecai's actions are a response to circumstances and surroundings, to the "anti-Semitism" of his day, and are conditioned by the dubious status of the Jew. The *nature* of Mordecai's response, however, is not determined by circumstances and environment but by his historic vision of Jewish destiny and commitment. Mordecai "bowed not down, nor prostrated himself before" Haman (3:2); he does not yield to the idolatry of his surroundings: "he had told them that he was a Jew" (3:4).

If we link this episode with the opening scene of the story, surfeited with luxury and voluptuousness, we soon realize that idolatry is not to be construed here in the narrow sense as a deviation from the worship of God, but in the larger sense as the rejection of a pagan civilization with its pomp and power and sensuality. In the opening scene, Ahasuerus, master and ruler "over a hundred and seven and twenty provinces, from India even unto Ethiopia," condemns his queen, Vashti, and "gives her royal estate to another" for refusing to appear at his feast "with the crown royal, to show the people and the princes her beauty." And his ministers, the seven princes of Persia and Media, who, with Ahasuerus, hold the fate of the world in the hollow of their hands, are busy flattering him and arranging for someone else to supplant Vashti.

Mordecai will not bow down nor prostrate himself before Haman, will not pay homage to the idolatry of empty pomp and brutal power. He is the "outsider"; he is the bearer of another destiny and the possessor of another heritage. "There is a certain people scattered abroad and dispersed among all the peoples in all the provinces of thy kingdom; and their laws are diverse from those of every people" (3:8)—and Mordecai is of this people. The laws of this people are "diverse" insofar as their content is holiness and their purpose is sanctification of life in the sight of God; they are not a weapon for worldly power, and they are not a codification of man's inhumanity to man.

There is no sweet and gentle humor in the *Book of Esther*, nor is there in it the negative humor of sheer hatred and malice. There is devastating satire in it and an exposure of the awful incongruity of enormous power—with life and death in the balance—vested in fools and scoundrels.

Jewish Humor as Irony: The Prophets

Circumstances and environments differ, and Jewish humor, like Jewish literature or philosophy, is not suspended in a void; it, too, has its roots in Jewish existence and springs out of the disappointments and satisfactions of people in the ordinary course of living. But if we refer to Jewish humor— or literature or philosophy or religion—in the singular, there must, then, be a certain quality in it, a characteristic that is constant and recognizable in Jewish humor *as such*.

We read in the *Book of Esther* that "Mordecai rent his

clothes, and put on sackcloth with ashes, and went out into the midst of the city, and cried with a loud and bitter cry" (4:1). It was a cry, a plea, for justice, which has resounded throughout the centuries, from Shushan in another era to Berlin in our own. It was a cry for justice, for the defense and preservation of his people and its destiny—and more, it was a cry for all the persecuted and downtrodden in the recurrent Shushans of the world. In *Deuteronomy* there is the Divine imperative: "Justice, justice shalt thou pursue" (16:20); and the commandment was part of the inheritance of the Mordecais of all the generations. Justice and righteousness were the refrain of the prophet's message, and it was righteousness—not merely a chamber in the Temple—that was Israel's Holy of Holies. Nietzsche wrote: "When Socrates and Plato began to speak of truth and justice, they were no longer Greeks but Jews."

It would, therefore, be altogether strange if righteousness were not a motif in Jewish humor: from Abraham's magnificent challenge: "Shall not the judge of all the earth do justly" (*Genesis* 18:25), to Sholem Aleichem's Tevye, as he confronts the peasants who are about to start a pogrom, with the naive and yet ultimate declaration: "There is a God in this world—not my God, your God, but our common God, everybody's God." Jewish humor is a humor of irony. It is irony as a way of telling the truth, of putting matters right, of extending a partial perspective into a more comprehensive one, of letting light in where there was half-darkness. The prophet's message is replete with irony, but it is not for degrading others so as to inflate one's own self-esteem (as Hobbes would have it), nor is it for the pleasure in beholding the stupidities and discomfiture of others without danger to the spectator (as Plato suggests in the *Philebus*), nor is it a gesture of corrective animosity for persons entangled in machine-like behavior (as Bergson describes it). The prophet's irony is directed against idolatry, against the allurements of pagan civilization. Its aim is to lift man up, not to push him down, to remind him of his commitments: "God hath a controversy with you."

Irony is no affront when it is a summons to our dignity and a spur to our latent possibilities. The prophet's irony is a way of telling the truth, of closing the gap between the human and divine perspective, of lessening and modulating the controversy between God and the people. It has been customary to acclaim the solemnity of the Jewish Scriptures, to acknowledge their high seriousness and their stirring pathos. But the humor of the Bible has usually been bypassed, perhaps because for many humor is still something presumably trivial and frivolous and hence not to be associated with the Bible. The humor of the Jewish Scriptures is the humor of irony, and it is not the opposite of high seriousness. It is complementary to it: another way of telling the truth, of putting matters right. It is not a humor for forgetting and evading, but for remembering: "Ye shall be holy for I your God am holy" (*Lev.* 19:2).

There is gentle irony in the vignettes about Jacob and La-ban as they engage in their ruses, trying to outwit each other. Much of the irony in the Joseph stories was carried over successfully in Thomas Mann's beautiful tetralogy (especially in *Joseph the Provider*). The nuances of humor in the episode where Rebecca deceives Isaac by substituting Jacob for Esau are unmistakable: there is an approximation here to the "comic mask" as Rebecca dresses up Jacob to resemble Esau. And the very name *Isaac* signifies laughter.

It is, however, in the laughter at idolatry that the humor of irony acquired in the Jewish Scriptures a depth and intensity as well as an artistry that are seldom matched elsewhere in literature, both sacred and secular. Elijah who heard "the still small voice" on the mountain in the wilderness and sensed in it the presence of God could also laugh in Samaria, the capital of Israel, with a laughter loud and thunderous as he taunted the pagan priests of Baal: "Cry aloud; for he is a god; either he is musing, or he is gone aside, or he is on a journey, or peradventure he sleepeth, and he must be awaked" (*I Kings* 18:27).

Elijah's irony with its laughter was not a solitary occurrence. It is audible again in Isaiah, where it is preceded by awe and reverence, for Isaiah "identifies" God as ineffable and without analogy in all Creation, and then leaps into irony as he depicts the hollowness of idolatry:

> *To whom then will ye liken God?*
> *Or what likeness will ye compare unto Him?*
> *The image perchance, which the craftsman hath melted,*
> *And the goldsmith spread over with gold,*
> *The silversmith casting silver chains?* (40:18–19)

The laughter does not cease, although the irony is milder and tinged with sadness, as Jeremiah, the prophet of so much sorrow, gives vent to it:

> *For the customs of the people are vanity;*
> *For it is but a tree which one cutteth out of the forest,*
> *The work of the hands of the workman with the axe.*
> *They deck it with silver and with gold,*
> *They fasten it with nails and with hammers, that it move*
>   *not.*
> *They are like a pillar in a garden of cucumbers, and speak*
>   *not;*
> *They must need be borne, because they cannot go.*
> *Be not afraid of them, for they cannot do evil,*
> *Neither is it in them to do good.* (10:3–5)

The method of irony in inveighing against idolatry is resorted to in the *Book of Psalms*, where the language is simple, and the statements are factual:

> *Their idols are of silver and gold,*
> *The work of men's hands.*
> *They have mouths, but they speak not,*
> *Eyes have they, but they see not . . .*
> *They that make them shall be like unto them;*
> *Yea, every one that trusteth in them.* (115:4–8)

The laughter of Elijah and Isaiah and Jeremiah has not subsided, despite persecution and martyrdom—the mocking of idolatry, the protest through irony against the injustice of coarse power, of man's degradation of man, and of the tarnishing of the "Divine image" in man.

Jewish humor does not abound in slapstick, in jokes about sex, in farcical comedy, in what is usually referred to as "broad" humor (although these, too, are "legitimate" types of comedy and are not wholly absent from Jewish humor). The Talmud is wary of jesting except at idolatry, and it is this kind of "jesting," this strain of irony, that has been the constant element in Jewish laughter from Elijah the prophet to Sholem Aleichem's Tevye. It must, however, be emphasized again that the continuous battle against idolatry was not solely a matter of theology. It was a scorning of pagan civilization with its cruelty and violence, with its adoration of the physical virtues, with its ruthless killing of people in war and of animals in the hunt, with its brutal system of slavery, with its cults of "sacred" prostitution, with its contempt for gentleness and compassion and impartial justice, and, above all, its arrogant ascription of infinitude to the finite—its deification of kings and emperors, its pantheons of amoral gods.

The passages from Elijah, Isaiah, Jeremiah and the *Book of Psalms* that have been cited could be paralleled with passages from these prophets and from others, such as Amos and Micah, incisive in their irony against the idolatry of wealth and lasciviousness and self-indulgence, against the injustice of oppressing and grinding down the poor and the weak and the unprotected laborer, against the neglect of the widow and the stranger in the gates. This, for the prophet, was the evil of pagan civilization penetrating into the Jewish kingdoms of Israel in the North and Judea in the South; this, for the prophet, was forgetting that religion and righteousness are one:

> *He judged the cause of the poor and needy;*
> *Then it was well.*
> *Is not this to know Me? saith the Lord.* (Jeremiah 22:16)

Jewish Humor as "Tragic Optimism"

The distinctive quality of Jewish humor is a will to righteousness. But why should the will to righteousness— which is a salient attribute of Judaism *as such*—require irony as its mode in humor? The answer has already been intimated. More explicitly it is this: So long as the actual and the ideal are disparate, so long as the hopes of the heart are not embodied in the contexture of things about us, there is work for man to do, and there is the urgency to stir the conscience to do the work. In classical Jewish terminology, its formulation would be thus: So long as the Kingship of God has not been established, so long as the Messianic expectancy has not been fulfilled, the world is in distress and needs to be mended, to be made whole and holy. Judaism has never accepted the proposition that this disparity is final; it has never yielded to the enticement of cutting off the ideal from the actual, the spiritual from the natural, of elevating the religious above— and, in effect, separating it from—the ethical.

The Jewish vision of life and human destiny attained primary expression in the Jewish religion, in the Messianic concept of a this-worldly redemption, and in Jewish humor with its irony. It is an irony that takes the measure of the distance between the actual and the ideal, between the idolatry we serve and the Kingship of God we strive for, between the injustice that prevails and the righteousness that we desire.

Jewish humor is, therefore, rooted in a tragic optimism: the world is moving toward the Messianic fulfillment, but "the future comes one day at a time." This optimism was tested and tried a thousand times—from the furnaces in Babylonia whose fires did not consume Daniel's three friends to the terrible ovens of Maidenek and Auschwitz whose fires devoured millions. The optimism of Judaism wavered now and then, and its light grew dim as the Jewish people was caught in the great contradiction, the persistent incongruity of its existence—the incongruity between what has been aptly called the Promise and the Pale, the Divine promise that Israel was to be a Chosen People, the betrothed of God, and the actuality of its condition as a dispersed people in a world too often hostile. There was no way of erasing the incongruity; it was wisdom to accept it. To discard the promise would have been tantamount to converting Jewish history into a somber farce, to deprive it of meaning; failure in the effort of accommodation to the world in the practical enterprise of living would have led inevitably to extinction. And so the optimism of Judaism remained firm and steadfast, but always with a tragic dimension to it: the world was not without purpose, and it was moving in the direction of the Messianic fulfillment, but in the drama of history the "Chosen People" was to act as the Suffering Servant of God.

The disparity between the actual and the ideal in universal history and the contradiction between the Promise and the Pale in Jewish history fell together as the fundamental incongruity of a world in which the beginning of redemption— *aschalta d'geulah*—is everywhere, but its consummation is yet nowhere. The optimism and its tragic dimension have been components of Jewish irony from Deutero-Isaiah to the milieu of Eastern Europe. For our grandparents, and for those before them, the Messianic expectancy was no vague and abstract conception; it was warm and vivid in their hearts and imagination and fortified them to bear much hardship. It is instructive to note how sublimity and irony mingled in the speech of the people on the Messianic theme: *Er vet kumen ven Moshiach vet kumen* ("He'll get here when the Messiah will arrive"); *Er vet nit farshpetikn a tog noch Moshiachn* ("He'll not be too late a day after the Messiah's coming"); *Host tzait biz Moshiach vet kumen* ("You have plenty of time till the arrival of the Messiah"). In this irony there is a clinging to the Promise, but not without a smile—a bit skeptical and a bit jovial. The irony and the smile are manifest in the wry remark of the *Maggid* of Kosenitz: "Dear God, if you do not want to redeem your people Israel, then at least redeem the Gentiles."

The smile and the irony are not confined to the Messianic expectancy; they reach out to God, too. Reinhold Niebuhr has written: "There is laughter in the vestibule of the temple, the echo of laughter in the temple itself, but only faith and prayer and no laughter in the holy of holies." Prayer and faith and awe *are* present in the Jewish Holy of Holies, but it is exactly because there is awe—"Know before Whom you stand"—that Abraham can plead with God: "Shall not the Judge of all the earth do justly." And several millennia later the compassionate Rabbi Levi Yitzchok of Berditchev can dare to engage God in a *din toreh,* in "litigation": *Vos hostu tzu dein folk Yisroel? Vos hostu zich ongezetz af dein folk Yisroel?* ("What have you against your people Israel? Why have you heaped afflictions upon your people Israel?") And in Peretz's folktale, *Berl Shneider,* the humble little tailor—without the prerogatives of a rabbi—can muster the courage and the impudence to quarrel with God for His indifference to the plight of the poor who are required, like the well-to-do, to abstain scrupulously from dishonesty, but, unlike them, do not always have food for their hungry children.

This irony expands into laughter, and the laughter splits into a myriad sparkling smiles. But it is also a "laughter through tears," as Sholem Aleichem's Tevye, with his piety undiminished and his faith unshaken, submits this "footnote" —in marvelous contrast to the "prayer and faith" in the Holy of Holies—to the traditional "theodicy": "We have, I tell you, a great God and a good God and a mighty God, and yet, let me tell you, I wish I had a blessing for each time the Master of the World polishes off a piece of work. Well, may the enemies have such a year." In Tevye's humor the tension of generations is for a moment resolved, and an equilibrium is restored between the piety and faith concentrated in the saying *Got un zein mishpot is gerecht* ("God and His decrees are just") and the complaints and indictments—in a mood of both superb insolence and sweet humility—of Levi Yitzchok of Berditchev, of Peretz's little tailor, of Sholem Aleichem's Tevye, of the many anonymous ones among the people.

High seriousness suffuses the whole of Jewish history. It is no fickle affair to contend with the idolatries of the world, to fasten upon it as a people's vocation, and it is no mean achievement to survive from era to era and from land to land in environments seldom hospitable and often antagonistic. Whatever the ingredients of humor may be, *contrast* is one of them. The high seriousness of Jewish existence—the discipline of the Law within the community and the restrictions, legal and civil, imposed from without—was bound to engender as a contrast a subtle and trenchant humor, but not so subtle or trenchant as to wipe out any chance of delight in it.

It was not with levity that the ancient prophet cried out

his protest against idolatry. But one can also guess that, as he painted a picture of idolatry with all the irony at his command, a smile passed across his face, and an ache was mitigated in his heart, and there was a brief respite of pleasure in the irony for its own sake. The pleasure was not drowned out but probably fortified by the high seriousness that inspired the prophet. It was pleasure in the play of contrast, in showing off the pretentious as being vapid and ludicrous.

Jewish Humor as Intermingling of "Is" and "Ought"

A world in which the actual and the ideal are disparate, in which righteousness has not yet been enthroned, is more than a house and less than a home: it is a house that is gradually being transformed into a home. If righteousness is the goal of history, as it is in the prophetic teaching, then there will be *estrangement* from the world as it is, and there will also be *involvement* in the world for what it may be if *we* will it. The estrangement and the involvement are correlative in "the long view," but in the routine of existence there are complications, and the Jew who will jest with a mild irony: *Er vet kumen ven Moshiach vet kumen,* will also intone the *Kaddish* prayer: "May He establish His kingdom during your life and during your days and during the life of all the house of Israel, even speedily and at a near time."

The complications are multiplied as one brings together this normative vision of the world as it should be with the empirical history of the Jews in the countries of the world. Somehow the political estrangement of the Jews on the stage of history as "outsiders" in the lands of their sojourn merges into the estrangement of the Jews not *from,* but *within,* a world where redemption has not yet worked itself out, but where the promise and the hope of redemption were as real to them as bread and water, as the grass in the fields and the wind in the air.

In one of the beautiful stories about Rabbi Levi Yitzchok of Berditchev, it is related that he was travelling with a group of Jews in a covered wagon. As evening approached they interrupted the journey for the appropriate prayers—*Mincha* and *Ma'ariv*. The driver, unaccustomed to idleness, began to grease the wheels and axles of the wagon while reciting the prayers from memory. Whereupon some of the passengers reproached him for mixing prayer with work. But the *Berditchever,* with a smile of gentleness in his eyes, retorted: "Oh, how wonderful it is! Even while this simple man is greasing his wheels, he is absorbed in prayer." This is a lovely story with a fine moral to it, but it may well be that there is much more to the story than the moral suggests. What the driver did is perhaps symbolic of the very essence of Judaism, surely in its prophetic version: Greasing the wheels of the wagon —this world of ours—so it may move in the direction of the Messianic fulfillment is the mission and destiny of Judaism.

But meanwhile the disparity between the actual and the ideal stares us in the face. And though we must not, out of impatience and despair, acquiesce in a *premature* redemption —surely not in the aftermath of Hitler and Stalin—we must not, at the other extreme, lose sight of the world as it will be in the Messianic fulfillment, and we must seek out the signs of redemption that are already discernible in it.

Rabbi Shneur Zalman of Ladi was arrested and kept in prison by the Czarist government. There is a story in connection with his release which illumines the concept of the actual and the ideal, and both the disparity and the bond between them. When he was let out his disciples were certain that it was due to a miracle. But, as usual, the proverbial Litvak interjects his doubts as he discusses it with one of the disciples: "A miracle? Most likely the governor was softened up with a nice juicy bribe." The disciple is taken aback, and then quickly, with a brightness and a dancing joy in his voice, replies: "Yes, what you say sounds reasonable enough, but there must be, don't you see, a *natural* explanation, too." This strikes us as totally crazy—a reversal of logic, even by the standards of the religious person who would define a miracle as supernatural. And if there is pleasure in such humor, as there is, and if we laugh or smile, it is precisely because it is such a reversal of logic, such a chaotic violation of meaning, in the style of Alice and the denizens of her Wonderland. It would seem to fit Kant's interpretation of laughter "as an affection arising from the sudden transformation of a strained expectation into nothing." Clearly there is fun and hilarity in the spectacle of topsy-turvydom, in mixing up the laws of logic and nature, and tossing about the categories of thought and reality—Aristotle's or Kant's—as children do with balls. It offers us an interlude of precious freedom, in a mood of playfulness, from the laws and restraints of our "normal" world.

But the highest humor is that which is not only a point of departure but also a point of return, which offers us a moment of precious freedom, a sweet and blessed holiday, only so that we may come back to our world as children come back to the home of their parents, which is their home too. They come back with eagerness, a gratefulness and a longing in their hearts, not because the occasion that took them away was disappointing but because it was a happy one, and now they want to be at home with those they love best and with the familiar things. Similarly, after the respite and the holiday, we come back to God's world which is our home and to nature's laws which are our anchor, and we are a trifle wiser and kinder for the holiday we have had. Nor is it surprising that after such a respite the scales should fall from our eyes, and we should see "a new heaven and a new earth."

There is, indeed, pleasure in the humor of topsy-turvydom, in the nullification of meaning as we encounter it in the coercive earnestness of communication with one another. But there is greater and richer pleasure in humor which has all this "and heaven too," which is an enchanting restoration of order and meaning as belonging to both the actual and the ideal worlds and forming the law of their continuity, of the growth of the one into the other.

To refer to a miracle as the *natural* explanation of an event is to confound not only common sense and science but also conventional religion itself. Such religion draws a line of demarcation between the natural and supernatural, and the line widens into a chasm without a bridge to connect them. For classical Judaism there is no absolute chasm between the natural and the supernatural, and the God of Judaism is a God of history. It is no unwarranted stretching of the doctrine of Judaism to link the ideal with the natural. The ideal is not the opposite of the natural but a possibility within things natural, and the redemption of the world is not outside history as a Divine initiative solely but as a drama and process within history. Although the ideal is only a possibility in things natural, it is nonetheless the natural in its fulfillment as the fruit is the fulfillment of the seed. It would be folly to settle for the world as it is without concern for the ideal as a genuine possibility in it; and it is right, in dealing with the world and events in it, to appraise them for what they are and for their approximation to what they may be in their fulfillment.

From the perspective of the world as it is the reasonable explanation for Rabbi Shneur Zalman's release was that of a nice juicy bribe for the governor. From the perspective of the world as it may and should be, under the aspect of righteousness, the reasonable explanation is that he was freed *without* a bribe, call it miracle or what you will, because he was innocent, and an innocent man should not be in prison. The humor of the anecdote lies in the childlike, but not childish, assessment of the world as though its ideal fulfillment were already an accomplished reality; and its irony reminds us, by means of this very confusion, of our distance from the redemption. Its summons is that we go on greasing the wheels of the wagon, or, in the bidding of Deutero-Isaiah: "Clear ye in the wilderness the way of the Lord, make plain in the desert a highway for our God" (40:3).

TEN

The Humor of Christ

ELTON TRUEBLOOD

Do not look dismal.

Matthew 6:16

The widespread failure to recognize and to appreciate the humor of Christ is one of the most amazing aspects of the era named for Him. Anyone who reads the Synoptic Gospels with a relative freedom from presuppositions might be expected to see that Christ laughed, and that He expected others to laugh, but our capacity to miss this aspect of His life is phenomenal. We are so sure that He was always deadly serious that we often twist His words in order to try to make them conform to our preconceived mold. A misguided piety has made us fear that acceptance of His obvious wit and humor would somehow be mildly blasphemous or sacrilegious. Religion, we think, is serious business, and serious business is incompatible with banter.

The critics of Christ have, on the whole, been as blind to His humor as have His admirers. Even Nietzsche, in deploring Christ's early death, wrote, "Would that he had remained in the wilderness and far from the good and just! Perhaps he would have learned to live and to love the earth—and laughter too." [1] The supposedly fierce critic was thus uncritical in that he did not bother to go beyond the stereotype to examine the evidence objectively.

The fact is that we have often developed a false pattern of Christ's character. Though we do not always say so directly, we habitually think of Him as mild in manner, endlessly patient, grave in speech, and serious almost to the point of dourness. The evidence for this is that we try to explain away any words or incidents in the Gospels which are inconsistent with such a picture. But, if we abandon this effort, and "sit down before the fact as a little child," with a minimum of presupposition, we come out with a radically different conception.

The supposed mildness is contradicted in a spectacular manner by the attack on the Pharisees. If the twenty-third chapter of Matthew were required reading, part of the stereotype would be broken, for few of us have heard in our day any attack so scathing, even in the midst of a political campaign. Christ apparently adopted from John the Baptist the choice epithet "brood of vipers" (Matt. 3:7 and Matt. 23:33), but He went on to manufacture stronger epithets of His own. Can a man be called a worse name than a white-washed tomb, full of putrid and decaying flesh? There is nothing mild about saying, as Matthew reports in two different contexts (Matt. 5:29, 30 and 18:8, 9), that there are situations in which a man ought to pluck out his eye and cut off his hand and throw them away. Nor is there mildness in Mark 9:43–48, which concludes with the violent double metaphor, "where their worm does not die, and the fire is not quenched."

The fiction that Christ was endlessly patient will not bear

[1] Translation of Nietzsche's "Live Dangerously" by Walter Kaufmann, in the latter's *Existentialism from Dostoevsky to Sartre* (New York: Meridian Books, 1956), p. 109.

examination. In His impatience with His inept disciples He is reported as saying, "How much longer must I endure you?" (Matt. 17:17, N.E.B.). In the parable of the Barren Fig Tree (Luke 13:6–9) we have a vivid account of the divine impatience. The clear teaching is that it is reasonable to be patient for a while, in order to give the unfruitful person or unproductive organization a chance, but that there is a limit to the required patience, and that, when we go beyond this limit, tolerance ceases to be a virtue. It is all right, we are told, to put on manure for one more year, but no longer.[2]

Christ's teaching to the effect that externals, including foods, cannot possibly make an inner or spiritual difference is stated with vivid emphasis as follows: "Listen to me, all of you, and understand this: nothing that goes into a man from outside can defile him; no, it is the things that come out of him that defile a man" (Mark 7:14, 15, N.E.B.). Since the boldness of this approach confused the literal-minded disciples, they asked for clarification and, this time, Christ was even more direct, speaking openly of the fact of evacuation. "He said to them, 'Are you as dull as the rest? Do you not see that nothing that goes from outside into a man can defile him, because it does not enter into his heart but into his stomach, and so passes out into the drain?' " (Mark 7:18, 19, N.E.B.). All evils, He thus taught, have internal origins. The deepest sins are spiritual rather than physical.

A prosy literalism not only misses the wry humor, when humor is present, but, what is worse, misses the point of the teaching. Christ taught in figures nearly all of the time, and everyone knows that no figure is to be accepted in its entirety. No one could suppose that when Jesus said He was the door,

---

[2] The parable of the Barren Fig Tree is unique to Luke and is in no way identical with the cursing of the fig tree (Matt. 21:18, 19 and Mark 11:12–14) which is reported as an event. The narrative may be a confusion of the parable.

He meant that He was made of wood. Most figures exist in order to illustrate single points, and to illustrate them with the requisite vividness. Thus each becomes patently absurd when it is pressed too far. The very fact that such figures are necessarily limited gives each one of them a little touch of humor. For example, there is sly humor, as well as deep meaning, in Christ's words about where to put a light. The message is about the necessity of witness, but the failure to make a witness is rendered laughable when Jesus asks, "Is a lamp brought in to be put under a bushel, or under a bed, and not on a stand?" (Mark 4:21). Since the lamp mentioned has an open flame and since the bed is a mattress, it is easy to see that in this situation the light would be suffocated or the mattress would be burned. The appeal here is to the patently absurd. The sensitive laugh, because they get the point.

The sly insertions are numerous indeed. In the midst of a serious discourse, the theme is lightened by the observation, "But know this, that if the householder had known at what hour the thief was coming, he would have been awake and would not have left his house to be broken into" (Luke 12:39). All of us know that it is easy to be smart when we are tipped off, and that to be forewarned is to be forearmed, but Christ delights us, in this case, by a fresh statement of the obvious. All of us know that we are sometimes more concerned with the social effects of our actions, in terms of reputation, than we are with intrinsic right and wrong, but we recognize this more vividly when Christ points out the tendency to cleanse the outside of the cup, rather than the inside (Matt. 23:25–26).

One reason for our failure to laugh is our extreme familiarity with the received text. The words seem to us like old coins, in which the edges have been worn smooth and the engravings have become almost indistinguishable. This is particularly true of the words of the Authorized Version. The words

seem so hallowed that they deepen the force of inherited as-
sumptions, which may actually be contrary to fact. In this
situation the newer translations are often helpful. These are
more likely to make us see the paradoxical character of what
has come to be accepted as common and unexciting. But we
need more than new translations; we need a definite act of
will. The main effort must be an effort on the part of the contemporary student to confront Christ as actually portrayed
rather than as we have imagined Him to be. Only then will
we feel the sharpness of His wit. We must do something to
liberate our minds from "the spell of familiar and venerated
words" in order to see their true significance. When we do
so it is impossible to argue with Edith Hamilton in her
trenchant dictum about the Gospels. "When they are read
with serious attention," she writes, "the kind of study one
gives to something to be mastered, the result is startling." [3]

A second reason for our widespread failure to recognize the
humor of the Gospels is their great stress upon the tragedy of
the crucifixion and the events immediately preceding it. The
events of the final days are told with such fullness that a
stranger to our culture, coming to the Gospels without prepa-
ration, might be excused for thinking of them as the story of
Christ's passion, with introductory passages added. The events
of Good Friday and Easter, because of their dramatic appeal
and profound significance, began, very early in Christian history, to occupy the center of interest. Because the tragic aspect
is intrinsically unhumorous, men came to see the sad picture
as the whole picture. When artists began to produce specula-
tive portraits of Christ they naturally stressed the somber
aspect. How many of the well-known efforts to portray Christ
show Him laughing or presenting a witty paradox? By enormous good luck the authors of the Synoptic Gospels were
able to preserve the authentic account which His simple fol-

[3] Edith Hamilton, *Witness to the Truth* (New York: W. W. Norton &
Company, 1948), p. 13.

lowers had provided, but, as the Fourth Gospel shows, the further men got from such sources, the less humor there was. The contrast between John and the Synoptics is, in this regard, striking indeed. The Apostle Paul, who never knew Christ in the flesh, appears to reflect none of Christ's humor. Indeed, the contrast in humor is one of the deepest contrasts between the Synoptic Gospels and the writings of Paul. Though Paul could be eloquent, he appears to have lacked Christ's gift of witty speech.

We have many reasons for being grateful for the production of the Synoptic Gospels, but one of the greatest reasons is that they provide a powerful antidote to the subsequent distortion. The Person they present has many contrasting features. He is a Man of Sorrows, but He is also a Man of Joys; He uses terribly rough and blunt language; He expresses blazing anger; He teases; He foregathers with a gay crowd. How, for example, could we ever miss the fact that His words and behavior surprised His contemporaries? We are told that "they were surprised that words of such grace should fall from his lips" (Luke 4:22, N.E.B.).

That Christ went with the gay crowd, including what the New English Bible calls "many bad characters," was extremely shocking to the religious leaders. Could there be any depth to His teaching if He failed to see how unworthy these laughing people were! "Now the tax collectors and sinners were all drawing near to him. And the Pharisees and the scribes murmured, saying, 'This man receives sinners and eats with them'" (Luke 15:1, 2). While Luke alone gives us the choice bit just quoted, all the Synoptics give the story of the feast at Levi's house. Mark's rendering is:

And as he sat at table in his house, many tax collectors and sinners were sitting with Jesus and his disciples; for there were many who followed him. And the scribes of the Pharisees when they saw that he was eating with sinners and tax collectors, said

to his disciples, "Why does he eat with tax collectors and sinners?" And when Jesus heard it, he said to them, "Those who
are well have no need of a physician, but those who are sick;
I came not to call the righteous, but sinners." [Mark 2:15–17]

That Christ did not fit the expected pattern was clear.
Those who gathered around John the Baptist, like those who
followed the Pharisaic party, engaged in solemn fasts, but
Christ did not do so. Both He and His disciples were notable
for their eating and drinking (Luke 5:33). Though only his
enemies called Him a drunkard, it is obvious that Christ drank
wine. It was His general reputation for gaiety which provided
the basis for one of His most humorous rejoinders, to the
effect that the critics could not be pleased. If people did not
like the abstemiousness of John, and if they also did not
like the gaiety of Jesus, what *did* they want?

"To what then shall I compare the men of this generation, and
what are they like? They are like children sitting in the market
place and calling to one another,

> 'We piped to you, and you did not dance;
> we wailed, and you did not weep.'

For John the Baptist has come eating no bread and drinking no
wine; and you say, 'He has a demon.' The Son of Man has come
eating and drinking; and you say, 'Behold, a glutton and a drunkard, a friend of tax collectors and sinners!' Yet wisdom is justified
by all her children." [Luke 7:31–35]

The sharp thrust of this final line is characteristic of
Christ's sly humor. He is willing to rest the case in terms of
human consequences. What happens in the lives of men and
women is the real test of His position or any other. His bad
reputation among the pious is a trivial matter, provided the
lives of ordinary people are enriched and glorified. "I'll judge

by my consequences, if you will judge by yours," He is saying in the most pithy manner.

Perhaps our greatest failure in creating a false picture of Christ has been a failure of logic. We assume that an assertion of sadness entails a denial of humor, but there is no good reason to suppose that such is the case. There is abundant evidence to show that contrasting elements of character, far from being mutually incompatible, are often complementary. The fact that Christ laughed does not, and need not, mean that He did not also weep. It is a well-known fact that humor often appears in the most noble spirits. Indeed, it is hard to find genuine classics without this combination. An excellent contemporary illustration of the fertile combination of seriousness and humor is provided by that inimitable journal, *The New Yorker*. Real humor, instead of being something merely light or superficial, depends upon profundity. "A humorous rejoinder," said Kierkegaard, "must always contain something profound." [4] Greatness is denied to those termed by Kierkegaard the "stupidly serious."

That mirth and compassion are compatible is one of the greatest lessons mankind can learn. Lincoln, before he read to the cabinet his draft of the Emancipation Proclamation, eased tensions by reading from a humorous book. The fact that he was a notable teller of funny stories did not hinder, in the least, his expression of profound pathos in the Second Inaugural. We can say of him, as Macaulay said of Addison, that he possessed "a mirth consistent with tender compassion for all that is frail, and with profound reverence for all that is sublime."

Boswell's *Life of Johnson* is generally regarded as the greatest of all biographical works, and part of the reason for this reputation is its remarkable ability to shift from the sublime

---

[4] Søren Kierkegaard, *Concluding Unscientific Postscript,* tr. by David F. Swenson (Princeton: Princeton University Press, 1941), p. 491 n.

to the laughable. One of the reasons why all Western philosophy is a continuation of the heritage of Socrates is that
the great Athenian exhibited precisely the combination in
which humor and seriousness strengthen each other. Who,
having once read the *Apology,* for example, can forget the way
in which Socrates, facing his accusers and recognizing that he
was doomed, made a laughable and preposterous proposal
about his penalty. The penalty he suggested was entertainment for life at the Prytaneum, a dining hall in Athens maintained at public expense.[5] It was at the Prytaneum that distinguished citizens were entertained. He even joked in the
hour of his death, when Crito asked how they should bury
him. " 'Any way you like,' replied Socrates, 'that is, if you
can catch me and I don't slip through your fingers.' He
laughed gently as he spoke, and turning to us went on, 'I can't
persuade Crito that I am this Socrates here who is talking to
you now and marshalling all the arguments. He thinks I am
the one whom he will see presently lying dead, and he asks
how he is to bury me!' " [6]

Far from laughter being incompatible with anguish, it is
often the natural expression of deep pain. Coleridge faced this
clearly when he tried to see why Hamlet jests when his companions overtake him. "Terror," he says, "is closely connected
with the ludicrous; the latter is the common mode by which
the mind tries to emancipate itself from terror. The laugh is
rendered by nature itself the language of extremes, even as
tears are." [7] It is not possible to have genuine humor or true
wit without an extremely sound mind, which is always a mind
capable of high seriousness and a sense of the tragic. This is
obviously part of the meaning of Socrates when, after a full

[5] *Apology,* 36E.
[6] *Phaedo,* 115C. Trans. by Hugh Tredennick (Penguin Classics, 154).
[7] Samuel Taylor Coleridge, *Writings on Shakespeare,* ed. by Terence
Hawkes (New York: G. P. Putnam's Sons, 1959), p. 158.

night of discussion with Agathon and his other friends, including even Alcibiades, he ended the symposium, at daybreak, by insisting that anyone who can write tragedy can also write comedy, because the fundamental craft is the same in each of them. Kierkegaard echoed this conclusion when he said that the comic and the tragic touch each other at the absolute point of infinity.

An appealing example which shows that wit and seriousness are wholly compatible in a single life is provided by Blaise Pascal. "Few men," said Landor, "have been graver than Pascal; few have been wittier." Indeed, we must say, in spite of our admiration for Bergson's famous essay on laughter, that the philosopher was wrong in saying that laughter is usually accompanied by an absence of feeling. "Indifference," he wrote, "is its natural environment, for laughter has no greater foe than emotion." [8] The probability is that Bergson would not have arrived at this conclusion if he had included the laughter of Christ in his researches.

Our logical mistake, which arises when we suppose that the assertion of Christ's sadness necessitates a denial of His humor, is the result of a superficial and therefore false application of the law of noncontradiction. This law, which is basic to all rational thinking, received its classic expression in Aristotle's *Metaphysics* (Book Gamma). It states that a thing cannot both be and not be at the same time and in the same sense. Only a confused mind could hold both that the earth is more than six thousand years old and that it is *not* more than six thousand years old. We do not know, in advance, which one of two contradictory propositions is erroneous, but we know that *one* of them is. All of this is extremely important, since, unless such a logical law is accepted, there cannot be any

[8] *Comedy,* being *An Essay on Comedy* by George Meredith and *Laughter* by Henri Bergson, Introduction and Appendix by Wylie Sypher (Garden City, N.Y.: Doubleday Anchor Books, 1956), p. 63.

rational discussion between human beings. There is no point in trying to be intellectually honest if inconsistency is acceptable. But once we accept the Aristotelian law we need to be very careful about claiming that propositions are contradictory when they are not. Contrariety and contradiction are vastly different conceptions. For example, there is a great contrast between the proposition "All men are wise" and the contrary proposition "No men are wise." Far from being contradictory, these may both be false and, as a matter of fact, *are* both false. In a slightly different logical context it can be said of laughter and tears that, though they are extremely different, they are mutually compatible, providing we consider a person's total character. The affirmation of one does not entail the denial of the other, for they are not contradictories.

Even our own experience in our own day should be sufficient to make us realize that laughter and a sense of concern are not really antithetical. We soon learn that we get better stories at a religious conference than we get anywhere else, and it is a commonplace that many Christian leaders are superlative tellers of humorous anecdotes. The late Rufus M. Jones was an example of this truth, but he did not stand alone. "The opposite of joy," says Leslie Weatherhead, "is not sorrow. It is unbelief." [9] It is not really surprising, therefore, that the Christian should laugh and sing; after all he has a great deal to laugh about. He understands, with George Fox, that, though there is an ocean of darkness and death, there is also an ocean of light and love which flows over the ocean of darkness.

Full recognition of Christ's humor has been surprisingly rare. In many of the standard efforts to write the Life of Christ there is no mention of humor at all, and when there is any, it is usually confined to a hint or two. Frequently, there is not one suggestion that He ever spoke other than seriously. It is to

[9] Leslie Weatherhead, *This Is the Victory* (Nashville: Abingdon Press, 1941), p. 171.

Renan's credit that he sensed the existence of the humorous element in the Gospels and called it striking, though he did not develop his insight in detail. Tennyson, in pointing out the paradox that humor is generally most fruitful in the most solemn spirits, said, "You will even find it in the Gospel of Christ." In several authors of the twentieth century we find a passing reference to the humorous side of Christ's teaching, though without development, in most cases. Characteristic is the reference of Harry Emerson Fosdick, "He never jests as Socrates does, but He often lets the ripple of a happy breeze play over the surface of His mighty deep." [10]

Many readers who have come to maturity in the present century owe their first recognition of Christ's humor to a brilliant English scholar, T. R. Glover, who, during the dark days of the First World War, published *The Jesus of History*.[11] Glover gave especial attention to the subject in some very striking pages of Chapter III, "The Man and His Mind." He recognized fully that it is only familiarity that has blinded us "to the gaiety and playfulness that light up his lessons." [12] One of the best passages in this remarkable book is the following:

A more elaborate and amusing episode is that of the Pharisees' drinking operations. We are shown the man polishing his cup, elaborately and carefully; for he lays great importance on the cleanness of his cup; but he forgets to clean the inside. Most people drink from the inside, but the Pharisee forgot it, dirty as it was, and left it untouched. Then he sets about straining what he is going to drink—another elaborate process, and the series of sensations, as the long hairy neck slid down the throat of the Pharisee—all that amplitude of loose-hung anatomy—the hump— two humps—both of them slid down—and he never noticed—

[10] Harry Emerson Fosdick, *The Manhood of the Master* (New York: The Association Press, 1958), p. 16.

[11] New York: The Association Press, 1917.

[12] *Ibid.*, p. 47.

and the legs—all of them—with whole outfit of knees and big padded feet. The Pharisee swallowed a camel and never noticed it. (Matt. xxiii, 24, 25.) It is the mixture of sheer realism with absurdity that makes the irony and gives it its force. Did no one smile as the story was told? Did no one see the scene pictured with his own mind's eye—no one grasp the humor and the irony with delight? Could any one, on the other hand, forget it? A modern teacher would have said, in our jargon, that the Pharisee had no sense of proportion—and no one would have thought the remark worth remembering.[13]

Glover showed that Christ was no Stoic, much as Chesterton showed that the understanding Christian is no Epicurean. It is quite possible that the face of Marcus Aurelius never changed, for his philosophy advocated superiority to emotion, but with Christ we are in another kind of world. His look showed anger and sorrow "at their obstinate stupidity" (Mark 3:5, N.E.B.). He was "moved with compassion" and He must have laughed, for those who tell jokes usually do.

Though a few books include references to the humor of Christ,[14] the most original and perceptive of modern writings on the subject is not in a book at all, but appeared in a most unlikely place, The American Mercury. The essay is by L. M. Hussey, and is called "The Wit of the Carpenter." [15] For some reason this has attracted very little scholarly attention and is seldom listed in bibliographies, even though it is executed with skill.

It is Hussey's hypothesis that the original followers of Christ reported what they did not appreciate or even under-

[13] Ibid., pp. 47–48.

[14] Laughter in the Bible by Gary Webster (St. Louis: Bethany Press, 1960) has one chapter called "Jesus' Use of Humor." There is a short article on "Humor" in The Interpreter's Dictionary of the Bible, Vol. II, pp. 660–62. Other books are Dudley Zuver, Salvation by Laughter (New York: Harper & Brothers, 1933), D. N. Morison, The Humour of Christ (London, 1931).

[15] The American Mercury, Vol. V., pp. 329–36.

stand, but that the speech was so pithy and so memorable that they found it easy to retain it and to convey it to those who eventually did the writing. Sober prose, as everyone knows, is hard to memorize or to repeat with any accuracy, whereas poetry, or the scintillating epigram, can be repeated with remarkable ease and faithfulness. The rough fisherman laughed and missed some of the nuances of the wit, but passed the wit on even more accurately for that reason. Referring to the persons who were Christ's first listeners, Hussey says, "I mean that by virtue of their naïveté they were literal-minded men—consequently of the sort to remember what they heard verbatim, and, unconscious of humorous im-plications, to set down their Teacher's sayings with almost mechanical verbal accuracy." [16] Literal faithfulness, Hussey speculates, was made possible by epigrammatic pungency of speech, which fixed itself indelibly in the memories of es-sentially illiterate men.

There is no doubt that this hypothesis has much in its favor. Certainly the epigrams have a freshness about them that it is impossible to believe is the result of the work of editors. Fur-thermore, we can frequently note a marked difference between the words attributed to Jesus and the clumsy attempts at justification or explanation. We have abundant evidence that the disciples failed, in a number of instances, to understand their Master.

A vivid illustration of such evidence appears when Christ says, "Beware of the leaven of the Pharisees and the leaven of Herod." His reference to the twin dangers of the Right and the Left was too advanced for the disciples. We can glow in his flaming impatience.

And they discussed it with one another, saying, "We have no bread." And being aware of it, Jesus said to them, "Why do you

[16] *Ibid.*, p. 329.

discuss the fact that you have no bread? Do you not yet perceive or understand? Are your hearts hardened? Having eyes do you not see, and having ears do you not hear? And do you not remember? [Mark 8:16-18]

A worse example of the failure of the Apostles to understand is shown in their argument about which one of them should be greatest, an argument which occurred in the most inappropriate setting, that of the Last Supper. If we may judge by John's account, the misunderstanding was so great that Christ undertook to correct it, not primarily by words which appeared to be wasted, but rather by the visible demonstration of washing their feet. Another sad evidence of misunderstanding came during Christ's final earthly appearance when, in spite of all that He had taught, they showed that they still had political expectations and asked, "Lord, will you at this time restore the kingdom to Israel?" (Acts 1:6). The contrast, Hussey claims, between the original word of Jesus and the reaction of His hearers is often apparent, because the disciples "set about to torture a literal significance from phrases first coined to blast utterly a literal intent."

The writer who has done most, in the twentieth century, to overcome the misapprehension that Christianity is a religion of sorrow and only of sorrow, is G. K. Chesterton. The paradox of the fundamental sadness of all Epicureanism was one of Chesterton's most revealing insights. Readers took notice when he showed them, in *Heretics*, the enormous contrast between the gay spirit of the early Christian and the pensiveness of an Omar Khayyám. People who had been complaining about Puritanism suddenly found that the shoe had been placed on the other foot. It was not hard for Chesterton to show that the characteristic man of classical antiquity was less boisterous than the Christian. The characteristic pagan philosopher believed in moderation, but the word does not appear in the New Testament, provided it is accurately translated. Even the most gifted of all the students of Socrates felt impelled, in his final work of maturity (a work in which the disturbing character of Socrates does not appear in the dialogue) to warn against both immoderate laughter and immoderate tears. The Athenian Stranger explains that "there must be restraint of unseasonable laughter and tears and each of us must urge his fellow to consult decorum by utter concealment of all excess of joy or grief, whether the breeze of fortune is set fair, or, by a shift of circumstance, the fortunes of an enterprise are confronted by a mountain of difficulty." [17]

The reader can see that the mood of the aged Plato, whatever his greatness, is far removed from the mood of Christ, which could include hot anger and great rejoicing. This contrast between the best of the classical spirit and the best of Christianity gave G. K. Chesterton his opportunity to elaborate a paradox and thus to challenge a generally accepted opinion. Though Chesterton shocked many of his contemporaries by showing, in *Heretics*, that Christianity is fundamentally a religion of joy, markedly in contrast to the melancholy mood of Omar Khayyám, it was in *Orthodoxy* that he completed his case. He tells us:

It is said that Paganism is a religion of joy and Christianity of sorrow; it would be just as easy to prove that Paganism is pure sorrow and Christianity pure joy. Such conflicts mean nothing and lead nowhere. Everything human must have in it both joy and sorrow; the only matter of interest is the manner in which the two things are balanced or divided. And the really interesting thing is this, that the pagan was (in the main) happier and happier as he approached the earth, but sadder and sadder as he approached the heavens.[18]

[17] *Laws*, V. 732C by A. E. Taylor, *The Collected Dialogues of Plato* (Bollingen Series LXXI, Pantheon Books, 1961).
[18] Chesterton, *Orthodoxy* (New York: Dodd, Mead & Co., 1927), pp. 294–95.

Chesterton is quite ready to concede that the men and women of the pagan civilizations could be gay about *some* things. Indeed, this is obvious. It is impressive, for example, to see how Aristophanes could make people smile about such important subjects as science and war. But Chesterton contends that it took something like the Gospel to make poor men experience "cosmic contentment." Men, who had come to know Christ, might be sad about the little things, but were tumultuously gay about the big things. "Giotto lived in a gloomier town than Euripides, but he lived in a gayer universe." Christianity fits man's deepest need because it makes him concentrate on joys which do not pass away, rather than on the inevitable grief which is superficial. The climax of Chesterton's great book is memorable:

And as I close this chaotic volume I open again the strange small book from which all Christianity came; and I am again haunted by a kind of confirmation. The tremendous figure which fills the Gospels towers in this respect, as in every other above all the thinkers who ever thought themselves tall. His pathos was natural, almost casual. The Stoics, ancient and modern, were proud of concealing their tears. He never concealed His tears; He showed them plainly on His open face at any daily sight, such as the far sight of His native city. Yet He concealed something. Solemn supermen and imperial diplomatists are proud of restraining their anger. He never restrained His anger. He flung furniture down the front steps of the Temple, and asked men how they expected to escape the damnation of Hell. Yet He restrained something. . . . There was something that He covered constantly by abrupt silence or impetuous isolation. There was some one thing that was too great for God to show us when He walked upon our earth; and I have sometimes fancied that it was His mirth.[19]

[19] *Ibid.*, pp. 298–99.

What is really strange about Chesterton, at this point, is his failure to see the open evidence of the humor of Christ, when he saw so much of it in the movement which stems from Him. Some of Christ's humor may have been "covered," but it is not true to say that all of it was of the hidden variety. Chesterton has put us greatly in his debt because of the way in which he has helped to restore a balance, but, if the evidence assembled in this book is correctly interpreted, we have to conclude that he did not go far enough.

The conception of Christianity in which compassion and joy were equally at home was given brilliant expression, a generation ago, in a pamphlet, published by the Epworth Press, called *God in Everything*. In this, Parson John writes to Miriam Gray,

Many of the religious people that I know, when they talk of religion, have a bedside manner and walk about in felt slippers. And if they speak of God they always tidy themselves first. But you go in and out of all the rooms in God's house as though you were quite at home. You open the doors without knocking, and you hum on the stairs, and it isn't always hymns either. My aunt thinks you are not quite reverent; but, then, she can keep felt slippers on her mind without any trouble.

Any alleged Christianity which fails to express itself in gaiety, at some point, is clearly spurious. The Christian is gay, not because he is blind to injustice and suffering, but because he is convinced that these, in the light of the divine sovereignty, are never *ultimate*. He is convinced that the unshakable purpose is the divine rule in all things, whether of heaven or earth (Eph. 1:10). Though he can be sad, and often is perplexed, he is never really worried. The well-known humor of the Christian is not a way of denying the tears, but rather a way of affirming something which is deeper than tears.

The consequences of Christ's rejection of the dismal are great, not only for common life, but also for theology. If Christ laughed a great deal, as the evidence shows, and if He is what He claimed to be, we cannot avoid the logical conclusion that there is laughter and gaiety in the heart of God. The deepest conviction of all Christian theology is the affirmation that the God of all the world is like Jesus Christ. Because the logical development is from the relatively known to the relatively unknown, the procedure is not from God to Christ, but from Christ to God. If we take this seriously we conclude that God cannot be cruel, or self-centered or vindictive, or even lacking in humor.

ELEVEN

Eutrapelia:
A Forgotten Virtue[1]

HUGO RAHNER

Did you ever practise eutrapelia? An odd question. Most of us have never even heard this strange Greek word, "eutrapelia," and scarcely anyone knows anything about the virtue which bears this name. But a person who is at all acquainted with the history of ethics and moral theology knows that eutrapelia is among the virtues mentioned in Aristotle's Nicomachean Ethics: it was there that Aquinas read about it and since then poor Eutrapelia has led a miserable existence in the standard books of moral theology, scantily adorned always with the same quotations that Aquinas knew, tired and reduced to a virtuous neutral attitude, upholding the mean in recreational play and joking.[2]

[1] Quotations from Aristotle and Cicero are given in the Loeb translations. The Fathers and St. Thomas Aquinas have been translated from the original language, in the light of Father Rahner's German renderings and abridgment.—*Translator.*

[2] Cf. *Salmanticensis Cursus Theologicus,* Lyons, 1679, III, pp. 785 f.; O. Schilling, *Lehrbuch der Moraltheologie,* Munich, 1928, II, pp. 14, 350; B. H. Merkelbach, *Summa Theologiae Moralis ad Mentem D. Thomae,* Paris, 1938, II, pp. 980 f.; H. Noldin, *Summa Theologiae Moralis,* Innsbruck, 1952, I, p. 260.

Let us try for once to remove the dust which has settled on this virtue. For it has the soft brightness of a noble and ancient gem, placed in the ivory bedecked cover of a Christian Gospel Book. It is a virtue of Greek *humanitas,* baptized in Christ. It is therefore neither antiquated nor a concept exclusive to the perpetually repeated Scholastic catalogue of virtues. If we contemplate it lovingly, we shall receive an answer to secret and heart-stirring questions as to how we are to give a mature Christian character to our modern existence, thrust as we are into the midst of this evil (and yet so lovely) world, into this noisy, merry (because mostly so mortally sad) world, from which a Christian may not seek refuge by imagining himself to be above it all.

The question that perpetually arises in such a train of thought is: may a Christian laugh, when he has heard our Lord's warning, "Woe upon you who laugh now; you shall mourn and weep" (Luke 6.25)? May a Christian go on merrily playing when a stern and strict choice has to be made for eternity? Is it right for him to relax, to ease the senses, when experience constantly reminds him how these same senses draw him down? All these are questions which the Fathers of the Church raised solemnly and seriously, which Aquinas tried to answer after mature and enlightened reflection, which were brought to a head in the bitter controversies between the Jansenists and the "devout humanists" with their ideas of a heaven on earth. They are questions which are raised in a completely new form today, when we are concerned with the thorny problem of the "Christian in the world," with discovering a mean between accepting and rejecting joyous, refreshing, relaxing things, between gravity and playfulness, crying and laughing. The Greeks knew and lived something of this ideal of the "serious-serene" man.[3]

[3] L. Radermacher, *Weinen und Lachen, Studien über antikes Lebensgefühl,* Vienna, 1947.

Great Christian thinkers adopted it and worked it up into the wise and lovely doctrine of "man at play". . . . As eutrapelia has become largely a forgotten virtue it will pay us to look into the school of the Greek and Christian sages, in order to hear what it is all about. What we shall learn there can give us strength and comfort.

We shall follow the example of Aquinas and first look up Aristotle's Nicomachean Ethics.[4] In his fourth book, the Stagirite speaks of the balanced mean in which every virtue consists and in which alone it maintains its true character and maturity. He then shows how this relates to joking and playing as activities which are just as necessary as seriousness and hard work for the development of a genuinely human life:

But life also includes relaxation, and one form of relaxation is playful conversation. Here, too, we feel that there is a certain standard of good taste in social behaviour, and a certain propriety in the sort of things we say and in our manner of saying them. . . . It is clear that in these matters too it is possible either to exceed or to fall short of the mean.

This mean Aristotle finds realized in the person who can be called "eutrapelos": the literal translation, "well-turning," shows at once what is meant. This person stands between two extremes, the description of which is particularly important as showing how Aristotelian ethics emerged from the cult and politics of the city-state—a description which Aquinas later took over. The one extreme is the "bomolochos," the poor wretch who hung about the altar of sacrifice in the hope of snatching or begging an odd bit of meat; in a broader sense, one who was ready to make jokes at every turn for the sake of a good meal and himself to be made the butt of cheap gibes.

[4] IV, 14 (1128a).

The opposite extreme was the "agroikos," the "boor," whose coarse stiffness was despised by the "asteios," the highly cultured Athenian citizen. Thus Aristotle says:

Those then who go to excess in ridicule are thought to be buffoons and vulgar fellows, who itch to have their joke at all costs, and are more concerned to raise a laugh than to keep within the bounds of decorum and avoid giving pain to the object of their raillery. Those on the other hand who never by any chance say anything funny themselves and take offence at those who do, are considered boorish and morose.

The "well-turning" person stands out against both extremes:

Those who jest with good taste are called witty or versatile—that is to say, full of good turns; for such sallies seem to spring from the character, and we judge men's characters, like their bodies, by their movements.

The philosopher sees a parallel in the development of Attic comedy, from the obscene ribaldry of the old to the refined wit of the new. The ideal is the man who practises eutrapelia, who observes the mean:

The buffoon is one who cannot resist a joke; he will not keep his tongue off himself or anyone else, if he can raise a laugh, and will say things which a man of refinement would never say, and some of which he would not even allow to be said to him. The boor is of no use in playful conversation: he contributes nothing and takes offence at everything; yet relaxation and amusement seem to be a necessary element in life.

This refined mentality of eutrapelia is therefore a kind of mobility of the soul, by which a truly cultured person "turns" to lovely, bright and relaxing things, without losing himself in them: it is, so to speak, a spiritual elegance of movement in which his seriousness and his moral character can be perceived. The object of eutrapelia is play for the sake of seriousness, as Aristotle once described it in an unforgettable chapter of the tenth book of the Nicomachean Ethics:[5]

It follows therefore that happiness is not to be found in amusements. Indeed it would be strange that amusement should be our End—that we should toil and moil all our life long in order that we may amuse ourselves. For virtually every object we adopt is pursued as a means to something else, excepting happiness, which is an end in itself; to make amusement the object of our serious pursuits and our work seems foolish and childish to excess: Anacharsis's motto, Play in order that you may work, is felt to be the right rule. For amusement is a form of rest; but we need rest because we are not able to go on working without a break, and therefore it is not an end, since we take it as a means to further activity.

This rather exclusive aristocratic ideal of mental refinement and culture, which was revived again by Cicero in his work, *De Officiis,* could not at first have much appeal to Christians. The notion of eutrapelia, as developed by Aristotle, is therefore not to be met with at all in the morality and asceticism of primitive Christianity. The reason for this may be found already in the fact that in the language of late antiquity "eutrapelia" had acquired very different overtones. "Eutrapelia" had almost become "bomolochia" and to describe a person as "eutrapelos" was to make him an object of contempt as a smart but garrulous windbag. Martial, for instance, gave to a clumsy and incompetent barber the nickname "Eutrapelos" to bring out the contrast.[6] It is evident that Aristotle's teaching had been forgotten.

[5] X, 6 (1176b).
[6] *Epigrams* VII, 83.

Moreover, the Christian in the light of revelation had become more perceptive of the dangers of the "world," abandoned to evil and under the dominion of Satan. How then could anyone want to be "hot for the world"? Thus the word which once had so sublime a meaning entered into the language of the New Testament with all the encumbrances imposed upon it by the linguistic development of Koine and the stern world-renunciation of the primitive Church.

Paul warns his Christians in the Epistle to the Ephesians (5.4) to avoid "ribaldry (*morologia*) or smartness in talk (*eutrapelia*)." It must always be a question of linguistic tact as to how we translate "eutrapelia" in this verse, but that it has a pejorative sense is already clear from the fact that Paul makes it equivalent ("or") to the chatter of fools. That is precisely how Jerome later understood it[7] and the Vulgate, as we know, translates it as "scurrilitas": namely, the vice of the *scurra*, the clown, the eternally jovial windbag. No: from the New Testament there was nothing to be done for Aristotle's Eutrapelia.

Clement of Alexandria, the first indeed to attempt to find an exact balance between Christian seriousness and a serene acceptance of the world, applies the word in the Pauline sense only when he is warning Christians against using "jocose (*eutrapela*) and unbecoming words" at their social gatherings.[8]

The Greek and Latin Fathers of the early Church were in fact always faced with the task of educating the naturally light-hearted and witty Christian, the product of the civiliza-

---

[7] *Comment. in Ep. ad Ephesios* III, 5 (PL 26, 520). On the exegesis of the Pauline "eutrapelia" cf. F. A. von Henle, *Der Ephesierbrief des heiligen Paulus*, Augsburg, 1908, pp. 259 f., and W. Bauer, *Griechisch-deutsches Wörterbuch zu den Schriften des neuen Testaments*, Berlin, 1952[4], Coll. 592 f.

[8] *The Tutor* II, 7, 53, 3 (GCS, Clement I, p. 189, 27).

tion of late antiquity, in the seriousness of Christian behaviour. We can understand it therefore when Ambrose,
for instance—incidentally, wholly in the spirit of his model,
Cicero—gives a warning against being too nimble in joking
and playing, even though this appears in an address mainly
to his clergy on whom he wants to impose the ancient Roman
and Christian discipline:

Joking should be avoided even in small talk, so that some
more serious topic is not made light of. "Woe upon you who
laugh now; you shall mourn and weep" (Luke 6. 25), saith the
Lord: are we then looking for something to laugh at, so that
we may laugh now but weep hereafter? I maintain that not only
loose jokes, but jokes of any kind must be avoided—except
perhaps when our words are full of sweetness and grace, not
indelicate.[9]

We can see him, dignified and stern, this Bishop of Milan,
presenting to his clergy his own ideal of Roman-Christian
rectitude, with that episcopal solemnity which made the
hypersensitive Augustine also feel that he was unapproach-
able:

The pleasures of the table, of playing and joking, break down
manly dignity and seriousness. Let us take care, when we are
seeking mental relaxation, not to dissolve all the harmony, the
concord—so to speak—of our good works.[10]

What Ambrose said to the clergy the equally strict
Chrysostom preached to the people of Constantinople and
Antioch, whipped up in every nerve with the lust for pleasure in the great city. We may read on this subject the sixth
homily on Matthew's Gospel which the "Golden Mouth"

[9] *De Officiis* I, 23, 103 (PL 16, 54 f.).
[10] *De Officiis* I, 20, 85 (PL 16, 49B).

delivered in Antioch in 390. Here we find ourselves in a world such as we have to reckon with today, in the gay city with its enticements to junketing, night life and unchastity disguised as merry-making.

This world is not a theatre, in which we can laugh; and we are not assembled together in order to burst into peals of laughter, but to weep for our sins. But some of you still want to say: "I would prefer God to give me the chance to go on laughing and joking." Is there anything more childish than thinking in this way? It is not God who gives us the chance to play, but the devil.[11]

These are harsh words; and they were not forgotten. Aquinas returns to the question. The preacher of penance has to exaggerate, for he knows that men are always more inclined to follow their pleasant bent towards baser things and that in this way alone he can establish a balance: thus nothing is more exposed to easy-going and deceptive indulgence than the sensitive mean of true eutrapelia. Aristotle felt this indeed, when he observed that the "bomolochos" was also frequently called "eutrapelos," the clown a wit, because the comic is enormously popular and most men are more enthusiastic about joking and ridicule than is fitting.[12]

It is of the greatest interest to see how, in the history of the christianization of the Greek eutrapelia, Aquinas made use of the material at hand from Aristotle and the Fathers of the Church. First of all then he interprets the above-quoted chapter from the fourth book in his commentary on the Nicomachean Ethics in this way:

There is some good in playing, in as much as it is useful for human life. As man needs from time to time to rest and leave off bodily labours, so also his mind from time to time must relax

[11] *Commentary on Matthew,* Homily 6, 6 (*PG* 57, 70D).
[12] IV, 14 (1128a).

from its intense concentration on serious pursuits: this comes about through play. Hence Aristotle says that man obtains in this life a kind of rest from his anxieties and preoccupations in playful conversation. . . . Those who go to excess in merry-making he calls *bomolochoi*, that is, "temple-plunderers," like the birds of prey who hovered about the temple in order to snap up the intestines of animals offered in sacrifice. So these people are always ready to seize anything which they can turn to ridicule. Such men are a nuisance through their efforts at all costs to raise a laugh. . . . But he says also that those who do not want themselves to make a joke and are annoyed by those who do, because they feel insulted, appear to be "agrii", that is, "boorish" and hard, because they are not softened by the pleasure of play.[13]

Here then the ancient doctrine of the Stagirite comes in a broad and full stream into a Christian book. Play and joking take their place in Christian morality; eutrapelia as the virtue of the mean here gains entry into moral theology and into asceticism.

Thus Aristotle shows what is the mean in playing. He says that those who exercise moderation in play are called *eutrapeloi*, "well-turning" (*bene vertentes*), because they are able to turn aptly into laughter what is said or done.

That is finely put: therefore the Christian may play; therefore also smiling, laughing, is a virtue. Here the way is prepared for the medieval theology of the merry Christian who sees the limits and inadequacy of all created things and for that very reason can smile at them: he knows the blessed seriousness of things divine. A person who does not understand this belongs to that class of whom Aquinas has aptly said: *non molliuntur delectatione ludi*, "they are not softened by the pleasure of play."

[13] *In decem libros Ethicorum Aristotelis ad Nicomachum*, lib. iv, lect. 16.

What is here presented mainly as an interpretation of Aristotle's text is developed by Aquinas in some illuminating pages of the second part of the *Summa Theologica,* where the question is raised: "Can there be a virtue in play?" Answering in the affirmative, Aquinas appeals to Augustine who at one time—still under the platonic influences of the early years of his conversion—spoke of relaxing the mind through play.[14] He discusses the severe words of Ambrose and Chrysostom of which we have already heard. It may help us to understand the clear teaching of Aquinas if we set out this article in a literal if somewhat abridged translation.[15]

First: It seems that there cannot be any virtue in play. For Ambrose says: " 'Woe upon you who laugh now; you shall mourn and weep,' saith the Lord. I maintain then that not only loose jokes, but jokes of any kind, must be avoided."

Second: Virtue is what God effects in us and without our co-operation. But Chrysostom says: "It is not God who gives us the chance to play, but the devil." Therefore there can be no virtue in play.

Third: Moreover, the Philosopher says that "the activities of play are not directed to any other end". But for virtue it is necessary deliberately to act for the sake of something else. Therefore there can be no virtue in play.

But against this we have what Augustine says: "I want you to spare yourself. For it befits a wise man to relax from time to time, to stop being intent upon the things he has to do." But such relaxation is obtained by joviality in words and deeds. Therefore, to indulge in these from time to time is fitting to the wise and virtuous man. The Philosopher also regards "eutrapelia" as the virtue which is exercised in play: we might speak of "gaiety" (*jucunditas*) or of "ready adaptability" (*bona conversio*).

---

[14] *De Musica* ii, 14 (PL 32, 1116A).
[15] *Summa Theologica* II–II q. 168 a. 2.

We must then answer: Man needs bodily rest, so that the body can be revived: he cannot go on working without interruption, since he has limited powers which are adapted to certain definite tasks. The power of the soul is likewise limited, adapted to certain activities. If, then, he imposes on himself an undue strain through some of his activities, he feels the effort and becomes tired. This is because the body also co-operates in the activities of the soul, since the soul—even the intellect—uses powers which operate through bodily organs. But sensible goods are connatural to man. Hence, when the mind is raised above sensible objects, because intent upon the operations of reason, there arises out of this a certain mental fatigue. . . . Thus man becomes more fatigued in mind, the more unreservedly he devotes himself to the activities of reason.

As bodily fatigue, then, is relieved by resting the body, so mental fatigue must be relieved by giving rest to the soul.

But, as we explained when dealing with the passions, the soul finds its repose in pleasure. Therefore, as a remedy against fatigue of soul, we must provide some pleasure, drawing the mind away for a time from its absorption in thought. So we read in the Conferences of the Fathers that some were scandalized to find the Apostle John playing with his followers. John told one of them, who was carrying a bow, to draw an arrow: he did this several times and John then asked whether he could keep on doing it without interruption; the reply was that the bow would break in the end. John therefore argued that man's mind would also break if the tension were never relaxed.

Sayings and deeds of this kind, in which nothing more is sought than the soul's pleasure, are known as playing and joking. It is therefore necessary to make use of them from time to time to provide repose for the soul. That also is what the Philosopher says: "Life includes relaxation, and one form of relaxation is playful conversation." From time to time then we must make use of some of these things.

In this respect, however, three things are to be avoided. First and most important, this pleasure must not be sought in immoral and harmful deeds or words. Hence Cicero says (*De Officiis* I, 29): "There is a kind of jest which is coarse, rude, vicious, indecent." Secondly, we must take care not to lose entirely gravity of soul. Hence Ambrose says: "Let us take care, when we are seeking mental relaxation, not to dissolve all the harmony, the concord—so to speak—of our good works"; and Cicero: "As we do not grant our children unlimited licence to play, but only such freedom as is not incompatible with good conduct, so even in our jesting let the light of a pure character shine forth." Thirdly, as in all other human actions, we must see to it that play and joking are suited to the person, time and place, and duly related to other circumstances, so that (as Cicero also expresses it) they are "worthy of the time and the man."

Therefore, there can be a certain virtue in play. The Philosopher calls it "eutrapelia" and says that a person is "eutrapelos," "well-turning," because he is well able to turn deeds or words into relaxation.

In answer to the first objection, therefore, we must say: It has already been observed that joviality must be suited to the circumstances and the persons. This is particularly important in regard to sacred doctrine, which is concerned with matters of the greatest import. It is from this field that Ambrose wants to exclude joking, not from human life altogether.

In answer to the second objection, we must say that Chrysostom's words are to be understood of those who are excessively addicted to play and especially of those who make pleasure in playing the whole meaning of life. They are described in the Book of Wisdom (15. 12): "They have counted our life a pastime." Against this attitude, Cicero writes: "Nature has not brought us into the world to act as if we were created for play or jest, but rather for earnestness and for some more serious and important pursuits."

In answer to the third objection, we must say that the activities of play as such are not directed to an end beyond themselves. But the pleasure derived from these activities provides a certain relaxation and repose for the soul. Therefore, in moderation, we may indulge in play. As Cicero again says, "We may, of course, indulge in sport and jest, but in the same way as we enjoy sleep or other relaxations, and only when we have satisfied the claims of our earnest, serious tasks."

That is the teaching of Aquinas on eutrapelia in joking and playing. May our reflections on the subject affect us as his own thought affected him when, in the next article of the *Summa,* he recalled wistfully an incident in the Lives of the Fathers and thus touched on a lovely and profound mystery of the grace of God which "plays" in the world: "It was revealed to Paphnutius that a certain joker would be his companion in heaven." [16] And in the same article, Aquinas had the courage—astounding at that time—to open the Christian gates also to actors, to the art of the theatre and to all their patrons, as did later the gentle Francis de Sales.[17]

In our opinion, this is again the time to think out afresh the forms and scope of true eutrapelia. Not everything in our civilization is in the hands of the devil and thundering from the pulpit is not always in place. Just because so many "bomolochoi" are active in our world and slip into the obscenities of ancient Attic comedy, we Christians are not obliged to become "agroiki," but must try to realize the Christian ideal of the serious-serene human being at play in his fine versatility, in eutrapelia, in that serene abandonment to the seriousness of God which, according to Theodor Haecker, lies very deep in the foundations of European-Christian civilization.

[16] *Ibid.,* a. 3 (*Vitae Patrum* viii, 63: PL 73, 1170).
[17] *Introduction to the Devout Life* I, 23.

TWELVE

Zen Humour

R. H. BLYTH

To say that the essence of Zen is humour sounds rather extreme, but is it a mere coincidence that the two are so often found together, in nations and in individuals? When I first read Dr. Suzuki's *Essays in Zen* I laughed at every koan he quoted; and indeed the less I "understood" the more I laughed. Whether this laughter was due to scorn or shame or bewilderment or some secret enlightenment is not the point. Zen has little to do with weeping. Zen is making a pleasure of necessity, wanting to do what you are doing, a perpetual realization that "all that we behold is full of blessings," that "cheerful faith" as Wordsworth calls it.

Again, much humour is concerned with the collision between the ideal and the real, with the emotional and intellectual contradictions of life, the personal, marital, social, and cosmic paradoxes. Profoundly considered, may not the strange joy of belly-laughter be due to a momentary joyful acceptance of that very contradiction? And is Zen anything but a continuance of this state, in which my will is the divine will? Is it not a steady illumination of which laughter is a flash, a spark? To continue the metaphor a little further, tinder is necessary to make a fire. It must be absolutely dry and lifeless, desireless, so that the spark may fall on it and burn it to an even more absolute nothingness. This is the state of mind just before enlightenment.

Let us assume then that Zen has a vital connection with humour, and before giving examples of their conjunction or identity in China, say once more what Zen is; this is better done by a subjunctive or imperative than an indicative sentence. When a thing and its meaning are undivided, indivisible, there is Zen. (A "thing" is an object, an action, even a sentence.) When there is a *total* activity, mind and body unseparated, when an action is done, not *by* somebody, *to* somebody, *for* a certain purpose, there is Zen.

Humour is found everywhere in literature; what is the relation between Zen and words? Zen is said to be "without dependence on words or letters." This is no doubt so, but we must not suppose that words and Zen are in any sense enemies. Emerson says that "words and deeds are indifferent modes of the divine being," and Dr. Suzuki Daisetz explains the relation between words and Zen in his own wonderful way: "An assertion is Zen only when it is itself an act and does not refer to anything that is asserted in it." [1] So we find, as we would expect, Zen in *Alice in Wonderland* and Lear's *Nonsense Verses*. Like humour, like poetry, Zen is not intellection, morality, beauty, or emotion, though they may be present at the same time.

We "see" Zen, we "feel" it in religion, for example the writings of Eckhart; in music, Bach everywhere, Mozart often, never in Haydn, in the last quartets of Beethoven; in nature, especially mountains and stones; in daily life, mostly in women, whose lack of brain and absence of morality gives them the Zen of nature. In art, I "find" Zen in Byzantine art,

---

[1] *Essays in Zen Buddhism,* 1st Series, p. 284.

its "fixed and unalterable truth in fixed unalterable images";
in Brueghel, with man and nature undivided, in Goya, fear
seen without fear; in Klee, truth never fixed, but always growing in the mind of the poet.

Zen is thus to be found in every place, in every time, but
the word and the intellectual realization of the one state of
mind in all its infinite varieties of manifestation, was created-
discovered in China. Supposed to have been brought from
India by Bodhidharma in 520 A.D., Zen is conspicuously and
preëminently and uniquely "humorous" and even witty. It is
possible to read the Bible without a smile, and the Koran
without a chuckle. No one has died of laughing while
reading the Buddhist Sutras. But Zen writings abound in
anecdotes that stimulate the diaphragm. Enlightenment is
frequently accompanied by laughing of a transcendental kind,
which may further be described as a laughter of surprised approval. The approval is continuous, it will even increase, but
the surprise, though it may not disappear, subsides, for as
Thoreau says, "The impressions which the morning makes
vanish with their dews, and not even the most persevering
mortal can preserve the memory of its freshness to midday." [2]

One of the more obvious examples of Zen humour, in the
ordinary sense of the word humour, is what is called *nenro,*
or *nenko,* which means "picking up and playing" with some
old saying of a master, and using it freely for one's own purposes. A form of this is the *chakugo,* or *agyo,* which we find
added to the *Hekiganroku.* Hakuin Zenji wrote a commentary on the *Hannya Shingyō* which he entitled *Dokugo
Hannya Shingyō, doku* meaning "poisonous." The idea of this
word and indeed of all humour, is that we are apt to be misled
by beauty, morality, so-called "truth," pleasant emotions, and
charming words. We need some shock to bring us back to a
reality which includes all that we hope for, but also ugliness

[2] *A Week on the Concord.*

and terror and so-called badness, and painful things. The "purpose" of the universe towards itself and ourselves is to do both, to bless and to damn, but the laughter which comes from being cursed is somehow deeper than the contented chuckle.

Our *sincerest* laughter with some pain is fraught,

our own pain and that of others.

Zen is the only religion in which laughter is not merely permitted but necessary. Take an example from Case 70 of the *Hekiganroku*.[3] Weishan (Isan), Wufeng (Goho), Yünyen (Ungan), three great disciples of Paichang (Hyakujō), 724–814, stand before him and are given the following problem:

Shut your gullet, close your lips, and say something!

This is of course not an exercise in ventriloquism. It is no different in its importance, its life-and-death-ness, from the triple question of Jesus to Peter, "Lovest thou me?" What Paichang asks his disciples to do is to live the truth before his eyes at this moment, uncircumscribed by speech or silence, to act absolutely, above the relativity of relative and absolute. What is odd and interesting also is the *chakugo* on the first sentence of the Case, "Isan, Goho, and Ungan were in attendance upon Hyakujō." It is, "Ha! Ha! Ha!" The Chinese ideogram for this is remarkable for its many mouths. What is the meaning of this laughing? Yüanwu[3a] is expressing his contempt for these four worthies paraded by Hsüehtou.[3b] They are more prepoceros than a rhinoceros. He scorns the teacher-pupil relation between them, for truth cannot be shared. There

[3] 70, 71, 72, are really all one Case.
[3a] Yüanwu (Engo) is responsible for adding "Introductory Words" to the Cases of the *Hekiganroku* (Blue Cliff Records) [Ed.].
[3b] Hsüehtou (Setcho) is the original compiler of the *Hekiganroku* [Ed.].

is the same laughter in the mouth of Yangchin (Yōgi), d. 1049 A.D., whose "sermon on the mount" is this:

He got up into his seat (a sort of pulpit), and exclaimed, "Ha! ha! ha! What's all this? Go to the back of the hall and have some tea!" He then got down.

Zen and poetry and humour have this in common, that there is no such thing as Zen, as poetry, as humour. They cannot be isolated, they cannot be defined, they do not have an ulterior significance; yet they are there or not there; they are distinct and indubitable; they alone are meaning.

According to Dr. Suzuki[4] the characteristics of enlightenment are irrationality, intuitive insight, authoritativeness, affirmativeness, a sense of the beyond, an impersonal tone, a feeling of exaltation, and momentariness. Laughter is breaking through the intellectual barrier; at the moment of laughing something is understood; it needs no proof of itself; it is in no sense destructive or pessimistic or concerned with sin or punishment. Laughter is a state of being here and also everywhere, an infinite and timeless expansion of one's own nevertheless unalienable being. When we laugh we are free of all the oppression of our personality, or that of others, and even of God, who is indeed laughed away. One who laughs is master of his fate, and captain of his soul:

Weep, and the world weeps with you;
Laugh, and you laugh alone.

The abruptness of humour and enlightenment is too obvious to need anything but an abrupt mention.

It is an odd and deeply significant thing that Zen begins (or is supposed to begin) with a smile. The story as given in the 6th Case of the *Mumonkan* is this.

[4] *Essays in Zen,* Second Series, page 16.

When the World-honoured One was on The Mount of the Holy Vulture, he held up a flower to the assembled monks. All were silent. Mahakasyapa the Venerable only smiled.

This story is found only in the *Daibontenmonbutsuketsugikyo,* which is considered to be entirely apochryphal. But this is itself in accord with the spirit of Zen, which is concerned with truth, not with facts. The use of a flower indicates the Indian mind; also the smile, which in China would be rather a grin or guffaw.

The next name in the history of Zen is that of Daruma, who seems to have had nothing very witty or amusing about him; it is odd that in Japan he has been transformed into a humorous figure almost against his will, a kind of doll with no legs that however much pushed over always regains its balance. Nevertheless, we find in the anecdotes of Daruma's sojourn in China that element of paradox, almost, one might say, the pleasure of contradiction, which characterises all those who like Zen, whether they are adepts or not. The story of Daruma's interview with the Buddhist Emperor Wu (converted to Buddhism in 517 A.D.) is a model of all succeeding *mondō,* Zen debates. It forms the 1st Case of the *Hekiganroku:*

The Emperor Wu of Liang asked Daruma, "What is the main principle of the Holy Teaching?" Daruma answered, "It is an Emptiness, with nothing holy about it."

The next great figure in Zen, Hui Neng (Enō), 637–713, was one of the most normal and uneccentric men of genius who ever lived, but even in him we find a perception of truth coupled with a strong sense of the ludicrousness of error. One example is the contest of the poems; another is when a monk quoted the following verse:

Wu Lun has a means
To cut off all thoughts;
The mind is not aroused by the external world;
The Tree of Enlightenment grows daily.

The Sixth Patriarch countered with the following:

Hui Neng has no means
To cut off any thoughts;
The mind is continually aroused by the external world;
How on earth can enlightenment grow?

There is the story of the enlightenment of Shuilao at the hands or rather the feet of his master Matsu (died 788 A.D.). He asked, "What is the meaning of Daruma's coming from the West?" Matsu immediately gave him a kick in the chest and knocked him down. Shuilao became enlightened, got up, and clapping his hands, laughed aloud. Taihui (1089–1163) tells us that when Shuilao was asked what his enlightenment was, he answered, "Since the master kicked me, I have not been able to stop laughing."

The usual posture for Zen monks to die in is sitting, that is, doing zazen, but the Third Patriarch, Seng Ts'an, died (in 606) standing with clasped hands. Chihhsien of Huanch'i, died 905 A.D., asked his attendants, "Who dies sitting?" They answered, "A monk." He said, "Who dies standing?" They said, "Enlightened monks." He then walked around seven steps with his hands hanging down, and died. When Teng Yinfeng was about to die in front of the Diamond Cave at Wutai, he said to the people round him, "I have seen monks die sitting and lying, but have any died standing?" "Yes, some," they replied. "How about upside down?" "Never seen such a thing!" Teng died standing on his head. His clothes also rose up close to his body. It was decided to carry him to the burning-ground, but he still stood there without moving. People from far and near gazed with astonishment at the scene. His younger sister, a nun, happened to be there, and grumbled at him, saying, "When you were alive you took no notice of laws and customs, and even now you're dead you are making a nuisance of yourself!" She then prodded her brother with her finger and he fell down with a bang. Then they went off to the crematorium. To these we may add Rui Loan Zenji, who entered his own coffin and died later, and Wan Nienyi Zenji, who got in the coffin before he was dead and pulled down the lid.

All this shows the Chinese understanding of the fact that death is *the* great subject for laughter as it is for tears. Yesterday, a young woman spoke to me about her mother who has not long to live. She loves her dearly, has not married because of her, and said, half-jokingly, half-seriously, "Mother has such a poor sense of direction I'm afraid she will never reach Heaven. I think I ought to die at the same time and be put in a double coffin together with her."

Wit is always laconic, and the best examples of all are perhaps those of Yün Men (Unmon), famous for his one-syllable answers:

A monk said to Yün Men: "If a man kills his father or mother he may repent before the Buddha, but if he kills a Buddha or a patriarch, to whom can he repent?" Yün Men said, "Clear!"

Perhaps the monk was thinking of the words of Confucius:

He that offends against Heaven has none to pray to.

In Christian terms it is the problem of Cowper and all super-sensitive people, "What shall I do if I have committed the unforgivable sin?" Or in the more common form, "How shall I undo the unundoable evil that I have done to others?" At first sight the reply of Unmon only makes the matter more confused. "Clear!" What is it that is clear? First, it is clear that we have here an insoluble problem brought forward by a monk who can never solve it because he is going round in a circle and asking what he shall do when he comes to the end of it. Second, everything is clear; it is clear that nothing is clear. Third, if I am clear, the universe is clear. If I have no object, no ambition, no choosing, everything is good. What is the humour in all this? Unmon's answer, "All clear!" is a burst of cosmic laughter which sweeps away all object and subject, all killing and repentance, all good deeds and Heavenly rewards.

We come last of all to the two great text-books of Zen,[5] the *Hekiganroku* (the *Piyenlu*), 1125 A.D., and the *Mumonkan (Wumenkuan)* shortly after 1228 A.D. The *Hekiganroku* with its hundred Cases is a sort of specialist's book for Zen adepts, totally incomprehensible to the uninitiated. It is not devoid of humour, but the amount of intellect in it makes it like the *Art of Fugue.* The *Mumonkan* is more like the *Forty Eight Preludes and Fugues,* and actually consists of forty-eight Cases. These cases exemplify all the different kinds of humour, and in *Haiku,*[6] nine varieties of humour are illustrated from the *Mumonkan* and the *Hekiganroku:* the laughter of disillusionment, studied idiocy, spontaneous idiocy, hyperbole, dilemma, scatalogical humour, dry humour, breaking with convention, pathos. To these we may add from the *Mumonkan,* the humour of pure contradiction, No. 4; of circularity, No. 9; of impossibility, Nos. 10, 46; of pure nonsense, No. 14; of Lear's nonsense, Nos. 16 and 48; the laughter of omnipotence, No. 22; of inconsequence, No. 24; of speechlessness, No. 32; extremes meeting, No. 48; a sort of practical joke, No. 40; mutual contempt, No. 31. The last case, No. 48,

---

[5] A short description of these will be found in Suzuki's *Essays in Zen Buddhism,* Second Series, pp. 217–229.

[6] Vol. I, pp. 219, 223.

consists of two parts, the first being an example of the opposite of "sudden glory"; the second is the "wild and whirling words" of transcendentalism:

The Zen Master Kan Fêng[7] was asked by a monk: "Buddha fills all the ten quarters of the world; one path leads to Nirvana (enlightenment); would you kindly tell me where this path is?" Kan Fêng took up his stick and drew a line with it, and said, "Here it is!"

Afterwards the monk brought up the matter with Yün Men (Unmon), who raised his fan and said, "This fan flies up to the thirty-third Heaven and hits the nose of the King there. Then the Carp of the Eastern Ocean tips over the rain-cloud with its tail, and it rains in torrents."

Kan Fêng goes to one extreme, Yün Men to the other, but both are true and both are humorous. The portals of Heaven are the garden gate. This pen I hold will cause a revolution. My love for my dog moves the sun and the other stars. God sneezes, and the universe is blown away. Compare this with the dilemma in *Alice in Wonderland* when we get the debate concerning the head of the Cheshire Cat. The executioner's argument is, "You couldn't cut off a head unless there was a body to cut it off from." The King's argument was, "Anything that had a head could be beheaded." The Queen represents Mumon himself, or rather, the Universe, when she says, "If something wasn't done about it in less than no time, she'd have everybody executed." Human beings are at every moment and in every place in this or some similar dilemma. The question is how always to act (and act we must) to please ourselves and others and God completely and perfectly.

[7] Disciple of Tung-shan (807–869).

THIRTEEN

The Dialectic of the Sacred and the Comic

M. CONRAD HYERS

It was one of the redeeming features of ancient and medieval monarchies to have recognized that every king needs a court jester, a part of whose function it is not only to make the king laugh but to make him laugh at himself. In the grotesque form of the jester, the king in all his pompous authority and power is revealed to his courtiers and to himself as also something of a clown. It is no accident of history that the king places this deformed or dwarfed or demented figure at his left hand not only to play the scapegoat as the butt of jokes but to play the role of the king himself in comic carica-ture. The sacredness of the royal person and the sacrality of his rule (whether by "divine right" or not) require the pro-fane person and mock rule of the court fool in order to pre-serve that delicate dialectical balance between holiness and humor, on either side of which, in the socio-political realm, are the pitfalls of tyranny and anarchy.

There is also the more subjective side of this necessity, and that is the need of the king for a comic alter ego, another less serious and more human self to step into. For it is in the person of the joker that the king jokes; in the person of the fool he becomes a fool. This not only reveals what he is, and prevents him from pretending to be what he is not, but allows him to be what he really is: a man like everyone else who participates with all his subjects in the frailties and follies of the human condition. The freedom of the court jester to violate all the proprieties and taboos of royalty, to flout pomposity and decorum, is vicariously experienced by the king as his own freedom, his personal emancipation from the rigid confines of his role and the loftiness of his pretension, the element of façade in his official self and station, and his overcoming of the contradiction in his person as both sacred lord and mortal man. Through the court fool the king preserves both his sanity and his humanity.[1]

As this familiar instance of the dialectic of the sacred and the comic illustrates, the comic stands in an essential relationship to the sacred, whatever its form or character, whether person or principle, role or ritual, spiritual teaching or moral ideal. The sacred needs the comic as much as the comic needs the sacred; for the comic apart from its basis in the sacred, or the sacred apart from the qualifications of the comic, are equal prey to distortion. As in the case of the king, if the sacredness of his person and role is taken too seriously to the exclusion of laughter, the door is opened to absolutism and despotism; but if the laughter does not presuppose a certain seriousness and sacrality, the door is opened to political chaos and social disruption.

In analyzing the various dimensions of this dialectic it is possible to isolate three levels on which the comic spirit moves in relation to the sacred, three moments that may or may not

[1] Cf. Enid Welsford, *The Fool: His Social and Literary History* (London: Faber & Faber, 1935).

exist simultaneously, but each of which is an essential element within the dialectic: innocence, ambivalence, and confidence. As will be argued, these moments correspond, in
terms of Christian myth, to the laughter of Paradise, of
Paradise-lost, and of Paradise-regained. The use of such a
mythological model is not arbitrary, nor simply a convenient
methodological tool; for the moods of comedy are, in fact,
precisely those that are symbolized by this mythical schema:
playful return to past innocence and immediacy, heroic/
iconoclastic response to present contradiction and anxiety, and
the realization or assurance of redemption and resolution.

Though the subsequent analysis of the three levels of the
comic is couched in terms of the Judaeo-Christian tradition,
the same interpretive structure could be used in explicating
the meaning and function of the comic spirit within any
religious context. The specific nuances and implications of the
dialectic of the comic and the sacred would, of course, vary
from one tradition to another; the over-all schema is nonetheless applicable to the dialectic wherever it occurs. For the
sake of continuity and facility, what is here presented, therefore, is an example of the serviceability of this particular
mythological model in interpreting the role of the comic,
using the Judaeo-Christian tradition as a point of reference.

The Play of Innocence

At the simplest level, comedy of whatever sort is a kind
of game that we play. It is a game in which the world is seen
from the perspective of the game, and as a game; i.e., it is
not taken with absolute seriousness, nor lived in with perpetual seriousness, but with a qualified and periodically suspended seriousness. Caillois' description of play is equally
applicable to comedy as a form of play: "It creates no wealth
or goods, thus differing from work or art. . . . Nothing has

been harvested or manufactured, no masterpiece has been created, no capital has been accrued. Play is an occasion of pure waste: waste of time, energy, ingenuity, skill, and often of money." [2] The thought of the results of humor, along with play, as being nonproductive and pure waste, or as being a form of abandonment to the immediacies of simple enjoyment, jars against our Calvinistic-Puritan-Capitalistic sensitivities. Yet if the initial and primary response to the holy is intensely serious, this intensity cannot be sustained indefinitely. Seriousness alone, even—if not especially—ultimate seriousness, is stultifying and creates its own sterile forms of bondage. We need not only to be acutely serious about certain things, but to laugh, to laugh even at our seriousness, to laugh at the things about which we become so serious and in which we become so seriously involved. We cannot be constantly serious about law, for instance, without suffocating the "spirit of the law" in the process—as the natural history of legalism abundantly demonstrates. In Santayana's words, "Where the spirit of comedy has departed, company becomes constraint, reserve eats up the spirit, and people fall into a penurious melancholy in their scruple to be always exact, sane, and reasonable. . . . Yet irony pursues these enemies of comedy, and for fear of wearing a mask for a moment they are hypocrites all their lives." [3]

Seriousness also intensifies anxiety. As in the case of anything of grave importance, the degree of tension and uncertainty generated by the *mysterium* and *tremendum* of the sacred (Otto) is unbearable for long periods of time and seeks a mechanism of withdrawal and release. There are two reasons

[2] Roger Caillois, *Man, Play and Games* (New York: Free Press of Glencoe, 1961), pp. 5–6. Caillois, however, both in the above and in *Man and the Sacred,* fails to deal adequately with the comic, either as a form of play and game or as a correlate of the sacred.

[3] George Santayana, *Soliloquies in England and Later Soliloquies* (New York: Charles Scribner's Sons, 1922), p. 138.

why the High Priest of ancient Israel entered the Holy of Holies but once a year: the one is that it represented the most sacred of places; the other that he could not possibly have stood it there year-round. The first reason is presented from the side of the sacred; the second from the side of the comic. In laughter, seriousness is made human and tolerable at the same time that it is preserved from stuffiness and prudishness. Humor apart from holiness may be irresponsible; but holiness apart from humor is inhuman.

Play is a human and therefore humane necessity; and humor is not only a form of play activity but a peculiarly human form of play activity. It may have its precursor in the grimaces and antics of the higher apes, but in the human species animal play becomes a unique mode of perceiving and responding to existence. The comic spirit and perspective represents the development of a specifically human capacity for playing with reality, and for seeing reality in terms of play. In identifying humor as a form of play, however, a distinction must immediately be drawn between humor as "play for play's sake," the sheer delight in play as its own justification, and humor as play for the sake of a more serious purpose—between the purely spontaneous playfulness of humor and the more serious and self-conscious intentionality of humor. All humor is play, but all play moves within the polarities of seriousness and frivolity, of sense and nonsense. In this regard, the comic and the aesthetic dimensions of perception and expression are strictly parallel: the play of humor is like the play of art, which on the one hand may involve a degree of purposiveness, and on the other hand may simply be an enjoyment of the sculpting or brush-play itself, a creation of form and color for the sake of creativity per se.

In its lightest and least serious moments, humor is one of the ways in which man frolics, perhaps plays the fool, behaves quite mundanely, acts with childish abandon, and delivers himself to the caprice of the instant. It is a leap into that "wild and careless, inexhaustible joy of life invincible." [4] The "weightier matters of the law" are set aside and another world, as it were, the world of play and game, is entered through the peculiar freedom of humor. It is the world of innocence prior to the knowledge of good and evil, beyond shame and guilt, immune from the ordinary proprieties and taboos, a world where there is neither the sacred nor the profane. The playfulness of humor is therefore its preservation of a delightful infancy, the recapitulation in adult form of childhood —a point stressed by Kierkegaard in rather melancholy terms: "The sadness in legitimate humor consists in the fact that honestly and without deceit it reflects in a purely human way upon what it is to be a child (directly understood), and it is eternally certain that this cannot return." [5] Without reducing humor to this level, or emptying it of its moment of return, one can nevertheless see in it an element of a lost innocence that is recovered in the unreflective immediacy and spontaneity of the comic spirit. It is a projection into that paradisal state of carefree abandonment, prior to the division of the world into the holy and the unholy.

In this retrogressive movement lies the peculiar form of profanation realized on this level of humor. Humor, as a form of play and of game, set in relation to the sacred becomes an act of profanation; for to be playful with respect to holy things, to look upon matters of ultimate concern from the perspective of the game, is to profane the sacred. But more than this, the sacred is profaned by annulling, in recovered innocence, the very distinction between the sacred and the profane. The tensions between the sacred and the profane,

[4] Joseph Campbell, *Hero with a Thousand Faces* (New York: Pantheon Books, 1949), p. 28.
[5] Søren Kierkegaard, *Concluding Unscientific Postscript* (Princeton: Princeton University Press, 1941), p. 533.

and the taboos enforcing them, are transcended through a momentary recapture of that state in which such categories do not exist—the state of freedom mythologically represented by the child Adam. It is a state in which none of the categories by which the world is divided up exist; for categories are the tools of order and rationality, of discrimination, whereas comedy moves within the freedom of irrationality, of suspended order, of nonsense. In the playful babblings of comedy lies the realization of that side of existence (objectively or subjectively considered) that stubbornly resists being rigidly fixed in any kind of sterile reasonableness or wooden eternal appropriateness. To put it as simply as possible: Who wants to make sense all the time? And yet in this very act of profanation, the comic leap into nonsense points in its own non-sensical way to the mystery of the sacred, the mystery of being itself, which cannot simply be reduced to logical syllogisms and rational forms, the mystery that cannot be exhausted by priestly definitions and delineations, or imprisoned by catechisms and programs, the mystery that cannot be contained and ordered by man.

Mythically this movement of comedy is also expressed in the paradigm of the periodic return of Creation to the primordial Void—as in the primitive seasonal festivals and their subsequent developments, the carnival, the New Year's celebration, the Mardi Gras, etc.[6] The serious Cosmos becomes, for a season, the playful Chaos; the play-character of all human activities and concerns is unveiled; and the way is opened for viewing the Creation itself as the "play" of God. It is on this level that the relationship between comedy and chaos is revealed: the comic represents chaos as the sacred represents cosmos. This is not, however, chaos in the threatening, demonic form of the abyss of nothingness—even though

[6] Cf. Mircea Eliade, *Patterns in Comparative Religion* (New York: Sheed and Ward, 1958), pp. 398 ff., 424–425.

comedy left to its own devices could enter this darkness—but the chaos of infinite potentiality and creative possibility, the chaos of uninhibited expression and indiscriminate form.

There is, after all, something enchantingly paradisal about chaos as well as cosmos; and it is to this paradise that we are returned through comedy. From the side of cosmos and the sacred, the negative, nihilating, "chaotic" character of chaos is seen; but from the side of the comic, chaos is seen positively as the womb of freedom, spontaneity, and immediacy. Through a comic inversion, the very lack of order and structure becomes paradisal, and the order and structure exemplified in the sacred cosmos becomes a prison and its taboos chains. The ambiguities inherent in the dichotomy between the sacred cosmos and the demonic chaos, and the demonic possibilities of the sacral order, are disclosed. The clown and the comedian—morphologically, if not historically, related as they are to the seasonal drama portraying the return of cosmos to chaos—are the quaint redemptors of the carnival who recapture that formless paradise of carefree naïveté prior to the often painful and alienating distinctions between man and animal, male and female, good and evil, sacred and profane. It is one of the many functions of comedy to recover this special freedom and simplicity of the child, or of primeval man—so well exemplified in the childish freedom and simplicity of the clown—before the emergence of order, differentiation, and discrimination, of duality and antinomy, of taboo, shame and guilt; in short, prior to the present cosmos. On the other hand the comic leap into nonsense and irrationality is not a complete or final return to chaos, but an interlude, a holiday. If it does become this it guarantees its own dissolution; for it must presuppose some substratum of sense and rationality in order to make the leap. There would be no point to or effectiveness in the comic twist if all were twisted. The factor of surprise that provokes laughter in the movements of the clown, or the termination of the joke, is predicated on the larger context of meaning and purpose. Thus in its own topsy-turvy way the comic leap points to the "leap of faith" itself.

Unfortunately, theologians and moralists have had much to say about man's responsibility to work, but little about his responsibility to play; many words about seriousness and sobriety, few about nonsense and laughter. Still it is really as much in play as in work, in the game as in serious activity, and especially in the play and game of humor, that man is differentiated from the rest of the animal kingdom. Christian theologians in particular have expended copious efforts on the subject of the "image of God" in man; yet for all these laborious and occasionally heated deliberations precious little has ever been said about humor as an aspect of the *imago dei*, let alone as a dimension of the religious situation before the divine. The impression is given that laughter is the creation of the devil or a fumbling demiurge, or that it is a pale substitute left to man after his expulsion from the more holy joys of paradise. In the representative terms of the Westminster Catechism, the chief end of man is the serious and awesome purpose of glorifying God and enjoying him forever. The ancient Greek peripatetics were at least as close to the true nature of things when they characterized man as the "laughing animal" (*zöion gelastikon*),[7] and saw in comedy the distinctive badge of humanity. The infant, in fact, around the age of one to three months, well before evidencing any of the more imposing and weighty characteristics of humanity—self-awareness, symbolization, speech, reason, abstraction, conscience, responsibility, religious concern, and the like—first of all smiles. Shortly thereafter he learns to laugh. This is one

---

[7] Lucian of Samosata, in "Sale of Creeds," described the peripatetic philosopher as one capable of distinguishing a man from an ass—the one able to laugh, the other not.

of the first manifestations of his humanity. It is something that the adult world often tries its best to smother under a blanket of seriousness and no-nonsense. Every parent is in great haste to have his child grow up and mature, to become serious, and often impatient with the carefree, playful world of childish impulse. Children have the remarkable talent for not taking the adult world with the kind of respect that we are so confident it ought to be given. They refuse to appreciate the gravity of our monumental concerns, while we forget that if we were to become more like the child, our concerns might not be as monumental. There is a certain refreshing element of profanation in the child's world of naïveté and mischief that blows like a gentle breeze through the stuffy pomposity of adulthood. Often with a simple question or a completely honest remark, perhaps with a quizzical smile or a whimsical laugh, a child can call into doubt the sanctimonious façade and sacrosanct presuppositions of an entire civilization.

Wordsworth's "Recollections of Early Childhood" speaks to the suppression of this delightfully human world of childish profanation, perhaps more than he intended:

> Heaven lies about us in our infancy!
> Shades of the prison-house begin to close
> Upon the growing Boy. . . .
>
> At length the Man perceives it die away,
> And fade into the light of common day.

The playfulness and innocence of humor is an essential part of the humanity of man, apart from which he does not mature but becomes inhuman. In this sense Jesus' insistence upon the necessity of becoming as little children takes on a new dimension; for without the grace of humor it is doubtful that any man can enter either the Kingdom of God or the Kingdom of Man.

Humor: Prophetic and Promethean

In addition to the purely playful level of humor, presenting a kind of neutral, oblivious face to the sacred, there is a profounder level that turns in more sophisticated and largely ambivalent expression toward the sacred. It is the comic stance in the midst of duality and contradiction, conflict and dilemma, doubt and anxiety, sin and guilt. It is not so much a humor that transcends the dichotomies and tensions of existence in a holiday of innocence, as a humor that moves within those dichotomies and tensions in comic reflection of them. It is, consequently, the comic mood that corresponds mythically with Paradise-lost. Rather than moving backward toward a relinquished immediacy and irresponsibility prior to the "fall," it remains within the present realities and confronts them comically.

As a direct response to, and reflection of, the ambiguities and relativities of existence, this level of humor in turn is ambivalent in its expression. In a way that is analogous to the double-response of fear (repulsion) and fascination (attraction) evoked by the awesomeness and mysteriousness of the sacred (Otto), the comic thrust is an act of profaning the sacred that moves away from and toward the sacred simultaneously. Just as the more serious reaction to the sacred is one of both shrinking back and drawing close, like the movement of the moth around the flame, so the comic response to the sacred is both withdrawing and aggressive. It does not leap simply and childishly into a sphere of playful immunity removed from, and as it were prior to, the distinctions between good and evil, justice and injustice, sacred and profane, but performs its comedy more self-consciously within an awareness of the problematic of the sacred in a context of estrangement and insecurity. The element of comic interlude is still present, but not as a temporary suspension of sacrality in the laughter of innocent abandon. It is laughter within the Adamic "knowledge of good and evil," and therefore shares reflectively in all the ambiguities and relativities of that knowledge.

The one side of this double-reflection may be designated as its prophetic character; the other as its Promethean character. On the one hand, humor is a mechanism of withdrawal and objectification; it is an act of separation, distancing, and detachment. The awesomeness and mystery of the holy, along with the anxiety it engenders, is temporarily suspended and relieved. And in this disengagement the objectivity and self-criticism that constitute the special virtue of the comic perspective are made possible. Sociologists have referred to this movement in terms of "role distance" and "backstage humor," a common phenomenon in relation to any serious role-playing activity.[8] Through humor one steps outside his normal identity or official image, his ordinary commitment and involvement, and achieves a certain freedom of detachment in relation to himself and his circumstances. What Sypher has said of the carnival may be said of the distancing effect of the comic withdrawal in general: "Those in the thrall of carnival come out, for a moment, from behind the façade of their 'serious' selves, the façade required by their vocation. When they emerge from this façade, they gain a new perspective upon their official selves and thus, when they again retire behind their usual *personae*, they are more conscious of the duplicity of their existence." [9]

[8] Cf. Erving Goffman's analysis of humor and role distance among surgeons (*Encounters* [Indianapolis: Bobbs-Merrill, 1961], pp. 115–132), and of backstaging and role performance (*The Presentation of the Self in Everyday Life* [Garden City: Doubleday, 1959]).

[9] Wylie Sypher, "The Meanings of Comedy," *Comedy*, Wylie Sypher, ed. (New York: Doubleday, 1956), p. 221.

On the other hand, Freud's analysis of humor as both an aggressive act, and one expressing rebellion against authority,[10] is equally applicable to the relationship of the comic to the sacred; for in humor the unquestioned authority of the sacred is questioned, the superior status of the holy is bracketed, and the radical distance between the sacred and the profane is minimized. The devotee who ordinarily assumes a posture of lowly prostration before that which is holy, now in laughter asserts himself and narrows the impassable gulf presupposed by the sacred. Instead of the more passive withdrawal and escape from the aweful majesty of the sacred, which at most is open to the charge of lack of involvement and commitment, this is an act that from the side of both the subject and the sacred constitutes a kind of trespass into the inner sanctum of holy things. It therefore opens itself to the charge of, not only levity and frivolity, but sacrilege and blasphemy. This is not, however, identical with sheer rebellion or antagonism, though it may degenerate into such, but an inevitable human response to sovereignty and intensity of whatever sort. If man cannot live by bread alone, neither can he live by holiness and propriety alone. In Freud's terms, the whole man includes the id as well as the superego; and in comedy the superego is either granted a leave of absence (the play of innocence) or made the object of comic withdrawal and aggression.

Prophetic Iconoclasm. It is because of the first side of this double response to the sacred—comic distance—that humor can become such a devastating weapon against the pride and pretension that claim to have elevated man and his understandings beyond the insecurities and fallibilities of the human situation. It is humor—in this case not innocently but reflectively—that restrains man from absolutizing any of the relativities of his existence. For that which is taken in all

[10] Sigmund Freud, *Jokes and Their Relation to the Unconscious,* James Strachey, trans. (New York: W. W. Norton, 1963), pp. 102 ff.

sincerity and good faith as being ultimate is taken as such by man; it is that which is ultimate and of ultimate importance to this or that human being. Even the interpretation of the sacred as the sphere of ultimate and unconditional concern (e.g., Tillich)[11] has an aura of ultimate and unconditional seriousness about it that man cannot give to his concerns without idolatry and fanaticism. And just as, from the objective standpoint, there is the question whether man ought to be unconditionally concerned about anything—as man— from the subjective standpoint there is the practical question whether it is possible for anyone, short of an unrelenting, if not insane, obsession, to be unconditionally concerned about anything. Laughter is therefore the lighthearted appendix to any "ultimate and unconditional concern" that preserves it from absolutism on the one hand, and at the same time from an intensification of anxiety over not having and possessing with complete security the ultimate and the unconditioned, or simply not being ultimately and unconditionally concerned about anything.

It is in this light that a comment like that of Harold Watts, though only too common, is so far from understanding the essential role of the comic spirit: "It is the trick of comedy to confirm all our superficial judgments; it must make us ignore those which we regard as profound and eternal." [12] Similarly, Allport refers to the function of humor as that of helping "to integrate personality by disposing of all conflicts that do not really matter." [13] The humorous remark or comic gesture, however, at its profoundest is the footnote attached to every pious and moral statement or act that reminds us of our humanity, our mortality, our finiteness and fallibility, our

[11] Paul Tillich, *Dynamics of Faith* (New York: Harper & Row, 1957).

[12] "The Sense of Regain: A Theory of Comedy," *University of Kansas City Review,* Vol. XIII (Autumn, 1946), p. 22.

[13] Gordon W. Allport, *The Individual and His Religion* (New York: Macmillan, 1950), p. 93.

foolishness. It is the bracketing placed around even the most serious and sacred moments of human existence that qualifies them as human moments, and the seriousness as human seriousness. It therefore has its own unique contribution to the religious situation. It may be a limited contribution, and one that unrestrained can also dissolve seriousness into cavalier frivolity; but it is an essential contribution nonetheless to the very sacrality of the sacred. Through the juxtaposition of awe and laughter, a certain necessary separation and distance from the sacred is achieved, providing that dimension of balance and perspective apart from which piety is in constant danger of becoming pride, devotion of becoming fanaticism, and the sacred the demonic. Inherent in the very seriousness and sacrality of religious concerns is the almost overwhelming tendency toward a tyranny of the sacred, to which the natural history of dogmatism gives abundant witness. Humor in relation to the sacred, therefore, has a critical iconoclastic function to perform, not simply with respect to the idolatrous possibilities of the convictions of others, but primarily of one's own.

That the theologian or ecclesiastic rarely takes up the role of comic profaner, at least publicly,[14] or gives a significant religious place to such a role, is generally the result of a completely negative interpretation of the profanation of the sacred. The sacred seems to demand only proclamation, not profanation; prophets and priests, not clowns and comedians. Yet insofar as man has no sacred objects or acts or conceptions that are completely within his possession and under his control (otherwise the basic elements of transcendence and revelation presupposed in the notion of the sacred are denied), and insofar as they are within his possession and under his control

[14] Of course privately, and in the company of other clerics, the phenomenon of "role distance" and "backstage humor" discussed by Goffman (loc. cit.) is probably as common among the clergy as any other professional group.

(and therefore subject to all the limitations of human nature), the profanation of the sacred is a necessity within the sacred itself. This is its ontological basis in the human situation, its specifically religious and moral *raison d'être*, as well as its psychological basis. It is the act by which man is prevented from absolutizing himself, his truths, his goodness, and even that which he holds most sacred. And it is the act by which his seriousness is restrained from becoming an anxious, or guilt-ridden, or dehumanizing obsession. There are, after all, in the variegated religious history of man few acts that have not been invested by some group with spiritual significance, few ideas that have not become the sacred truths in some tradition, few objects that have not been at some time considered holy. It was, in fact, this sacrilization of everything from pebble to phallus—and without any apparent common denominator suggestive of holiness—that led Durkheim to seek an interpretation of the nature and power of the holy in sociological rather than religious terms.[15] Though the various forms of humor in relation to the sacred may appear blasphemous, true blasphemy is not to be found in the profanation wrought by humor as such, but ultimately in the absence of humor. For at the heart of the comic spirit and perspective is the acceptance of the prophetic warning against idolatry, and against that greatest blasphemy of all, the claim to possess or to be as God. The clown and comedian—in this sense prophets in their own right—symbolize the comic relativizing of the category of the holy. They pose the problematic of the sacred by playfully and indiscriminately endowing everything with holiness, or—which is the same—endowing everything with profanity. In their momentary suspension of sacrality is the playful reminder that nearly everything at one time or another in the millennia of man has been exalted to the pinnacle of the sacred. It calls in question the absoluteness

[15] Emile Durkheim, *The Elementary Forms of the Religious Life* (1915).

of human interpretations of the sacred by intimating that anything can, and almost everything in fact has, become invested with the aura of a holy concern; and therefore that nothing can be given the finality of a sacredness that is inviolable and eternal, which is completely beyond the pale of humor.

Humor is not all playfulness in the purer sense of play for the sake of play. There is an important element of seriousness in humor, in this case a genuinely prophetic seriousness. In the comic play with holy things, there is at work the more profound purpose of pointing to the play element in all matters of human concern, whether art, music, literature, politics, law, custom, philosophy, morality, or religion—and thus of restraining the ever-present temptation to confer upon them a finality that nothing human enjoys. As Huizinga has masterfully demonstrated, there is a fundamental dimension of play in all cultural enterprises, including the most sacred rites and forms, moral codes and religious beliefs.[16] It is, at least in part, in play that the primal dramatizations of human behavior, myth and ritual, have their origin and basis; and out of play that all forms of culture derive, and as play—no matter how seriously undertaken and considered—perpetuate themselves. The holy ritual of the Catholic mass, to take a single example, for all its richness of meaning and symbolism and power, and for all the sacredness of its revelatory and redemptive significance for the communicant, is nevertheless at the same time a form of human play and game.[17] To forget or to deny this is to open up the rite to the possibilities of pride and pretension and idolatry against which the prophet has always

[16] Johan Huizinga, *Homo Ludens* (Boston: Beacon Press, 1950). "In all the wild imaginings of mythology a fanciful spirit is playing on the borderline between jest and earnest" (p. 5).

[17] For a classic development of the theme of "the playfulness of the liturgy," see the essay of the same title in Romano Guardini, *The Spirit of the Liturgy* (1935), recently reprinted in *The Church and the Catholic and The Spirit of the Liturgy* (New York: Sheed & Ward, 1967), pp. 171–184.

contended. Though Huizinga does not draw or develop this particular conclusion, it is one of the functions of the playfulness of the comic, not only to participate in the play element that underlies all things human, from the least to the most sacred, but to be a perpetual reminder of it.

Humor is also a reminder of the essential awkwardness of the human situation, an awkwardness that is only intensified in the religious situation. The awkward person or awkward act or awkward posture has been a basic part of the repertoire of comedy, whether portrayed by clown or comedian. The existential predicament of man, however, and above all of man as he approaches the sacred, is the epitome of awkwardness. It is upon the tension generated by the ambiguities and contradictions of this predicament that comedy draws, and which it reactualizes and symbolizes on a more trivial plane— e.g., the endless falls and misfortunes of the circus clown, the caricatures of the cartoonist, the deflation of haughty splendor in slapstick routines, etc. On the one hand, there is an intrinsic awkwardness about man's being and position in the cosmos as such, an awkwardness that is comical, as well as serious and often tragic. The glory and pathos of the human situation to which Pascal referred so poignantly in his *Pensées* also has its humorous side: suspended between heaven and earth, eternity and time, the infinite and the finite, spirit and flesh, rationality and impulse, good and evil, the grandeur and misery of man is laudable, lamentable, and ludicrous alike. The real clown, finally, is Everyman—to which fact the painted face of the clown points emblematically. This awkwardness, on the other hand, reaches its climax in the religious situation as man attempts to deal with matters of ultimate concern, and with the most fundamental questions concerning his existence. It is an awkwardness the comic side of which has never been adequately summarized in traditional philosophical or theological categories.

To take the case of the theologian whose office it is to

articulate the implications of the faith and life of a particular
religious community, the theologian who now, say, in his
thirtieth year undertakes to give considered thought to the most
encompassing issues of all, who ventures in fact systematically
to explore the nature of God in his relatedness to the world,
to develop a methodology appropriate to its divine object,
perhaps even to engage in a respectable "science of God":
whether he self-consciously recognizes it or not, he is in the
clumsiest of positions, and the importance of his office notwithstanding, his figure is to this extent the ridiculous figure
of the clown. The words of Yahweh to Job—in the midst of
earnest reflection on the most tortuous of theological problems,
and after having sought with his fellow theologians over the
space of thirty-seven chapters to interpret the relationship of
the ways of God to the fortunes of men—best express the
humorousness as well as pathos of the religious situation:
"Where were you when I laid the foundations of the world?"
(Job 38:4). It is as if a celebrated theologian of the church
had just completed the final declarations of his one, two,
three, or perhaps twelve volume systematic on nature, man,
and God, expecting to hear the words, "Well done, thou good
and faithful servant," only to hear instead, "Where were you
when I laid the foundations of the world?" [18]

To take oneself seriously, therefore, as a human being, and
as a human being in relation to the sacred, is to laugh; for it
is the seriousness of one who is awkward and often contradic-

[18] One cannot help thinking here of Karl Barth's remark concerning his
prodigious theological efforts: "The angels laugh at old Karl. They laugh
at him because he tries to grasp the truth about God in a book of Dogmatics. They laugh at the fact that volume follows volume and each is
thicker than the previous one. As they laugh, they say to one another,
'Look! Here he comes now with his little pushcart full of volumes of the
Dogmatics!'" *Antwort* (Zollikon-Zurich: Evangelischer Verlag AG, 1956),
p. 895, trans. Robert McAfee Brown, George Casalis, *Portrait of Karl
Barth* (Garden City: Doubleday, 1963), p. 3.

tory in his finiteness, his fallibility, and his folly. It will also mean other things, of course: to be humble, forgiving, repentant, etc. But even here there is an inner relationship between humor and the more "serious" virtues. It was a most unfortunate omission on the part of medieval Christianity not to have included humor and humorlessness in its moral glossary of the seven cardinal virtues and the seven deadly sins. Humility includes the ability to laugh at oneself and the refusal to take oneself too seriously. Laughter may open the way to forgiveness; for in laughter hostilities are softened, just as forgiveness allows enemies to laugh together. Repentance ends in laughter, and repentance needs laughter to preserve itself from moroseness and self-chastisement. Humility, forgiveness, repentance, even love without humor, are easy prey to distortion, as also on the darker side are moral and religious attitudes toward sin, shame, and guilt.

Sin, for example, is not only sinful and therefore to be treated piously, but stupid and therefore to be treated comically. The face of the sinner is also the mask of the harlequin; sinful folly is also comic folly. This the clown and comedian have always understood. The irony of evil lies in its foolishness and folly. Thus in the comic figure the sacrificial scapegoat of the cultus is replaced by the clown who in his own awkward way brings about redemption from sin, interpreted as foolishness. In laughter, as well as in repentance, sin is purged, guilt is released, and shame is taken away. The evil deed is personified comically and made the object of ridicule, and in this manner exorcised. Demons are driven off through laughter as well as through prayer. As Karl Barth remarks in his *Dogmatics,* "Sinister matters may be very real, but they must not be contemplated too long or studied too precisely or adopted too intensively. . . . The very thing which the demons are waiting for, especially in theology, is that we should find them dreadfully interesting and give them our serious and perhaps systematic attention." [19] Sin, like right-eousness, is to be taken seriously, but not too seriously. Satan as well as the saint is thus a legitimate subject for comedy; and the Devil has quite naturally been cast in this role in Christian circles—e.g., the popular representation of him in a red suit, with forked tail and horns, and with an impish glint in his eye. Indeed the comic hero is often one who is both saint and sinner, angel and demon, as was his mytho-logical counterpart, the Trickster. [20] In the duplicity of his character and role he brings an essential qualification to the potential oppressiveness of both the holy and the unholy. The counterpart of the profanation of the sacred is the profanation of the demonic. There is an awkwardness about both our good and our evil; man is incapable of being either completely divine or completely demonic. Thus the man who boasts of his depravity is as funny as the man who parades his purity. It is here that the source of the common ambiguity in the character of the clown or comic hero is to be found; he is, after all, Everyman.

The extreme forms of the doctrine of "total depravity," and especially the extended deliberation and elaboration on the subject, in Augustinian and Reformed theologies are instances of such a misguided ultraseriousness in relation to the demonic —a misunderstanding that is not unknown in the realm of "unfaith" as well. A philosopher like Sartre, for example, only inverts this form of theological ultraseriousness when he labors the element of Absurdity at the heart of reality, and describes the profoundest levels of human existence in the categories of

[19] Church Dogmatics III/3 (Edinburgh: T. and T. Clark, 1960), p. 519. Barth, however, does not in any formal sense apply the same dialectic of the sacred and the comic to the whole of theology.

[20] For an analysis of the Trickster motif, see C. G. Jung, "On the Psy-chology of the Trickster-Figure," The Collected Works of C. G. Jung, Vol. IX/1 (New York: Pantheon Books, 1959), pp. 255–274.

nausea, anxiety, abandonness, and despair.[21] A large part of the sickness of Roquentin in Sartre's *Nausea* is not only that he finds no fragments of meaning and purpose in life, but precisely that he finds no fragments of comedy, only nausea and disgust over the dirty hodgepodge of chaotic phenomena around him, and despair at the tragic absence of the good, the true, and the beautiful. He is unable to laugh at life, or to laugh at himself and his anguished philosophy of life. He takes himself as seriously in his despair as the dogmatic theologian in his faith or the self-righteous man in his election to heavenly reward. *Nausea* is a French tragedy without a comic epilogue. The comic perspective is as much lacking here as among the somberest of theologians who find all sorts of divine purposes and meanings at the heart of things, or who discourse, also *ad nauseum,* on the wickedness of man in parallel categories of fallenness, depravity, unbelief, and rebellion. This radicalizing of meaninglessness, this final death of faith and hope, becomes a new form of seriousness, a new ultimate—the Absurd—which desperately needs the comic spirit. The clown and the comedian also deal with the Nihil and the Surd, but comically.

Promethean Rebellion. In contrast to the movement of withdrawal from the sacred, which permits the freedom of distance and detachment, there is also on this same level the opposite movement of approach that permits another kind of freedom, the freedom of invading and handling the sacred in ways that ordinarily would be taboo. The comic spirit on every level expresses freedom in relation to the sacred; in this case, however, it is not the freedom to move backward into a sphere of immunity prior to the distinction between sacred and profane, nor the freedom to step outside the sacred in reflective disengagement, but the freedom to bridge the dis-

[21] Jean-Paul Sartre, *Existentialism* (New York: Philosophical Library, 1947).

tance ordinarily required by the sacred, the freedom to challenge the authority and sovereignty of the sacred. It is not the nostalgic humor of comic asylum, the spontaneous frolic for the sake of frolicking, nor the constraining humor that stands apart in comic detachment, but an aggressive humor that asserts its freedom in spite of its bondage, its guilt, and its sacred ties. The paradigm here, therefore, is not that of playful innocence, or of prophetic iconoclasm, but of Promethean rebellion. The mode of this particular relationship to the sacred is analogous to the freedom available to the court jester vis-à-vis the supremacy and dominion of the king. One of the liberties to which the jester is privy is the license to profane the sacredness of the person and rule of the king, to mock the niceties and conventions of royalty, to transgress the code of the court, even to proclaim himself king. On the one hand, this provides the king with the perspective of comic distance; on the other hand, it provides the court, and symbolically the kingdom, with a harmless avenue for venting animosity and rebellion.

Such humor is clearly not innocent, but operates self-consciously within the knowledge of good and evil. As the other side of an ambivalent response to the sacred, and to the estrangements of Paradise-lost, it becomes a Promethean assertion of freedom in relation to divine order, to the inevitabilities of fate, to constituted authority, to custom and law, to structure and cosmos of whatever sort. The aura of rebellion therefore clings to it; for it is the assertion of the freedom of the will, the autonomy of the human spirit, the integrity of the individual. The creative principle within chaos pits itself against the restrictive principle within cosmos. It is, however, a comic rebellion; and this is its virtue. Laughter has a kind of immunity that outright aggression and trespass do not. The laughter is, of course, serious to a certain extent, in that all comedy on this level has an undercurrent of seriousness about it. But it is not completely serious, for the rebelliousness of the act is sublimated in laughter; and like all comedy, as typified in the person of the court fool, its distinctive trait is folly. This characteristic is of special importance, not only in relation to sacred concerns, but in relation to other human beings who might, for whatever reason, arouse antagonism and hostility. Through humor, aggression can be redirected into socially accepted and relatively innocuous channels.[22]

This Promethean thrust of humor, like its prophetic counterpart, is evident not only in relation to the sacred, but the tragic and demonic. The comic hero cries out in oblique protest against the inequalities and injustices of life, the inescapable dilemmas of human existence, the evils and enigmas of Paradise-lost. Laughter is not only gaiety and lightheartedness; it may also express the harsh struggle against hopelessness and despair, the "courage to be" (Tillich) in the threat of nonbeing. It is this dimension of the comic spirit, in particular, that is represented in the farcical episodes interspersed within the larger drama of some of the ancient Greek tragedies, as in Euripides' *Alcestis,* or in the comic interludes (*Kyogen,* lit. "mad words") often found between the performances of the classic Japanese no plays.[23] Especially is this to be found in the radical juxtaposition of the tragic and the comic effected in the Greek satyr play, appended to sober

[22] Cf. Konrad Lorenz, *On Aggression* (New York: Harcourt, Brace & World, 1966), in which on ethological grounds the origin of laughter is seen as a process of ritualizing aggression, similar to the various mechanisms for ritualizing aggression developed among a variety of animal species. Laughter is interpreted as the specifically human mechanism for redirecting threatening movements and for releasing tensions generated by frustrated aggressive impulses. One is reminded of the thesis, advanced at the turn of the century by Anthony Ludovici in *The Secret of Laughter,* that the smile was originally a sublimation of the menacing act of baring the teeth.

[23] Cf. Shio Sakanishi, *Japanese Folk-Plays: The Ink-Smeared Lady and Other Kyogen,* 2nd ed. (Rutland, Vt.: Charles E. Tuttle, 1960).

dramatic productions, as in Sophocles' *Ichneutai* or Euripides' *Cyclops*, where comedy parodies the tragedy that has preceded it. Through humor a postludic qualification is given to the heavy seriousness and somberness of the tragedy as the sacred themes of the drama and the fundamental laws of fate and human destiny are, in effect, profaned. The tragic hero is now seen through the mask of the comic hero, and the comedy in the human situation is revealed. At the same time the intensity of pathos is given release and temporary resolution. Tragedy, as with any serious modality, needs comedy to preserve equilibrium and perspective; comedy humanizes tragedy in the same way that it humanizes the sacred. The dismal and fated conclusion of the tragic flaw or circumstance is partially overcome in a comic flourish. This is its prophetic side. The tragedy, however, is also transcended in another, distinctively Promethean sense, corresponding specifically to its tragic character: the comedy of the satyr play is an expression of man's stubborn refusal to give tragedy and fate the final say. In the very act of profaning the tragic an otherwise inexorable destiny is surmounted. The fate that cannot be transcended, or the arbitrary will of the gods that cannot be overturned, is transcended and overturned in an heroic gesture of the human spirit. Incongruous though it may seem, man has the last laugh.

The same heroic quality of the comic spirit is more concretely visible in the remarkable phenomenon of Jewish humor; for the Jews, like the American Negroes, have developed a genius for comedy in the midst of a history of tragedy.[24] It is hardly a coincidence that a high percentage of comedians in the United States, especially in relation to their proportions in the population statistics, are Jewish and Negro. Their

---

[24] Cf. Viktor Frankl's discussion of the role of humor in a Nazi concentration camp: *Man's Search for Meaning: An Introduction to Logotherapy* (New York: Washington Square Press, 1963), pp. 68 ff.

humor is the "satyr play" that qualifies the enormity of some of the darkest hours in Western civilization. Humor is not only possible in relation to the more superficial and innocent incongruities of life; it may also express a certain heroic defiance in the face of life's most crushing tragedies, an unquenchable nobility of spirit that refuses to allow fate to have the last word—to be absolute. And in this sense, in fact, a preliminary victory has already been won over cynicism and despair. Where there is humor, there is still hope. The human spirit has not been utterly vanquished. As long as humor exists, the will to live and the determination to continue the struggle, even against insuperable odds, has not been finally destroyed. Within the seeming inappropriateness of the comic mood, therefore, lies a profound affirmation of life in spite of its blackest moments. Comedy celebrates life by mocking its absurdities, by forcing its tragic twists into comic twists. Seriousness alone—for all its desire to deal positively and concretely with life—ends in abstraction from life, if not in a sense of futility.

It is in this sense that comedy holds a redemptive potentiality; for all its playfulness and rebelliousness and profanity, a sacred character. In the midst of the demonic and the absurd, the comic spirit leaves the door open to faith and hope. Comedy is therefore closer to the deep springs of religion than tragedy. The tragic perspective terminates in unredeemed and unredeeming conflict, in bitter defiance without resolution and without hope; while comedy is a prefiguration of anticipated joy, a return to chaos as a prelude to a new cosmos, a comic suspension of meaning and plunge into irrationality as a transition into a fuller meaning and higher rationality that is to come. The dialectic of the tragic and the comic, like that of the sacred and the comic, moves toward a synthesis beyond both moments, whether in the eschaton of the prophet or the eternity of the mystic. The existential situation of Paradise-lost is obstinately resisted as the final movement in the human drama. As Sypher has so suggestively put it: "The tragic action . . . runs through only one arc of the full cycle of the drama; for the entire ceremonial cycle is birth: struggle: death: resurrection. . . . Consequently the range of comedy is wider than the tragic range—perhaps more fearless—and comic action can risk a different sort of purgation and triumph. If we believe that drama retains any of the mythical values of the old fertility rite, then the comic cycle is the only fulfilled and redemptive action. . . . Is this the reason why it is difficult for tragic art to deal with Christian themes like the Crucifixion and the Resurrection? Should we say that the drama of the struggle, death and rising—Gethsemane, Calvary, and Easter—actually belongs in the comic rather than the tragic domain?" [25]

It is, of course, quite true that comedy tends to reduce everything with which it deals to the dimensions of the farce, to treat matters of ultimate consequence as trivia, and therefore that it seems to point inevitably in the direction of the absurdity of all things. The clown and the comic hero appear to be only the calloused protagonists of chaos. Unlike tragedy, or any serious structure, there is no requirement imposed upon comedy to be rational and intelligible, to conform to a plot, to make sense. Comedy makes the most of the elements of surprise and chance. It twists and distorts; it exaggerates and understates; it defies proportion, balance and common sense; it grins and grimaces where one should be solemn or sad. It

[25] Sypher, *op. cit.*, p. 220. Allusion is being made here to the thesis advanced by F. M. Cornford that the origins of Greek comedy, as well as tragedy, are to be found in the ritual drama of the seasonal fertility rites, which portrayed the death of the old God, the old King, the old year, the momentary return to chaos, and the rebirth of the new cosmos. *The Origin of Attic Comedy* (London: Edward Arnold, 1914). Cf. Mircea Eliade, *Cosmos and History: The Myth of the Eternal Return* (New York: Harper & Row, 1959).

is for this reason that the worst thing that can happen to a joke is for it to be explained to someone who has failed to laugh; rational explanation is the one thing that is inappropriate. Comedy has its own logic; but it is a logic that employs the elements of irrationality and absurdity to the full. It is this that provides the delicate mechanism of the "comic twist," the sudden, unpredictable, and nonsensical turn of events, contortion of the face, or wrenching of language that precipitates laughter. But if comedy were to take irrationality and absurdity as ultimate, this would prove its own undoing. Comedy must presuppose order and meaning in the very act of not taking it with absolute seriousness.

The Laughter of Confidence

In this we have a clue to another dimension of humor, a dimension that points beyond chaos and Paradise-lost, that transcends the conflicts and contradictions of existence, and therefore that belongs more in the category that is known in mythical terms as Paradise-regained. A correlation has previously been drawn between comedy and chaos over against cosmos and the sacred. Comedy plays upon absurdity and returns its participants to the freedom of nothingness; it reveals incongruity and delights in the nonsensical. This, however, is absurdity and nonsense set in relation to a transcendent ground of meaning and reason; it is chaos in the overarching context of cosmos, the comic intermission that presupposes the sacredness of the larger drama itself. But if the sacred cosmos is destroyed, then comedy is in danger of destruction as well. A dominant theme in much of modern literature—as also in art, poetry, music, and philosophy—has been precisely this loss of faith in any ultimate sense and purpose in life, any all-embracing frame of reference in relation to which life is to be seen and measured, any mythical scenario and religious ethos that informs and unconsciously structures one's day-to-day being, and the consequent belief in the essential meaninglessness, if not absurdity, of existence. As a result it has become increasingly difficult to use any of the traditional categories of tragedy and comedy, drama or farce, to characterize the work of playwrights from Chekhov to Sartre to Beckett to Albee. Without any fundamental sacral order, the situation becomes completely ambiguous. As in watching a performance of Beckett's *Waiting for Godot,* one does not know whether to laugh or cry. Far from giving greater profundity to the drama, or intensity to the humor, both profundity and intensity are dissolved; for there is no longer any distinction between the profound and the trivial. In an absurd world, everything is flattened out. There can no longer, except arbitrarily, be any hierarchy of meaning, value, and purpose, no difference between a tragic and a comic event. Both the seriousness of the sacred and the pathos of the tragic, as well as the humorousness of the comic, have been undermined. Life may continue to have its proximate purposes and assigned meanings, its relative tragedies and its little jokes, but essentially life simply is, without tragedy or comedy, the sacred or the profane.[26] As in Robbet-Grillet's *Jealousy* where nothing significant happens because nothing is either significant or insignificant, distinctions no longer apply; for the irrationality and incongruity that lies at the root of both tragedy and comedy—the resolution of which lies in the *mysterium* of the sacred—itself has been absolutized.

It is in this sense that genuine comedy points, in its own

[26] The laughter of despair is well-expressed by Ionesco: "In a world that now seems all illusion and pretense, in which all human behavior tells of absurdity and all history of absolute futility; all reality and all language appear to lose their articulation, to disintegrate and collapse, so what possible reaction is there left, when everything has ceased to matter, but to laugh at it all?" Eugène Ionesco, *Notes and Counter Notes,* trans. by Donald Watson (New York: Grove Press, 1964), p. 163.

left-handed way, in the direction of faith. Comedy presupposes faith in a sacred order, or depth dimension of being, at the same time that it represents a persistent refusal to absolutize it and to take it with absolute seriousness. Humor thus in clownish fashion calls attention to faith in an ultimate meaning and purpose in things that transcends both tragedy and comedy, both the harsh and ludicrous incongruities of existence. For all of its levity and frivolity, it is an affirmation of light rather than darkness at the heart of reality, of meaning rather than absurdity at the center of the mystery of Being. The same humor that profanes the sacred is also a prophetic voice raised in the wilderness, a comic figure or "holy fool" dressed like John the Baptist in camel's skin and eating locusts and wild honey, making straight the way. In its own outrageous manner it is an agent of redemption; for in its very opening up of the sacred cosmos to the profane chaos, it bears witness to a faith in the ontological priority of cosmos over chaos. Precisely in its nonsense and folly it celebrates the primacy of the rational over the absurd and the meaningful over the meaningless.

On the second level, humor corresponds with the existential predicament of Paradise-lost as the correlate of the relativity of faith and the ambiguities of the human situation. A third dimension has now been opened up, however, which is a laughter within the confidence of faith. It is to this that the previous level points, and from it that it seeks resolution and fulfillment. Humor corresponds not only to the insecurity of faith, as human faith, but to the security of faith as well, as that which points beyond itself. It is not only a double reflection of the problematic of the sacred, the sacred that man in all his finiteness and fallibility acknowledges as such, but of the ultimacy of the sacred. If there were no element of confidence and finality in faith, it would not be faith but despair. It would not represent the humble recognition, within the frail act of faith, of the relativity of all finite perspectives, but the nihilistic relativity of cynicism. It would be an attempt to suspend humor in mid-air, the subsequent result of which could only be that of its falling flat on its face in its moment of achievement.

Though laughter often arises out of the tensions generated by insecurity, in its most mature form laughter arises within the freedom of security. Humor at its profoundest, therefore, is more than the comic side of doubt and anxiety, of ambiguity and dilemma, of incongruity and tragedy. It is more than an act of withdrawal from the sacred, or of aggressively bridging the gap that separates from the sacred. It is humor within the assurance of faith that the distance will be, or has already to some extent been, closed. Humor not only presupposes distance but familiarity. We do not, for example, joke readily with total strangers. Rather we experience the greatest freedom to indulge in frivolous tête-à-tête in the company of those with whom we have established some relationship; and the degree to which we have this freedom is the degree to which we have achieved a basis for mutual confidence and trust. In this sense, too, humor has an intrinsic relation to the sacred; it presupposes a familiarity with the sacred, a basis in the sacred, a relationship sufficiently established to permit the freedom of humor.

As that which is grounded in the sacred, humor is also the laughter within the joy of faith. It is not the hollow laughter of cynicism and despair, but the gay laughter of belief in an ultimate ground and resolution of meaning, purpose, and value in life. This is not a humor within the anxiety outside of faith, but alongside the anxiety within faith. As such it is motivated not simply by the element of tension within faith, as human faith, but by the element of trust as the distinctive mark of faith. It is therefore the lightheartedness that accompanies hope and assurance, the carefree laughter granted by the freedom of faith. Here it is more than the freedom of playful innocence, more than the freedom of prophetic iconoclasm and Promethean rebellion. It is the freedom of confidence. Something of this side of the comic spirit is captured in the ancient custom in Greek Orthodox circles of setting aside the day after Easter as a day of laughter and hilarity, a day in which joking and jesting are appropriate within the sanctuary because of the big joke God pulled on Satan in the Resurrection. Cosmos has been victorious over chaos, faith over doubt, trust over anxiety; and man is now truly free to laugh with the laughter of higher innocence. Humor becomes the play of joy.

As a result of the element of profanation in humor, and the fact that humor suggests a lower order of spirituality than joy, this particular dimension of the relationship of the sacred to the comic is often not recognized, even though in a sense it is the most important of all; for it is at this point that both the primordial basis of the comic in the sacred and the eschatological fulfillment of humor in hope is revealed. William Hamilton, for instance, in commenting upon the recent increase of interest in humor on the part of the ecclesiastical world, has remarked: "We must now seek more passionately than ever to banish humor from the Holy of Holies. Our defenses of humor have been a pathetic attempt to keep in step with a secular culture that has nothing else. . . . In a world redeemed by Christ, humor becomes joy." [27] Yet though joy and humor are certainly not synonymous, neither are they alien. Humor is not displaced by joy, but is one of its forms of expression. To be caught up in the exultation surrounding the sacred, and in the confidence and assurance of faith, is not to annul humor but to give it its proper basis. Joy does not exclude humor any more than holiness excludes laughter. The

[27] "Humor: Plausible and Demonic," *The Christian Century*, Vol. LXXVI (July 8, 1959), p. 807.

element of surprise that characterizes all comedy is by faith transmuted to that higher plane to which C. S. Lewis alludes in his spiritual autobiography: one is "surprised by joy." [28]

It is here that the playful, carefree humor of childish immediacy and abandon is joined by the mature humor within the celebration of the sacred. The laughter that takes place in a zone where, as it were, there is neither the sacred nor the profane, a sphere of simple immunity from the proprieties that circumscribe the sacred, is now completed by the laughter from the side of the sacred, the laughter that takes place in the surety and thanksgiving of faith. What, on the one hand, is the recaptured paradise of innocent play in the freedom prior to the knowledge of good and evil is, on the other hand, the play of Paradise-regained on the further side of the knowledge of good and evil, the play in the freedom of acceptance and restoration that follows repentance and faith—in Christian terms, the playfulness that corresponds to the time before the fall and the time after redemption. In between is the humor that corresponds neither to the one kind of freedom nor the other, but to the relativities and anxieties of the human condition as such—the ambivalent humor of Paradise-lost, whose freedom becomes the act of withdrawal or aggression. All three forms of humor are moments within the dialectic of the sacred and the comic, and each, in a way peculiar to itself, is essential to faith and the sacred.

[28] *Surprised by Joy* (New York: Harcourt, Brace & World, 1955).

FOURTEEN

On Being with It:
An Afterword

CHAD WALSH

The writing of an essay, let alone a book, about the comic
is in itself a comic adventure; for one is inevitably involved
in the awkward double predicament of trying to take the
comic seriously and the serious comically, and most likely
being successful in neither to the dissatisfaction of all. To
write seriously about the comic is to fail to practice what one
preaches; and yet to practice what one preaches is to fail
to be taken seriously. Such a dilemma, embarrassing enough
in itself, is only intensified when the announced topic is
religious humor, and above all when this religious humor has
the distinction of being analyzed in an *academic* context. Here
the contradiction reaches such a pitch that one is inclined to
bow the knee in despair, were it not for the fact that this, too,
is one of the comic absurdities that man has managed to fall
into.

Such a pile-up of apparent incongruities, however, only
underlines the extent to which holiness and laughter have

become separated in the schizophrenia of common parlance and scholarly discourse. If even would-be advocates of the comic spirit are themselves conspicuously fearful of displaying such in the face of the "enemy," this only reveals how deep-seated in our culture is the assumption that humor is less responsible than seriousness, if not outright boorish or devilish. The problem with most essays on the comic, consequently—and the present collection is no exception—is that they proceed in a solemnity of tone and style that seems more suited to earning a degree in philosophy or being nominated to a bishopric than to inviting men to celebration and laughter. This vague and persistent uneasiness about humor—like a minister timidly trying out a mild off-color joke at a vestry meeting—reflects all too faithfully the ethos of a Christendom that (perhaps even more in its Protestant than in its Catholic manifestations) is ill at ease with laughter in the temple, preferring to concede merriment to Satan's citadel, or at least to the country club and the pool hall.

The theological basis for the scarcity of lighthearted, if not raucous, moments (even in a book recommending them) is best stated by one of the theologians I most esteem, but who in this instance is guilty of what I believe to be a profound misunderstanding of man's stance before God:

Insofar as the sense of humour is a recognition of incongruity, it is more profound than any philosophy which seeks to devour incongruity in reason. But the sense of humour remains healthy only when it deals with immediate issues and faces the obvious and surface irrationalities. It must move toward faith or sink into despair when the ultimate issues are raised.

That is why there is laughter in the vestibule of the temple, the echo of laughter in the temple itself, but only faith and prayer, and no laughter, in the holy of holies.[1]

[1] Reinhold Niebuhr, "Humour and Faith," *Discerning the Signs of the Times* (New York: Charles Scribner's Sons, 1946), pp. 130–131.

Reinhold Niebuhr speaks as a Christian, more specifically as a Protestant and neo-orthodox theologian, overwhelmed by the transcendence and otherness of God, but with no sense of the baroque. I recall one early novel by Aldous Huxley in which a character is converted to the Roman Catholic Church, and promptly (1) gains weight, and (2) composes a book of humorous verse about the Crucifixion. This episode is not calculated to amuse most Protestants, and perhaps the number of Roman Catholics who chuckle at it without inhibition is strictly limited also. But Huxley's character is, I insist, an authentic Christian.

The eternal dialogue of the sacred and the comic comes more easily to the Jew, whose folklore is full of instances in which ordinary men and Yahweh himself engage in altercations and bargaining sessions reminiscent of a used-car dealer and a reluctant customer trying to come to a meeting of minds. As for those faiths outside the biblical tradition—Zen Buddhism, for example—the distinction between the divine and the profane has a way of not arising, as though everyone were a Harvey Cox from birth, and sees nothing incongruous about laughing uproariously at the moment of supreme illumination.

A great part of the malaise afflicting Christianity today, particularly in its Protestant forms, is that it has forgotten (or never learned) how to laugh. Like Niebuhr, it fails to realize that even (maybe especially) in the holy of holies men are *set free* by the ultimate presence of God, so that in that fellowship they can offer whatever gifts they come bearing, including the gift of humor. Mythologically speaking, in heaven God and the redeemed sit around tape recorders, sharing the incongruities and absurdities of their experiences, and compiling a celestial equivalent of *Joe Miller's Jest Book.*

Charles Williams, the late British writer whose novels and poems explore the many mansions of earthly and celestial love, was much sought out by the young asking his advice about the love of man and woman. Often the inquirers expected him to emphasize the solemn and sacramental quality of the mysteries in bed, but they were not prepared for his insistence that sexual love demanded, as its proper mode, gaiety, playfulness, and laughter. And yet it is obviously true. The most profound union of bodies and souls does not come from reciting the *Te Deum* during the preliminary and climactic moments, but rather from playing jokes on each other's bodies and making unexpected explorations, rather like children investigating a new doll's house.

The comic is not a wart on the human soul but a part of the soul, and the soul is diminished if the comic is excised by any kind of spiritual X-ray. The man or woman who passes into the holy of holies and ceases to laugh is bringing into God's presence a mangled creature, one who is less than the full being that God intended him to be. The comic is an essential part of our humanity, a distinctively human trait that sets us apart from other mammals as sharply as does the c.c. content of our brains. Why should God wish comedy to go into the deep freeze just because he reveals himself? God himself is the primal humorist. The sculptor who guided evolution toward the hippopotamus has the impish playfulness of a Dada artist, and the God who chose to become man indulged in as absurd and baroque a gesture as any scientist who finds a way to turn himself into an alley cat and live among his fellow felines while still remembering the gleaming test tubes and the intellectual excitement of the laboratory.

The Christian faith is very funny. (It is also very solemn, but that is not in dispute.) It is funny because of the incongruities in it, and its total lack of monochrome dignity. The frivolous have rightly cracked jokes about a God who seemed to take a more than spiritual interest in a carpenter's wife. The birth of a divine son in a stable is touching but also funny, suggesting a farce in which a presidential candidate is assigned to the most disreputable motel in the red-light district of a city, and there receives the visitation of the TV cameramen and commentators. The Crucifixion (as Huxley's convert rightly saw) is solemn, hideous, and comic all at the same time. The comedy lies in the solemnity of the crucifiers who so humorlessly sought to do one thing while actually doing the quite different thing intended by God. The crucifiers meant to put an end to the visible activities of a rabble-rousing rabbi, and succeeded in inaugurating a new age in which all certainties are transvalued to the background music of divine laughter.

Many of the contributors to this book emphasize the value of the comic as an antidote to man's pretensions—and rightly so. The overzealous, the fanatic, the excommunicator and executioner—these are nearly always serious, contemptuous of frivolity and giggles. Such solemnity, accompanied often by neurotic self-examination and overscrupulosity, can bar the road to God more surely than any repertoire of dirty jokes and blasphemous pranks. Laughter, particularly when inspired by a recognition of the off-color humanity that we share, is a great leveler of barriers between man and man, and between man and God. By laughter we acknowledge the human condition and get outside the solitary prison of the self. In one of my early poems, "Spiritual Biography," I think I said this better than my prose could state it:

> No sooner said or done, the word or deed,
> Than memory mythologized it. He'd
> Convey it safely to his room and test
> It for the sins so subtle when confessed
> They rang like virtues. Morning-after heads
> And crude carnality of bouncing beds
> Were not for him. He ate Augustine's pears
> And classified their seeds in frequent prayers.

(Father O'Brien heard his voice with terror,
And ladled penances by trial and error.
"Sweet Mary, give me Micks that beat their wives,"
He said, "or Wops too free with carving knives.")

He died, he died. It was as he expected—
Not welcomed home nor finally rejected.
His stay in Purgatory lasted ages;
His monologues would fill ten thousand pages;
St. Peter's agents, whom he often met,
Invariably reported back, "Not yet."
The population ebbed and flowed, and he
Progressed in conscience and seniority
Until one day a spirit newly come,
And reeking still of nicotine and rum,
Told him a good one of a farmer's daughter.
He laughed. He paled. He laughed again. The water
Of clear humility rained down his skin,
Dissolved the lucent sheath of subtle sin.
(St. Peter's sides were aching when he let him in.)[2]

A sense of humor reminds us that we are odd hybrids indeed: mammals with angelic (and demonic) aspirations; it
reminds us of the still odder fact that God made us this way
for reasons that presumably seemed good to him though
opaque to us; it reminds us finally that God is as absurd as we
are, for he insists on entering into the deepest fellowship with
us hybrids, and in fact goes to totally preposterous extremes
(Red Sea, Bethlehem, Calvary) to lure or drag us into this
fellowship. All these absurdities must be as funny in heaven
as they are on earth. They are as funny as the incongruity
between the ecstasies of human love and the mammalian
physical equipment by which that love is expressed.

[2] Chad Walsh, *Eden Two-Way* (New York: Harper & Row, 1950), pp.
38–39.

Incongruity and absurdity: these rightly call for the laughter of faith. But I am haunted by the feeling that incongruity and absurdity are not the total sources of the comic as it plays its role in the midst of the sacred. The great mystics and poets have sought symbols for the ultimate revelation and state of being, and have often found it in the dance—not the ballroom dancing of a few decades ago when one cheek clung possessively to another, and not the more recent dancing in which solitary figures gyrate and occasionally meet each other like whaling ships passing at visible range in the Pacific. No, the divine dance of the mystics and poets is more a tribal activity or a square dance, with each participant weaving in and out, a complex pattern in which each ultimately enters into relation with all, according to the intricate and joyfully accepted conventions of the game. There is the divine music to guide their feet, but in the midst of the music they laugh, they exchange quick jokes and pleasantries; wink speaks to wink and hand speaks to hand. In this celestial dance there is no canceling out of tragedy and cruelty and stupidity, but somehow all these are engulfed in the dance at last; even Calvary, even death by cancer, are steps in the dance.

As a poet, I suppose I constantly think of literary analogies. The overly solemn attitude toward the comic (Niebuhr, for instance) reminds me of French classical drama, its single-minded insistence on nobility of thought and language, its almost total unwillingness to admit that even the most elevated hero or heroine must take time out to go to the bathroom. Shakespeare has always been difficult for the French, as he would have been for the Greeks. When I speak of Shakespeare, I mean the man who wrote for the popular stage more than three and a half centuries ago and whose plays (including the tragedies) are both funnier and dirtier than anyone, except literary specialists who know the slang and innuendos of the Elizabethan period, is aware. To take one simple example, when Hamlet says to Ophelia, "Get thee to a nunnery," he is advising her to enter a convent and preserve her purity. But any groundling knew the slang meaning of nunnery, "whorehouse," and responded appropriately to the double take: the tormented Hamlet was simultaneously calling her a slut. This is an example of the verbal level, but the juxtaposition of the serious and the funny occurs as well in situations, such as the drunken porter scene in *Macbeth*. It is at its most comic—and poignant—when the wrecked but redeemed Lear seems for a moment more grieved by the death of his fool than by the condition of Cordelia. In short, Shakespeare presents the fullness of the human condition in a way that Racine and even Sophocles do not. There is, I think, a valid analogy that carries over to religion. The believer who does not laugh within the holy of holies is deficient not merely in humor but in his awareness of that glorious absurdity that we label the sacred.

In all this, happily, I have the feeling that I am speaking in the context of a vanishing world, my world, the world of high seriousness and lofty pretension. It is a world that received one of its starts in ancient Jerusalem, but a stronger impetus in the academies of Plato and Aristotle. It is the world that invented science, circled the moon, devised the laws of syllogistic logic, set the computer in motion. It is a world that thinks in terms of categories, and demonstrates that A is different from B, and C is different from both. That world is dying in a revolution more fundamental than the confrontation of the have-nots with the haves, or the dark-skinned with the light-skinned. The ultimate worldwide revolution of our times sets the hippies in confrontation with the squares. The holy mad men, the poets, are returning as though Plato had never banished them, and all categories are dissolving into an undifferentiated flux of experience.

The signs of this ultimate revolution are everywhere. In

the college students carrying paperback books on Zen. In the drug cult. In the new morality. In be-ins, love-ins. In young people who not so much *will not* as *can not* point a gun at a strange soldier and pull the trigger. In the kind of non-linear perception that Marshall McLuhan has described.

And in the arts. The arts changed first, then the hippies came; life has a way of imitating art. In the arts the categories are collapsing. What is one to call a device (a neutral term) that goes through intricate motions propelled by batteries, that flashes lights in stylized or random motions, that has a tape recorder intoning nonmetric verse to the beholder, or rebroadcasting comments recorded from casual bystanders? Nor is the melange of the arts all. A work of art is becoming a moment's thing, often made of material not meant to be more eternal than bronze, as fragile perhaps as a cereal box or pound of butter.

Most of all, the arts are losing their high seriousness. When a sculptor visits the local junkyard and returns to the studio with materials for his next oeuvre, he produces a work that has a built-in dialogue between the serious and the playful, the esthetic and the comic.

The revolution of the destruction-of-categories (even that of male and female, as witness the attire of the young) is so much about us that we see it only by fits and starts and as through a glass, very darkly; mostly we try not to see it at all, or to convince ourselves that only a few misguided souls are involved and they will soon see the light and make their peace with the Establishment. But in reality, the Establishment is suffering a traumatic crisis of inner confidence. University boards of trustees, the lords of Wall Street, even the joint chiefs of staff seem much more certain of their power than they actually are.

Already the lines of the new age are dimly visible, though lines is not a good figure of speech. Perhaps one should say

configurations or swirls. It will not necessarily be a world in
which logic and science and technology vanish. More probably, these will remain as useful tools. By developing them
and moving into a cybernetic civilization, it will be possible for
machines to do most of the routine thinking and work, and
men and women can turn to more interesting matters.

The "real life" will become non-Euclidian, nonlinear to
use McLuhan's term. It will give the emotions, even the
senses, a dignity they have not had since Plato. The smell of
a flower, the touch of skin against skin, will at least rank
equal with the solution of a quadratic equation. Personal relations will count for more than abstract bureaucratic charts
of organization. Time will seem to move in a different way,
more like a circling eddy than a grim stream advancing compass straight toward one cold sea. Everything will be sacred,
and everything will be funny.

It will be a very religious age, though probably the word
"religion" will be rarely spoken. It will be an age in which
oriental religion (still basically pre-Aristotelian) will have a
built-in advantage, largely free as it is of the either/or thinking that Christianity (with a Hellenic assist along the way)
has acquired. Religion will be not the separate day, the
separate place, the wholly other, but rather an angle of vision,
a dimension, to be found everywhere. Many are seeking it
today with sex or drugs. It is quite conceivable that others
will seek it with bread and wine, once Christians liberate
themselves from certain hang-ups, notably a logic-chopping
mode of discourse, and the tendency to treat the sacred as
though it were gold ingots stored in the vault of a Swiss bank.
(One doesn't laugh, I imagine, in a Swiss bank.)

If this picture of the future (the near future) is even approximately correct, then the essays in this book become still
more important. They are pioneer efforts to rip away the
mask of solemnity that religious people have long worn, worn

so long that the living flesh of the human face has imitated the mask. The essays, for the most part, are cautious efforts. The course of history may quickly overtake and pass them. But in their tentative way, they open the door a few inches. They prepare the way for a time when humanity's free laughter will be counterpoint to God's, and men will come into the holy of holies with hymns of praise—and jokes about a traveling salesman and the farmer's daughter—and jokes about the Crucifixion—on their lips.

Appendix: Christian Sobriety

ROBERT BARCLAY

PROPOSITION XV
Concerning Salutations and Recreations, &c.

Seeing the chief end of all religion is to redeem men from the spirit and vain conversation of this world, and to lead into inward communion with God, before whom if we fear always we are accounted happy; therefore all the vain customs and habits thereof, both in word and deed, are to be rejected and forsaken by those who come to this fear; such as taking off the hat to a man, the bowings and cringings of the body, and such other salutations of that kind, with all the foolish and superstitious formalities attending them; all which man hath invented in his degenerate state, to feed his pride in the vain pomp and glory of this world: as also the unprofitable plays, frivolous recreations, sportings, and gamings, which are invented to pass away the precious time, and divert the mind from the witness of God in the heart, and from the living sense of his fear, and from that evangelical spirit wherewith Christians ought to be leavened, and which leads into sobriety, gravity, and godly fear; in which as we abide, the blessing of the Lord is felt to attend us in those actions in which we are necessarily engaged, in order to the taking care for the sustenance of the outward man.

I. Having hitherto treated of the principles of religion, both relating to doctrine and worship, I am now to speak of some practices which have been the product of this principle, in those witnesses whom God hath raised up in this day to testify for his truth. It will not a little commend them, I suppose, in the judgment of sober and judicious men, that taking them generally, even by the confession of their adversaries, they are found to be free of those abominations which abound among other professors, such as are swearing, drunkenness, whoredom, riotousness, &c.; and that generally the very coming among this people doth naturally work such a change, so that many vicious and profane persons have been known, by coming to this truth, to become sober and virtuous; and many light, vain, and wanton ones to become grave and serious, as our adversaries dare not deny: yet that they may not want something to detract us for, cease not to accuse us for those things which, when found among themselves, they highly commend; thus our gravity they call sullenness, our seriousness melancholy, our silence sottishness. Such as have been vicious and profane among them, but by coming to us have left off those evils, lest they should commend the truth of our profession, they say, that whereas they were profane before, they are become worse, in being hypocritical and spiritually proud. If any before dissolute and profane among them, by coming to the truth with us, become frugal and diligent, then they will charge them with covetousness: and if any eminent among them for seriousness, piety, and discoveries of God, come unto us, then they will say, they were always subject to melancholy and to enthusiasm; though before, when among them, it was esteemed neither melancholy nor enthusiasm in an evil sense, but Christian gravity and divine revelation. Our boldness and Christian suffering they call obstinacy and pertinacity; though half as much, if among themselves, they would account Christian courage and nobility. And though thus by their envy they strive to read all relating to us backwards, counting those things vices in us, which in themselves they would extol as virtues, yet hath the strength of truth extorted this confession often from them, That we are generally a pure and clean people, as to the outward conversation.

But this, they say, is but in policy to commend our heresy.

But such policy it is, say I, as Christ and his apostles made use of, and all good Christians ought to do; yea, so far hath truth prevailed by the purity of its followers, that if one that is called a Quaker do but that which is common among them, as to laugh and be wanton, speak at large, and keep not his word punctually, or be overtaken with hastiness or anger, they presently say, O this is against your profession! As if indeed so to do were very consistent with theirs; wherein though they speak the truth, yet they give away their cause. But if they can find any under our name in any of those evils common among themselves (as who can imagine but among so many thousands there will be some chaff, since of twelve apostles one was found to be a devil), O how will they insult, and make more noise of the escape of one Quaker, than of an hundred among themselves!

II. But there are some singular things, which most of all our adversaries plead for the lawfulness of, and allow themselves in, as no ways inconsistent with the Christian religion, which we have found to be no ways lawful unto us, and have been commanded of the Lord to lay them aside; though the doing thereof hath occasioned no small sufferings and buffetings, and hath procured us much hatred and malice from the world. And because the nature of these things is such, that they do upon the very sight distinguish us, and make us known, so that we cannot hide ourselves from any, without proving unfaithful to our testimony; our trials and exercises have here-through proved the more numerous and difficult, as will after appear. These I have laboured briefly to comprehend in this proposition; but they may more largely be exhibited in these six following propositions:

1. That it is not lawful to give to men such flattering titles, as Your Holiness, Your Majesty, Your Eminency, Your Excellency, Your Grace, Your Lordship, Your Honour, &c., nor use those flattering words, commonly called COMPLIMENTS.

2. That it is not lawful for Christians to kneel, or prostrate themselves to any man, or to bow the body, or to uncover the head to them.

3. That it is not lawful for a Christian to use superfluities in apparel, as are of no use, save for ornament and vanity.

4. That it is not lawful to use games, sports, plays, nor among other things comedies among Christians, under the notion of recreations, which do not agree with Christian silence, gravity, and sobriety; for laughing, sporting, gaming, mocking, jesting, vain talking, &c., is not Christian liberty, nor harmless mirth. . . .

Let us consider the use of games, sports, comedies, and other such things, commonly and indifferently used by all the several sorts of Christians, under the notion of divertisement and recreation, and see whether these things can consist with the seriousness, gravity, and Godly fear, which the gospel calls for. Let us but view and look over the notions of them that call themselves Christians, whether Papists or Protestants, and see if generally there be any difference, save in mere name and profession, from the heathen? Doth not the same folly, the same vanity, the same abuse of precious and irrevocable time abound? The same gaming, sporting, playing, and from thence quarrelling, fighting, swearing, ranting, revelling? Now how can these things be remedied, so long as the preachers and professors, and those who are the leaders of the people, do allow these things, and account them not inconsistent with the profession of Christianity? And it is strange to see that these things are tolerated every where; the inquisition lays no hold on them, neither at Rome, nor in Spain, where in their masquerades all manner of obscenity, folly, yea, and Atheism is generally practised in the face of the world, to the great scandal of the Christian name; but if any man reprove them in these things, and forsake their superstitions, and come seriously to serve God, and worship him in the Spirit, he becomes their prey, and is immediately exposed to cruel sufferings. Doth this bear any relation to Christianity? Do these things look any thing like the churches of the primitive Christians? Surely not at all. I shall first cite some few scripture testimonies, being very positive precepts to Christians, and then see whether such as obey them can admit of these forementioned things. The apostle commands us, That "whether we eat or drink, or whatever we do, we do it all to the glory of God." But I judge none will be so impudent as to affirm, That in the use of these sports and games God is glorified: if any should so say, they would declare they neither knew God nor his glory. And experience abundantly proves, that in the practice of these things men mind nothing less than the glory of God, and nothing more than the satisfaction of their own carnal lusts, wills, and appetites. The apostle desires us, 1 Cor. vii. 29, 31: Because the time is short, that they that buy should be as though they possessed not; and they that use this world, as not abusing it, &c. But how can they be found in the obedience of this precept that plead for the use of these games and sports, who, it seems, think the time so long, that they cannot find occasion enough to employ it, neither in taking care for their souls, nor yet in the necessary care for their bodies; but invent these games and sports to pass it away, as if they wanted other work to serve God in, or be useful to the creation? The apostle Peter desires us, "To pass the time of our sojourning here in fear," 1 Pet. i. 17. But will any say, That such as use dancing and comedies, carding and dicing, do so much as mind this precept in the use of these things? Where there is nothing to be seen but lightness and vanity, wantonness and obscenity, contrived to draw men from the fear of God, and therefore no doubt calculated for the service of the devil. There is no duty more frequently commanded, nor more incumbent upon Christians, than the fear of the Lord, to stand in awe before him, to walk as in his presence; but if such as use these games and sports will speak from their consciences, they can, I doubt not, experimentally declare, that this fear is forgotten in their gaming; and if God by his light secretly touch them, or mind them of the vanity of their way, they strive to shut it out, and use their gaming as an engine to put away from them that troublesome guest, and thus make merry over the Just One, whom they have slain and crucified in themselves. But further, if Christ's reasoning be to be heeded, who saith, Matt. xii. 35, 36: That "the good man, out of the good treasure of the heart, bringeth forth good things; and an evil man, out of the evil treasure, bringeth forth evil things," and that "of every idle word we shall give an account in the day of judgment," it may be easily gathered from what treasure these inventions come; and it may be easily proved, that it is from the evil, and not the good. How many idle words do they necessarily produce? Yea, what are comedies but a studied complex of idle and lying words? Let men that be-

lieve their souls are immortal, and that there will be a day
of judgment, in which these words of Christ will be accomplished, answer me, how all these will make account in that
great and terrible day, of all these idle words that are necessarily made use of about dancing, gaming, carding, and
comedies acting? And yet how is it that by Christians not
condemning these things, but allowing of them, many that are
accounted Christians take up their whole time in them, yea,
make it their trade and employment? Such as the dancing-
masters and comedians, &c., whose hellish conversations do
sufficiently declare what master they serve, and to what end
these things contribute. And it cannot be denied, as being
obviously manifest by experience, that such as are masters of
these occupations, and are most delighted in them, if they be
not open Atheists and profligates, are such at best as make
religion or the care of their souls their least business. Now
if these things were discountenanced by Christians, as inconsistent with their profession, it would remove these things:
for these wretches would be necessitated then to betake themselves to some honest livelihood, if they were not fed and
upholden by these. And as hereby a great scandal and stum-
bling-block would be removed from off the Christian name,
so also would that in part be taken out of the way which
provokes the Lord to withhold his blessing, and by occasion
of which things the minds of many remain chained in darkness, and drowned in lust, sensuality, and worldly pleasures,
without any sense of God's fear, or their own souls' salvation.
Many of those called fathers of the church, and other serious
persons, have signified their regret for these things, and their
desires they might be remedied; of whom many citations might
be alleged, which for brevity's sake I have omitted. . . .

IX. But they object, That men's spirits could not subsist,
if they were always intent upon serious and spiritual matters,
and that therefore there is need of some divertisement to re-

create the mind a little, whereby it being refreshed, is able with greater vigour to apply itself to these things.

I answer; Though all this were granted, it would no ways militate against us, neither plead the use of these things, which we would have wholly laid aside. For that men should be always in the same intentiveness of mind, we do not plead, knowing how impossible it is, so long as we are clothed with this tabernacle of clay. But this will not allow us at any time so to recede from the remembrance of God, and of our souls' chief concern, as not still to retain a certain sense of his fear; which cannot be so much as rationally supposed to be in the use of these things which we condemn. Now the necessary occasions in which all are involved, in order to the care and sustentation of the outward man, are a relaxation of the mind from the more serious duties; and those are performed in the blessing, as the mind is so leavened with the love of God, and the sense of his presence, that even in doing these things the soul carrieth with it that divine influence and spiritual habit, whereby, though these acts, as of eating, drinking, sleeping, working, be upon the matter one with what the wicked do, yet they are done in another spirit; and in doing of them we please the Lord, serve him, and answer our end in the creation, and so feel and are sensible of his blessing: whereas the wicked and profane, being not come to this place, are in whatsoever they do, cursed, and their ploughing as well as praying is sin. Now if any will plead, that for relaxation of mind, there may be a liberty allowed beyond these things, which are of absolute need to the sustenance of the outward man, I shall not much contend against it; provided these things be not such as are wholly superfluous, or in their proper nature and tendency lead the mind into lust, vanity, and wantonness, as being chiefly contrived and framed for that end, or generally experienced to produce these effects, or being the common engines of such as are so minded to feed one another therein, and to propagate their wickedness, to the impoisoning of others; seeing there are other innocent divertisements which may sufficiently serve for relaxation of the mind, such as for friends to visit one another; to hear or read history; to speak soberly of the present or past transactions; to follow after gardening; to use geometrical and mathematical experiments, and such other things of this nature. In all which things we are not so to forget God, in whom we both live and are moved, Acts xvii. 28, as not to have always some secret reserve to him, and sense of his fear and presence; which also frequently exerts itself in the midst of these things by some short aspiration and breathings. And that this may neither seem strange nor troublesome, I shall clear it by one manifest instance, answerable to the experience of all men. It will not be denied but that men ought to be more in the love of God than of any other thing; for we ought to love God above all things. Now it is plain, that men that are taken with love, whether it be of a woman, or of any other thing, if it hath taken a deep place in the heart, and possess the mind, it will be hard for the man so in love to drive out of his mind the person or thing so loved; yea, in his eating, drinking, and sleeping, his mind will always have a tendency that way; and in business or recreations, however intent he be in it, there will but a very short time be permitted to pass, but the mind will let some ejaculation forth towards its beloved. And albeit such a one must be conversant in those things that the care of this body and such like things call for; yet will he avoid as death itself to do those things that may offend the party so beloved, or cross his design in obtaining the thing so earnestly desired: though there may be some small use in them, the great design, which is chiefly in his eye, will so balance him, that he will easily look over and dispense with such petty necessities, rather than endanger the loss of the greater by them. Now that men ought to be thus in love with God, and the life to come, none will deny; and the thing is apparent from these scriptures, Mat. vi. 20, "But lay up for yourselves treasures in heaven." Col. iii. 2, "Set your affection on things above," &c. And that this hath been the experience and attainment of some, the scripture also declares, Psalm lxiii. 1, 8; 2 Cor. v. 4.

And again, That these games, sports, plays, dancing, comedies, &c., do naturally tend to draw men from God's fear, to make them forget heaven, death, and judgment, to foster lust, vanity, and wantonness, and therefore are most loved, as well as used, by such kind of persons, experience abundantly shows, and the most serious and conscientious among all will scarcely deny; which if it be so, the application is easy.

Bibliography

General Anthologies

Corrigan, Robert, ed., *Comedy: Meaning and Form*. San Francisco, Chandler Publishing Co., 1965.

Enck, John J., Forter, Elizabeth T., Whitley, Alvin, eds., *The Comic in Theory and Practice*. New York, Appleton-Century-Crofts, 1960.

Lauter, Paul, ed., *Theories of Comedy*. New York, Doubleday & Co., 1964.

Religion and the Comic

Blyth, R. H., *Oriental Humour*. Tokyo, Hokuseido Press, 1959.

———— *Zen and Zen Classics*, 4 vols. Tokyo, Hokuseido Press, 1962–65.

Chotzner, Joseph, *Hebrew Humour*. London, Luzac & Co., 1905.

Connolly, Francis X., D'Arcy, Martin, and Ulanov, Barry, *Literature as Christian Comedy*. West Hartford, Conn., St. Joseph College, 1962.

Good, Edwin M., *Irony in the Old Testament*. Philadelphia, The Westminster Press, 1965.

Huizinga, Johan, *Homo Ludens*. Boston, Beacon Press, 1950.

Jónsson, Jakob, *Humour and Irony in the New Testament*. Rekyjavík, Iceland, Bókaútgáfa Menningarsjóds, 1965.

Jung, C. G., "On the Psychology of the Trickster Figure," *The Collected Works of C. G. Jung*, Vol. IX/1. New York, Pantheon Books, 1959, pp. 255–274.

Kierkegaard, Søren, *Concluding Unscientific Postscript,* trans. David F. Swenson. Princeton, Princeton University Press, 1941.

―――― *The Concept of Irony*. New York, Harper & Row, 1966.

Lynch, William F., S.J., *Christ and Apollo*. New York, Sheed & Ward, 1960.

McGregor, Geddes, "Faith, Doubt, and Laughter," *Christian Doubt*. London, Longmans Green, & Co., 1951, pp. 65–73.

Oliver, E. J., *Hypocrisy and Humor*. New York, Sheed & Ward, 1960.

Rahner, Hugo, *Man at Play*. New York, Herder & Herder, 1965.

Trueblood, Elton, *The Humor of Christ*. New York, Harper & Row, 1964.

Vos, Nelvin, *The Drama of Comedy: Victim and Victor*. Richmond, John Knox Press, 1966.

Wagoner, Walter, ed., *Bittersweet Grace: A Treasury of Twentieth-Century Religious Satire*. New York, World Publishing Co., 1967.

Watts, Alan, *Beyond Theology*. New York, Pantheon Books, 1964.

Webster, Gary, *Laughter in the Bible*. St. Louis, Bethany Press, 1960.

Zuver, Dudley, *Salvation by Laughter*. New York, Harper & Brothers, 1933.